INTRODUCTION

WHY DID WE PRODUCE THIS BOOK?

For a couple of reasons. First, we wanted to provide a little inspiration to students sweating over their application essays to highly selective colleges. We've heard too many freaked-out high schoolers with outstanding academic and community service records, enviable SAT and ACT scores, and impressive sports achievements complain that they didn't know what to write about or at least didn't know where to start. So we decided to prove to them that there are a million different ways to approach the essay and that if students reflect on what's most important to them, they will indeed have something to write about. Our evidence is enclosed herewith: actual essays that got real, breathing high school students— kids with crushes and acne and big feet—into the colleges of their dreams.

These kids wrote about scores of things, from their love of horses to the shortcomings of being short to their theories of how the quality of life for all men everywhere would rise significantly if engineers could only figure out how to make testicles detachable. There are essays with sad themes—stories of family tragedy and civil war. There are some with funny ones—stories of puberty's late arrival and of public humiliation. There are stories of achievement and of failure, of love and death, of a relationship with God and a lack thereof.

You win some . . .

The essays you'll find in these pages were written by students of diverse backgrounds and for a wide variety of colleges. And like most collections of prose by many authors, the essays in this collection display a range of creativity and sophistication with the written word. Some are so good that they will intimidate you; others will make you say to yourself, "Hey, I could write something like that." Some are so strange and unexpected that you will wonder how on earth some of the most discriminating colleges in the country accepted into their freshman classes the people who wrote them. And those are just the essays written by admitted applicants.

Pardon me? Does that mean that there are profiles in this book of applicants who were *not* accepted to these selective schools, too?

Yes.

. . . You lose some

What's the use of including those? Fortunately, the answer to this question is our second reason for producing this book: to help you educate yourself about the regularities and irregularities of selective college admissions—how different parts of your application are evaluated by different college admissions offices. We've not only provided the essays written by almost ninety selective college applicants; we've also included their SAT I and II scores, ACT score, high school GPA, race, gender, and their hometown and state, all of which competitive schools may take into consideration when making admit decisions. Sure, you can find average SAT scores and GPAs of last year's freshman class in most college guides, but what you'll find here are the *complete profiles* of real applicants who are currently enrolled in, or have recently graduated from, the most selective undergraduate schools in the nation. To top it off, we've also included interviews with admissions officers at thirteen stellar schools to help shed a little light on what happens on the other side of the admissions fence.

What can you learn from this book?

We don't comment on any individual essays, applicants, or admissions results, so we won't try to direct your responses toward any specific form or content. We simply present the information to you and let you do what you will with the evidence (except plagiarize it). But after considering the figures for each student who was accepted to the college of your choice (and for most colleges, we provide the profiles of several students), you'll start to get an idea of what you need—in terms of academic competitiveness, essay quality, racial or geographic differentiation, whatever—to gain acceptance to it. What's more, we provide what we call "overlap," or all of the other schools to which each student applied and the ultimate results of those applications. By studying these results, you can start to gauge what your own success rate will be at the various mega-selective colleges in America. Even if you're not applying to any school included in this book, the quality of the essays and the strength of the students' overall applications can be used to measure your own writing and credentials.

Beyond its usefulness, this book is also a celebration of the human aspect of the application—and it's a good read, to boot!

We also hope that this book will help prepare you to encounter both success and failure with your college applications. You're going to be a bit perplexed when Harvard accepts, Columbia waitlists, and Stanford rejects you. As you'll see, even wunderkinds—we've profiled plenty of them—get denied admission to top-flight schools.* In fact, very few of the

---

*Last year's break-in of Yale's online admissions database by a Princeton admissions officer ignited questions of whether some mega-selective schools make admissions decisions based on their knowledge (or belief) that one or more of their competitors have already admitted an applicant they have in common. We believe that this was an isolated incident and that these elite colleges' admissions offices are almost unwaveringly on the up-and-up. They certainly are interested in finding out who their competitors are, and to whom they may lose yield (the percentage of admitted students who enroll in a college) and why, but they can and usually do find this out through perfectly legitimate and ethical means.

COLLEGE ESSAYS THAT MADE A DIFFERENCE

The Princeton Review

COLLEGE ESSAYS THAT MADE A DIFFERENCE

Random House, Inc.
New York
www.PrincetonReview.com

Princeton Review Publishing, L. L. C.
2315 Broadway
New York, NY 10024
E-mail: bookeditor@review.com

ISBN 0-375-76344-9

Editorial Director: Robert Franek
Editor: Erica Magrey
Designer: Scott Harris
Production Editor: Julieanna Lambert
Production Coordinator: Scott Harris

Manufactured in the United States of America.

9   8   7   6   5   4   3   2

ACKNOWLEDGMENTS

This book would not have been possible without the dedication of many fine members of The Princeton Review crew, most notably Robert Franek and Erik Olson, whose intense involvement was instrumental in the book's development. A shout-out also goes to John Katzman and Pat Vance for believing in this book and giving us the opportunity to turn it into a reality, Scott Harris and Julieanna Lambert for transforming the manuscript into a killer book, David Soto and Yojaira Cordero for their assistance on multiple occasions, and Ali Fernandez and Chey Ramos for their patience and understanding.

The following admissions officers kindly set aside time to speak with us about the particular aspects of their institution's undergraduate admissions process, offering invaluable insight: Alyssa Sinclair, Carol Lunkenheimer, Janet Rapelye, Jennifer Wong, Jim Miller, Joel Bauman, John Latting, Lorne T. Robinson, Margit Dahl, Matthew Swanson, Rob Moore, Tom Parker, and Virginia Harrison.

The folks most vital to this book, of course, are the contributors—eighty-nine amazing students who took the time out of their busy lives to stay in touch and answer my questions. To each student who participated in this project (chosen for publication or not): Many thanks for your patience, hard work, and generosity. We commend you for having the guts to lay it all out there for the benefit of future generations of elite college applicants.

Erica Magrey

CONTENTS

students you'll encounter in this book got into every college to which they applied. So what should this mean to you? It means that failure is a part of life, even when you've busted your hump working on whatever it was that ultimately failed. But there's a flip side to this sort of self-consoling thinking. After reading this book, you'll know that even if you do get a rejection letter, there's no reason to feel completely bereft. A few fat envelopes are probably wending their way to you.

Why'd they do it?

So why would students allow us to publish their essays, test scores, grades, and personal biographical information? They realize the intrinsic value of sharing their stories: little glimpses of perspective for the elite college hopeful. Many said they were honored to have been chosen for publication and to have been given the chance to help the next generation.

Which schools did we accept submissions from, and why?

We accepted submissions from current students at, or recent graduates of, any college that received a selectivity rating of 95 or higher in the 2002 edition of *The Best 345 Colleges*. Although we acknowledge that many students applying to less selective schools also have excellent grades and write first-rate admissions essays, we decided that a short list would be more useful and manageable. Our search did not yield results from two schools that met our selectivity requirement, so we were left with a list of forty-three outstanding institutions:

Amherst College	Harvard College
Barnard College	Haverford College
Bates College	Johns Hopkins University
Boston College	Macalester College
Bowdoin College	Massachusetts Institute of Technology
Brown University	Middlebury College
California Institute of Technology	New College of Florida
Carleton College	Northwestern University
Claremont McKenna College	Pomona College
Colby College	Princeton University
Columbia University	Rice University
Cornell University	Smith College
Dartmouth College	Stanford University
Davidson College	Swarthmore College
Duke University	Tufts University
Georgetown University	United States Air Force Academy

United States Coast Guard Academy   Washington University in St. Louis

United States Naval Academy   Wellesley College

University of Chicago   Wesleyan University

University of Notre Dame   Williams College

University of Pennsylvania   Yale University

Washington and Lee University

How did we choose which applicants to include?

We had an overwhelming response to our call for submissions, and in the end we had no choice but to turn down some amazing applicants. Our goal was to provide you with the best possible cross-section of top applicants—a group of students who applied to different schools, submitted essays on a range of themes, had varied academic records, and were dealt a mixture of admissions decisions. We did not aim to produce cookbook recipes, line-by-line instructions of what to do and not to do in your application to X University. Rather, we wished simply to show you how real students fared in the admissions jungle.

HOW TO USE THIS BOOK

Essay Fundamentals

We want to emphasize the role that grammar plays in essay excellence, so we composed a short review of the essentials. We also discuss the essay's importance in an application.

Q&A with Admissions Officers

We interviewed admissions folks at thirteen top schools and discussed the essay, the application as a whole, and the specifics of how the admissions ship is run at each school. Their responses will give you some insight into what happens after your application is signed, sealed, and delivered.

The Applicants

Each student profile is broken down into swallowable chunks. First, we give you the name of the student and a photograph, if one was provided. We then offer a short paragraph, composed by the applicant, summarizing major accomplishments and activities that were highlighted on the application. Next, we show you the student's stats, or statistical record (test scores, GPA), and demographic information (hometown, gender, ethnicity). We list the schools that the student applied to, as well. Finally, you will see the student's application essay in its original condition (e.g., no typos corrected), listing in which applications the essay was included. In a few cases, we printed more than one essay written by a given student; Princeton's application, for example, requires four short essays, so we wanted to make sure we included the complete set.

We did not group the applicants into any categories or organize them by school; you will find them in alphabetical order by first name.

While you read, you may want to consult each school's profile, either in *The Best 345 Colleges* or on our website, www.PrincetonReview.com. In each school profile, you will find information about students who applied in the most recent academic year, including the average SAT and ACT scores of the freshman class, the number of applicants, and the yield (the percentage of students accepted who enrolled). We also break down the application elements into hierarchical categories—which components of the application each school considers very important factors, important factors, and other factors; you'll see which of these categories the essay falls into for each college.

Where They Got In

This is an index of the admissions decisions each student received. Try putting yourself in the position of the admissions officer; in some cases, you may be surprised by the admissions staff's decisions. This index is also alphabetized by the student's first name.

Each student also provided a few sentences to fill us in on what they've been doing since application season—where they go to school, what they major in, and whatever else they're up to these days.

Index of Essay Themes

Admissions officers joke about common essay themes, so we decided to break the essays down into our own categories. Have a look and see who else wrote about Music & Musicians, and on what page you may find his or her profile.

EDITOR'S NOTE

Though it goes without saying, don't plagiarize the essays in this book. Different colleges ask different essay questions. Some simply ask for a personal statement. Others want you to answer several short essay questions in addition to writing a longer, more thoughtful essay. Requested lengths will vary. In any case, your response should be in your own words. We encourage you to note buzz words, structures, and themes that you really like. But draw the line at copying phrases, whole sentences, or paragraphs. There's a chance you'll get busted, which would mean you couldn't get into college at all. Plus, plagiarism is wrong, so you'd have to walk around with that yucky guilty feeling for the rest of your days.

PART 1

ESSAY FUNDAMENTALS

GRAMMAR AND PUNCTUATION

Like any good writing, your college application should be clear, concise, candid, structurally sound, and 100 percent grammatically accurate.

Clarity and conciseness are usually the products of a lot of reading, rereading, and rewriting. Without question, repeated critical revision by yourself and by others is the surest way to trim, tune, and improve your prose.

Candor is the product of proper motivation. Honesty, sincerity, and authenticity cannot be superimposed after the fact; your writing must be candid from the outset. Also, let's be on the level: you're probably pretty smart and pretty sophisticated. You could probably fake candor if absolutely necessary. But you shouldn't. For one thing, it's a hell of a lot more work. Moreover, no matter how good your insincere essay may be, we're brazenly confident that an honest and authentic essay will be even better.

Structural soundness is the product of a well-crafted outline. It really pays to sketch out the general themes of your essay first; worry about filling in the particulars later. Outlines don't come out perfectly the first time (for most of us mortals, at least). Many people like to start by spitting out ideas onto paper in the form of "bubble outlines"—they'll write down the names of things that they're passionate or know a lot about, circle the ones that they really think describe who they are, then connect with lines ideas that complement one another. Others, like whiz-kid movie director Paul Thomas Anderson, start writing lists of things that they like or have done, lists and lists and lists, until an overall theme starts to take shape. If you go about it this way, you have the details of your essay written down even before you decide what your theme will be. The idea is to get thinking, get your thoughts onto paper, then settle down to attack the task of building a formal outline. Pay particularly close attention to the structure of your essay and to the fundamental message it communicates. Make sure you have a well-conceived narrative. Your essay should flow from beginning to end. Use paragraphs properly and make sure the paragraphs are in a logical order. The sentences within each paragraph should be complete and also flow in a logical order.

Grammatical accuracy is key. A thoughtful essay that offers true insight will stand out unmistakably, but if it is riddled with poor grammar and misspelled words, it will not receive serious consideration. *It is critical that you avoid all grammatical errors.* We just can't stress this enough. Misspellings, awkward constructions, run-on sentences, and misplaced modifiers all cast doubt on your efforts. Admissions officers will wonder, how much care did you put into the essay's composition?

GRAMMATICAL CATEGORY	WHAT'S THE RULE?	BAD GRAMMAR	GOOD GRAMMAR
MISPLACED MODIFIER	A word or phrase that describes something should go right next to the thing it modifies.	1. Eaten in Mediterranean countries for centuries, **northern Europeans** viewed the tomato with suspicion. 2. A **former greens keeper** now about to become the Masters champion, **tears** welled up in my eyes as I hit my last miraculous shot.	1. Eaten in Mediterranean countries for centuries, **the tomato** was viewed with suspicion by northern Europeans. 2. **I was a former greens keeper** who was now about to become the Masters champion; **tears** welled up in my eyes as I hit my last miraculous shot.
PRONOUNS	A pronoun must refer unambiguously to a noun and it must agree (singular or plural) with that noun.	1. Though **brokers** are not permitted to know executive access **codes, they** are widely known. 2. The **golden retriever** is one of the smartest breeds of dogs but **they** often **have** trouble writing **personal statements** for law school admission. 3. Unfortunately, both **candidates** for whom I worked sabotaged their own **campaigns** by taking a **contribution** from illegal **sources.**	1. Though **brokers** are not permitted to know executive access **codes, the codes** are widely known. 2. The **golden retriever** is one of the smartest breeds of dogs but **it** often **has** trouble writing **a personal statement** for law school admission. 3. Unfortunately, both **candidates** for whom I worked sabotaged their own **campaigns** by taking **contributions** from illegal **sources.**
SUBJECT/VERB AGREEMENT	The subject must always agree with the verb. Make sure you don't forget what the subject of a sentence is, and don't use the object of a preposition as the subject.	1. **Each** of the men involved in the extensive renovations **were** engineers. 2. Federally imposed **restrictions** on the ability to use certain information **has** made life difficult for Martha Stewart.	1. **Each** of the men involved in the extensive renovations **was** an engineer. 2. Federally imposed **restrictions** on the ability to use certain information **have** made life difficult for Martha Stewart.
PARALLEL CONSTRUCTION	Words in lists in the same sentence need to be similar in form to the other words in the list.	1. The two main goals of the Eisenhower presidency were a **reduction** of taxes and **to increase** military strength. 2. **To provide a child** with the skills necessary for survival in modern life is **like guaranteeing their** success.	1. The two main goals of the Eisenhower presidency were **to reduce** taxes and **to increase** military strength. 2. **Providing children** with the skills necessary for survival in modern life is **like guaranteeing their** success.
COMPARISONS	You can only compare things to exactly the same things.	1. The **rules** of written English are more stringent than **spoken English.** 2. The **considerations** that led many colleges to impose admissions quotas in the last few decades **are similar to the quotas** imposed in the recent past by large businesses.	1. The **rules** of written English are more stringent than **those of spoken English.** 2. The **considerations** that led many colleges to impose admissions quotas in the last few decades **are similar to those** that led large businesses to impose quotas in the recent past.
PASSIVE/ ACTIVE VOICE	Choose the active voice, in which the subject performs the action.	1. **The ball was hit by the bat.** 2. After months **were spent** trying to keep justdillpickles.com afloat single-handedly, **resignation was chosen by me.**	1. **The bat hit the ball.** 2. After **I spent months** trying to keep justdillpickles.com afloat single-handedly, **I chose to resign.**

Good writing is writing that is easily understood. You want to get your point across, not bury it in words. Don't talk in circles. Your prose should be clear and direct. If an admissions officer has to struggle to figure out what you are trying to say, you're in trouble. Also, almost every college requires freshmen to complete a course or two in composition, even if you plan on majoring in a subject that isn't writing-intensive, like chemistry. If you can demonstrate that you have good writing skills, you'll have a serious edge in these required courses.

Get to the point in three pages. Don't be long-winded and boring. Admissions officers don't like long essays. Would you, if you were in their shoes? Be brief. Be focused. And if there is a word limit, abide by it.

Buy and read *The Elements of Style*, by William Strunk, Jr. and E. B. White. We can't recommend it highly enough. In fact, we're surprised you don't have it already. This little book is a required investment for any writer. If your major involves much writing, it will become your best friend. And if you decide on a profession that requires you to put pen to paper on a daily basis, you will refer to it forever.

Have three or four people read your personal statement and critique it. Proofread your essay from beginning to end, then proofread it again, then proofread it some more. Read it aloud. Keep in mind, though, that the more time you spend with a piece of your own writing, the less likely you are to spot any errors. You get tunnel vision. Ask friends, boyfriends, girlfriends, professors, brothers, sisters—somebody—to read your essay and comment on it. Have friends read it. Have an English teacher read it. (More than one admissions officer told us that a teacher was the best person to read your essay.) Have an English major read it. Have the most grammatically anal person you know read it. We don't care. Just do whatever it takes to make sure your personal statement is clear, concise, candid, structurally sound, and 100 percent grammatically accurate.

WHAT COLLEGES WANT TO SEE IN YOUR ESSAY: WRITING ABILITY AND INSIGHT INTO WHO YOU ARE

The admissions officers reading your essay want it to prove to them two things. First, they want it to show that you can write at a college level, which means that you have a command of the English language and can use it to craft a cogent written statement. They're not interested in your vocabulary skills, though, so give the thesaurus to your mom and have her hide it. You should be able to write your essay without fancy words whose meaning you don't understand. (And it is so painfully obvious to admissions officers when you don't; they're almost embarrassed *for* you.)

Admissions officers are interested in seeing that you understand sentence and paragraph structure and can pace a narrative. Oh yes, and that you know what a narrative is in the first place. In case you're a little unsure, a narrative is simply a story. And unless you're William Faulkner (who didn't even graduate from college), the story you tell to the admissions officer through your essay needs to be brief, flow logically from one event to the next, and have a convincing conclusion. People usually act consistently (even if they're consistently inconsistent), and their pattern of actions more times than not leads to consistent outcomes. You'd have to be a darn clever wordsmith, for example, to convince a reader that a chain smoker could enter the New York City Marathon and win it just because he "had a lot of heart." Your essay should not require the admissions officer to suspend disbelief. So keep it brief and coherent.

This does not mean that you should edit your essay down to nothing, or let someone else edit it down to nothing. It shouldn't *sound* like a marketing piece. It should sound like the way you would talk (when you speak with correct grammar, of course).

An additional point we hope you will pick up on is that no matter how impressive your grades and test scores and extracurriculars are, admissions decisions by these top-flight schools involve subjective elements that you can't control. But don't try to be someone else in your essay, someone whom you think they want to see. That's the job of a con artist, and it almost never works in the admissions office. Besides, conning people leaves you feeling all icky inside. Why bother?

Time and again admissions officers tell us that they want to see students write their college essay about something they, the students, actually care about. Write about something you do, not something you would do if you were president of the United States (unless specifically asked to do so). They aren't interested in reading about your plan for eliminating AIDS from the world. They're interested in hearing how and why you spent every Wednesday afternoon for the last two years teaching an underprivileged kid how to use a computer, even on days when you didn't want to or didn't think you had time. They're even interested in why you're passionate about Spider-Man comics.

But notice the "why." The essay isn't just an opportunity for you to riff in an effort to show that you're a crank who would bring some much-needed uniqueness to campus. It's an opportunity for you to convey to the admissions committee insight about who you are. This means the essay absolutely must include the "why." There are no exceptions. Why do you love Spider-Man? Is it something he is or isn't? Is what he does somehow an allegory for selfless service to others? If you're an artist, is it the care with which every frame is crafted? The detail? If you're a cultural anthropologist, is it Spidey's continued ability to resonate with readers, both old and young? The point is, your essay should show that you have thought about why you love what you love, believe what you believe, or are what you are. The "why" in your essay will show that you know how to reflect and analyze, both of which are wicked important attributes to have in college.

TOPICS THAT WORK; TOPICS THAT DON'T

Opinion differs from college to college regarding what are good essay topics and what aren't. You can read about these differences of opinion in Part 2 of this book, which is devoted to the interviews we conducted with many deans, directors, and assistant directors of admissions at elite colleges.

There are a few topics that almost invariably send shudders down admissions officers' backs. These include sex, drugs (especially *your* sex life or drug use), or violent events in which you participated. Admissions officers also tire of reading travelogues and stories of how you recovered from a sports injury. Want to make them groan? Rehash the extracurricular activities that you already listed on the section of the application devoted to them, or editorialize on the top news item of the day. Swearing isn't usually effective, either. They appreciate humor, but if you're not funny in person, you shouldn't try to be so on paper. This is why you should have someone else read your essay: if your humor doesn't elicit the right response from your teacher, it most likely won't get the reaction you're looking for in the admissions office.

Admissions officers also don't want to read the essay you wrote for another school. If you're using the same essay for all schools to which you're applying and you refer specifically to the school, you should make sure to replace the previous school's name with the current one. It's only common courtesy.

What *do* they like to read about? Curiosity, passion, and persistence. These are the sorts of attributes that great college students have. These great students go on to be great alumni. Colleges that have great students and great alumni tend to attract quality applicants, and on the cycle goes. But you shouldn't *tell* the admissions office that you are curious, passionate, or persistent; you should *show* them. Let your narrative do this. How? Check out some of the essays inside.

SO HOW MUCH DOES THE ESSAY COUNT, ANYWAY?

As Jim Miller, dean of admissions at Bowdoin College told us, "A great essay could heal the sick but couldn't raise the dead." We know of no college whose admissions office places more weight on the essay than they do on your high school GPA. Almost without exception (the exception being those colleges who don't require test scores, like Bates College), the two most important factors in your application are your GPA and standardized test scores. If you are reading this very early in high school, make getting good grades your top priority. When it comes time to take the SAT or ACT, prepare well for it, take it once, and kick its ass. If you're reading this in the fall of your senior year and your GPA is in the toilet, this book is going to be of little use to you.

The consensus among most admissions officers is that the essay can both help and hurt you, but it can help you more. That is reason enough to put your best effort into writing it. It is, after all, the one part of your college application over which you have total control. This book is our way of preparing you to do take command of that process with authority.

PART 2

Q&A WITH ADMISSIONS OFFICERS

HERE'S THE DEAL

We interviewed admissions officers at thirteen selective schools about undergraduate essays and applications. They told us the specifics of how their staff reviews applications; they discussed essay themes, plagiarism, and deferrals, among other things; and they offered writing tips to college applicants. The following professionals dedicated their time to answering our questions:

Tom Parker, dean of admissions at Amherst College

Virginia Harrison, associate dean of admissions at Bates College

Jim Miller, dean of admissions at Bowdoin College

Jennifer Wong, director of admissions at Claremont McKenna College

John Latting, director of admissions at Johns Hopkins University

Lorne T. Robinson, dean of admissions and financial aid at Macalester College

Alyssa Sinclair, assistant director of admissions at Middlebury College

Joel Bauman, dean of admissions at New College of Florida

Carol Lunkenheimer, dean of admissions at Northwestern University

Rob Moore, assistant director of admissions at the United States Coast Guard Academy

Janet Rapelye, dean of admissions at Wellesley College

Matthew Swanson, assistant director of admissions at Williams College

Margit Dahl, director of undergraduate admissions at Yale University

Q&A

WHAT THEMES CONTINUALLY COME UP IN ESSAYS?

Amherst: We give four or five different options. I look for an experience or interaction that they have had that led them to a particular value or interaction, a reflection.

Bates: My trip to "blank." That might be China. That might be California. That might be France. Tragedy. My three-day solo in the wilderness. Sports injury. What I learned from being on a team. Another category would an opinion about something—usually political or social. Any one of them could be a great essay or weak.

When we refer to the "My Trip to France" essay, that's a category that means the writer thought going on a trip was enough to carry the essay. And of course, it's not. If you're able to go on a trip to somewhere, you ought to have good material to write about, and it should be specific to your experience, so talking about jitters in the airport and about your plane ride is not enough.

The sports injury essay usually doesn't work. It's too generic.

Sometimes it gets broadcast to applicants that tragedy is a good topic. So when applicants try to create a tragedy or write about tragedies that they are only marginally involved in—those are not good essays.

Any essay might be very strong if the individual allows the voice to come through. When we're reading essays we're trying to hear the voice. We're specifically hoping the writer is speaking to us about something that matters to them.

Bowdoin: Travel abroad, and for some reason there has been a run on grandparent illness or death.

Claremont McKenna: General autobiographical stuff, overcoming hardships, greatest accomplishments.

Middlebury: We see a fairly broad range; however, a few common themes include outdoor trips—NOLS or Outward Bound—recovery/growth after a season-ending athletic injury, lesson learned on service trips to South American countries and during international travel in general, and important family members or milestone family events—divorce, moving, illness, etc.

New College: We offer two essay prompts, and students are expected to respond to both.

1. Why are you interested in attending New College?

2. Identify, on one or two sentences, an issue of importance to you. Then advocate a policy or position in connection with this issue. Write as if you were advocating your position to someone in authority who might be able to carry out your recommendation.

For the first, the most common responses discuss our use of written evaluations rather than grades, our small average class size, and the great freedom we offer in course selection.

For the second, common themes are standardized testing—usually against—September 11, affirmative action, and environmental issues. These essays often reflect the hot topics of the day and current events.

Northwestern: We change the questions every year, partly for variety's sake, but also so we can use questions that ask for reflection. Bottom line: We're looking for an answer to the question with thought and analysis; most of our questions have that component to them. We actually post our essay questions on our website as of July 1 if students want to work on them early.

USCGA: The service academy is different, smaller. Everyone always talks about the ocean. We're looking for people who want to be a part of the institution; people who play sports, have a good technical background, and can illustrate those things in their essays.

A common theme: Half of the applicants use a sports theme, a varsity sport. "We won the state championship." We want them to show leadership and potential in the common essay.

We also see, "Oh, I love the ocean." Essays aren't that important. They make sure the students can write, but the essay won't make or break an application.

Wellesley: We use the Common Application; students have a choice so we see a wide variety of topics. We're looking for how well they write and for a command of the English language.

Williams: Many essays focus on a service-oriented spring break trip. Another common topic involves students rehashing the awards they've won or the titles they've held. A fair amount of essays are written about a book that might have influenced an applicant or about an important or influential relative. Most conspicuously, I ready many essays about athletic involvement or accomplishment. These topics are not necessarily dead-end routes to a good essay; it's just that they are fairly common topics and run the risk of being cliché if not carefully written.

Yale: The most common ones are probably [about] the things that students do the most in high school. Our essay topics are very open and we let them talk about things that are very meaningful. We're not one of those colleges that asks for offbeat topics and asks applicants to come up with a creative answer. We certainly get ones about important people, grandparents, family experiences, that sort of thing.

There are terrible essays on wonderful topics and wonderful essays on very ordinary topics. The topic itself does not make the essay.

What writing tips would you give to the majority of your applicant pool?

Bates: If a student has rushed through an application, it shows. It cannot be superficial. Often your first draft will be superficial; then you start over and go down another layer.

Give it time. You owe it to yourself to give it time. Do several drafts. Keep to a minimum the number of other people you let read it and edit it, because it gets polished away to nothing. You don't want it to be slick. Do not use words you do not normally use—it shows!

The essay is just one piece in the application and in the decision. I'm trying to take the hype off of the essays—the transcript is so much more important.

Bowdoin: Proofreading is wicked important.

Claremont McKenna: Please use your own "voice," especially when writing your personal statement. This should not be an exercise in packing in as many SAT-prep words as possible! Write about something that you care about, something that gives us a window into your perspective/experience.

Johns Hopkins: Get your pen and paper or saddle up to the word processor; the important thing to keep in mind is, don't write as if there is a correct answer. Don't be too cautious. It seems to me that we work hard to craft questions that prevent that, but we see students who are too cautious. Be adventurous intellectually—write unconventionally. Applicants have more freedom than they think, and it's in their interest to use that flexibility.

Macalester: Be yourself. Use your own voice. "Own" your essay rather than letting someone else tell you what to write. Address any questions the admissions committee may have about your application up front. Tell your "story," if you have one.

Middlebury: Most students should "write what they know," and not worry about being completely original in their subject matter. In most cases we care more about how a student writes about a topic than the topic itself.

New College: Once you've written your essays, *let them sit for a few days*. It's very tempting to hit the send button or drop them in the mail, but it's definitely a good idea not only to proofread for mechanical errors, but also to consider whether there is a real *point* to each essay. Are they well developed? Do the ideas flow logically? Our college writing consultant points out that she can teach someone how to use semicolons, but she can't teach them how to think.

We're looking for some sort of organized, well-reasoned argument, without typos or grammar errors—looking for the ability to reason and think clearly and make a reasoned argument on some topic. The greater the evidence of thoughtfulness, the better. The essay should show some level of sophistication, technical skill, and reasoning ability.

Northwestern: Answer the whole question. For example, we have a question that asks what an applicant would do with five minutes of airtime; what would you talk about and why? Kids don't answer the why part, they go on about the subject but there's no analysis, no reflection.

USCGA: Some will take a pencil and write something really quick and it's not thought out. When students takes the time, that helps.

Wellesley: Students should proofread their essays. There is no excuse, with word processing tools, for spelling and grammatical errors. Essays done at the last minute look that way. This is their moment to say something good or positive and sell themselves, not complain about their SAT scores.

Williams: Stress to them on the one hand to remember it's not an English paper. It should be written in a voice that is their own, which means it can have its own syntax and structure and need not be something they would turn in as a paper in school. I'd also advise that they use it as an opportunity to expand the admission officer's sense of who they are rather than reiterate what has been seen in the application already.

Yale: Just try and be as honest and open about themselves as they can be. We are trying as hard as we can to get a feeling for who this person is. The pieces of paper really do represent them pretty well. And students control a piece of that through their student essays.

WHO SHOULD EDIT THEIR ESSAY?

Amherst: Parents are awful, friends are awful, and people who advise kids for money are awful. The best person is a teacher.

Northwestern: If you're a kid whose mom might be an English teacher, ask her. Or ask your best friend or sibling. Always a good idea to have someone else read to see if your essay sounds like you.

Yale: These are essays that they need to write. Not their mother or their guidance counselor or a website. I think it's perfectly all right for a parent or friend to read the essay, but they shouldn't do it with a red pen in hand.

What do you hate to see—grammatically and content-wise?

Amherst: Cutesy stuff. I look for sincerity. The ability to think abstractly produces the best essays, frankly; balancing experience and talking vividly about an experience that transpired.

A not-funny kid trying to be funny. The heavy hand of some college consultant.

Bowdoin: When applicants write in the passive voice—don't know why—we'd rather not see that. Content-wise, impersonal stuff doesn't help your case; something more personal is preferable. Our questions are open-ended.

Claremont McKenna: I hate seeing essays written in overblown language—it's not impressive, it's fake. Good grammar, of course, is always a plus. Essays on the "current event du jour" are often pretty shallow and uninsightful. If you want to write on an event, try something closer to your community. You'll educate your audience, and the issue is probably something you feel more strongly about.

Johns Hopkins: There are two things that I see regularly, two "lines" that are crossed. (1) Ideological issues are best left aside. An applicant who gets too much into specific political issues just might be thrusting these views on someone who disagrees, and then [the reader] has to work at remaining objective. We train our staff to take students on their own terms, but we're all human. I don't see why an applicant would test the waters. (2) Sometimes students come across as immature. Showing a sense of humor is great, but don't use humor in your college application that you wouldn't use with your parents!

Macalester: Misspellings, poor grammar, and typographical errors really get in the way of reading an essay, so attention to detail is important.

Middlebury: Individual admissions officers would respond differently to this, but we all seem to agree that any essay focusing on a boyfriend or girlfriend, no matter how well written, is a very poor choice. The use of profanity, even for "effect" may be viewed as reflecting poor judgment. We don't expect perfection when it comes to grammar, but careless mistakes, especially misspelled words, suggest that students may not be putting much effort into their applications.

New College: Essays that were clearly written for other schools definitely strike a wrong chord—we try to be mature about it, but there you have it. Essays that were obviously written off the cuff are also irritating. We like to see a sense of perspective, so we don't want essays that are emotional but not reflective. Grammatically, students need to show a certain level of responsibility and effort. There's no real excuse for grammar errors, particularly with the spelling and grammar checks available to most students.

Northwestern: Swear words.

USCGA: Essays that are three lines long and poorly written. Almost don't like to see an essay that is too well written—that's written by parents.

Wellesley: Gratitude goes a long way and ingratitude falls flat. We're looking for maturity. Some students think that in order to stand out they need to shock us. We call it the Oprah effect. They shouldn't tell us everything. Overcoming adversity with grace is great, but sometimes telling of a horrific case leaves the committee hanging. Students should sift through their experiences and ask themselves whether the admissions committee needs to hear about this. We're looking for readiness to enter college and intellectual curiosity.

Williams: As far as content, I don't like to see a regurgitation of the activities chart on page three of the application. I do not like to see essays that are too self-congratulatory without revelation [or] essays that are basically academic papers, even if they are intelligently written. I like to see an essay that is well-written, interesting, and in some way surprising. A good essay will make me want to read it a second time.

Yale: Forced creativity or forced humor or sort of self-consciously trying to be different. By itself, is that going to keep somebody out? No. But it doesn't help their cause.

If a topic feels forced, they just need to put that pencil down. Students ask themselves, What does that college want to hear? And we keep telling kids that you're 180 degrees in the wrong direction if you're asking yourself that question. They do need to sit in the driver's seat and ask, What should this school know about me?

This is not the time to be particularly shy; on the other hand, you don't want to go at it with a great deal of braggadocio. You don't want to start every paragraph with the letter *I*. They should be asking themselves, What kind of essay is going to get them as close to what I'm like?

WHAT DO YOU LOVE TO SEE?

Amherst: Pure pleasure, genuine intellectuality.

Bowdoin: Things that are personal and simple. People try to get complex. Things that are meaningful come across that way as you read them.

Claremont McKenna: Students who take some calculated risks in their essays, and in doing so, really show their personality.

Johns Hopkins: We start at the beginning. The first sentence is read carefully, then the first paragraph is closely read, and then it's open-ended from there . . . if it's high quality, we'll examine everything. The very first sentence should accomplish a lot . . . the essays I remember do that—similar to a short story. Some students don't dive right in; they try to set up their case, crafting what turns out to be dry prose. They don't have time to do that.

Macalester: I enjoy reading direct, honest, concise writing.

Middlebury: Ideally, we love to see truly fine writing that reflects mature thought, a mastery of the language and mechanics, and a topic that reveals a great deal about the applicant simply because it tells a good story. Essays of that caliber are fairly rare, so we also enjoy pieces that possess the elements mentioned above but may not have them in equal share.

New College: We love to see a clear sense of engagement—that the student hasn't just fulfilled her or his obligation to submit an essay, but has really thought about it and obviously cares about the topic. We also get a big kick out of colorful metaphors—although these, in and of themselves, will probably not make the difference in an admission decision.

Northwestern: Writing with a natural voice. Don't be formal if you're not formal. If you're funny, be humorous. We're trying to get a sense of what you're like; stay with your natural voice.

USCGA: Someone who wants to be a coast guard officer and wants to be successful.

Wellesley: I'm a complete sucker for the grandparent essay, i.e., what I learned from them, what they taught me, what they taught my family. In my twenty-two years in admissions, I haven't read a bad grandparent essay. I like to hear about gratitude for someone in your life, such as a family member or favorite teacher.

Williams: A truly unique voice, a subtle and interesting revelation, a successful essay about failure.

WHAT BORES YOU?

Amherst: Students playing the college application process too safely . . . it's refreshing to see a kid being him- or herself—you don't have to climb Mount Kenya . . . as long as it's sincere.

Bowdoin: The rehash of the editorial, like nuclear disbandment. Trite conclusions. The travel abroad conclusion: "No matter where we are, we're all the same." The travelogue to Italy: "We went here and there."

Claremont McKenna: Not a fair question! If I'm bored, that's my problem; it should not affect the applicant.

Macalester: Indirect, misleading, meandering writing.

Middlebury: We always encourage students to write what they want us to know about them. The least compelling essays are those that seem to be written to impress an admissions office; they tend to lack authenticity.

New College: It's pretty dreary to read an essay on a "hot topic" that does little more than restate the obvious arguments.

Northwestern: The class trip to Europe. We don't tend to have repetitive stuff, since we change questions.

USCGA: Students often say the same thing. I ran three miles today. I love the ocean.

Wellesley: I don't want to see a laundry list of extracurricular activities—the information from the third page of the Common Application. It does not help to receive this list. Take one or two activities from this list and explain why they're important. Take that next step. Simply listing activities is not enough.

Williams: Essays that aren't very curious. Essays that rely too heavily on humor, particularly, puns and jokes I've heard before. Funny essays can be quite effective, but only if there's substance below the cleverness.

Yale: Superficiality. There are many students who, for whatever reason, do not go beyond the superficial. They'll tell us what they've been doing [and] keep it fact-based. But they don't get it to a reflective level.

WHAT MISTAKES DO YOU SEE SO OFTEN THAT THEY DON'T COUNT AS A STRIKE AGAINST AN APPLICANT?

Amherst: It does count against you. The hastily and poorly done essay is pretty close to irrevocable.

Bowdoin: The misspelling of the word *pursue* and the use of *that* instead of *who* when referring to a person.

Macalester: Mistakes are mistakes. When they're made, they're noticed.

Middlebury: If we catch them, I can't think of an instance where errors wouldn't be noticed, but that doesn't mean that they will eliminate a student from contention. Punctuation errors or "spellcheck" mistakes—using *form* instead of *from,* etc.—are frustratingly typical, but a few isolated instances in one application will not keep a student from the admit list. It is the cumulative effect of the application that gets noted. If there are so many careless mistakes that the application feels rushed, then those errors will influence the readers and the committee in a negative way.

New College: Essays that were clearly written for other schools—we really *do* try to be mature about it.

USCGA: One we do get a lot is when another institution's name is in our place. We see it more often with letters of recommendation from a teacher, but sometimes we do see an applicant make this mistake.

Wellesley: There is no answer to this; mistakes do count. You're applying to an institution of higher learning. We have professors reading the essay, so you should write your essay as if a professor is reading it.

Students think they need to use big words with more than four syllables. We have what we call the thesaurus essays, and sometimes they are so turgid we're left wondering, who is this person?

Know how to spell *perseverance* and *camaraderie*, if you're looking for specifics to this question.

Williams: One spelling error won't necessarily turn me against the essay's author, but essays obviously written and edited in haste do make me wonder about the applicant.

WHAT TOPICS ARE RISQUÉ?

Bowdoin: Humor is tough, sexual experiences are not a good idea. A fair number of applicants will elevate themselves by degrading their peers: "unlike my peer." You don't want to do that or trash a teacher.

Claremont McKenna: Depends on the reader. Students should write about whatever they think will give the admissions committee some kind of insight. I wouldn't want to squelch creativity!

Macalester: I really don't want to know about their sex lives.

New College: We try to avoid giving the student a formula for gaining our approval. The student should just choose a topic that she or he finds meaningful and interesting.

USCGA: It's subjective—we have three faculty members. One might think it's risqué; one might love it.

Wellesley: Don't tell us about your first kiss. Applicants should know this writing is aimed at adults, not their peers. It's a formal process. This essay can be more colloquial than another assigned paper, but it should not border on obscene.

An example: Some students will paraphrase a conversation they've had. One student did this and used profanity throughout. The result was distasteful and inappropriate for a college essay.

Williams: In general, I find students to be overly timid in their choice of essay topics. It is unappealing to see students flaunting risqué subject material strictly for shock value.

Yale: I think it's not so much the topic as it is the degree to which they deal with a topic; I don't think that there's any individual topic that can't be dealt with. I think some kids do take risks in essays. They don't always work, but I appreciate the courage to try. Don't waste 50 percent of your essay space with a poem; it's ultimately going to serve you a little better to write some prose.

WHAT EXPERIENCE WOULD YOU LIKE STUDENTS TO WRITE ABOUT MORE OFTEN?

Bowdoin: It doesn't have to be about victories where you overcome a difficulty or surmount an issue. Oftentimes, you can succeed in an essay without writing about winning [by] writing about failure.

Claremont McKenna: Things that genuinely matter to them . . . . I know there's pressure to sound "impressive," "worldly," "community-oriented," etc., but experiences about things that immediately impact students tend to evoke stronger and more interesting essays.

Johns Hopkins: Students assume we want to know about them personally—and we do—but we want the essay to be a window on their lives, their community, school, teachers, what their situations are. Students rarely reflect on their schools or neighborhoods, but more on family and friends. We want to learn about the context of the application. Where is the student coming from? We prefer the essay to talk about one's own situation; it helps us balance the traditional admissions measures—grades, scores, etc.—in the application.

Middlebury: This strikes me as a matter of personal taste, but some of the most effective essays I've read focus on place—a region where a student was raised or a summer home that has significance, etc. When done well, these essays are powerful indicators of a student's sense of self and his awareness of the influences that have shaped him. Having said that, these essays are enjoyable because they are rare. If everyone wrote about place then I'm sure it would seem overdone.

USCGA: A student who wanted to find out about the Coast Guard so he went to a base, or an applicant whose father was in the Coast Guard and that inspired the student.

Wellesley: I like hearing about anything that they're grateful for in preparation for college: a coach, a parent, a grandparent, an experience, travel, a job.

Williams: In general, the failures, the unresolved conflicts, the uncertainties in these young people's lives.

IS THERE ANYTHING ABOUT AN ESSAY THAT MAKES YOU UNABLE TO TURN THE APPLICANT DOWN?

Amherst: When it's real intellectually. One particular student had the combination of a great essay and a reading list, which overcame a good but not great record; in this case the essay might outweigh other factors—these are the 10 percent group.

Bowdoin: Keep it narrow, get readers' attention right away, and stay on task, on point.

Johns Hopkins: There are essays that are compelling, that make the difference. So students should know that essays should be taken seriously. If a student puts effort into essays, they should help his or her chances.

The remarkable thing about essays is that there's no ceiling on quality, unlike SAT scores or GPAs. A great essay can carry a student. A poorly done essay might do the opposite. It can certainly determine the initial path an application takes through the process.

Macalester: No.

Middlebury: No. The most compelling essay must be accompanied by the rest of the "package."

New College: Not that any of us can recall.

USCGA: I can only think of one—a student from England, and he was the best writer, an American. He had so many old literature references, had a 1500 SAT. But he ended up having a 2.5 or 2.0 his first semester here.

Wellesley: No. The meat is the transcript—the grades and test scores. The essay is important, but it is never the sole decision-maker.

What's the most ridiculous achievement you've ever seen listed on an app? Most ridiculous essay topic?

Bowdoin: Voted best in charades.

Was this student admitted?

I don't think so.

Claremont McKenna: A young woman wrote about how she collected her hair into a massive hairball.

Middlebury: Again, there is a myriad of answers to this question but when students list "awards" that have nothing to do with achievement, it does give the reader pause. The role of Prom King or Queen is a good example of a nonachievement that students might highlight. Ridiculous essays can include such topics as "How I'm like a salad—a mixture of lots of harmoniously blended ingredients."

New College: We don't think it's appropriate to answer this, but suffice to say that we came up with some pretty funny responses before coming to this conclusion. We're certainly not averse to humor in the application.

USCGA: One applicant telling one of her lifeguard experiences where she saved a life and she won a community award, and then at the end of the essay, she said she was just kidding. The first time I thought it was humorous, but she tried it again on the second essay. She wasn't accepted.

Williams: Surviving a plane crash.

A young lady's description of her home taxidermy business. Her subjects were collected from roadkill. She was accepted and is a pretty remarkable, well-rounded person.

What kind of essay book would you recommend for students? What would be most helpful for students in terms of preparation?

Amherst: Don't like them.

Bowdoin: Don't know of any.

Claremont McKenna: Not familiar with any specific books.

Johns Hopkins: I would give them examples of good writing. Just as a composer wouldn't deny borrowing themes from predecessors, it's appropriate to learn from the work of good writers. In terms of technique for writing a good college essay, I'd look at the short story as a model.

Macalester: I don't recommend essay books for students. The end result of reading any such book is that essays all start to sound alike—i.e., they're not the *only* people reading those books. Students' essays should be individual works of their own creation. What works for one person doesn't necessarily work for another.

Middlebury: Using a "how to" book could take away an essay's authenticity and personality. Rather than investing in an essay book, a good grammar reference or a guidebook that helps students avoid common grammar pitfalls could be of more use.

New College: We try to explain that our expectations may be different than those of their high school—we try to describe to the student what analysis means as opposed to expository writing. We try to encourage a more thoughtful, analytical approach to writing. This is conveyed through personal contact, and we also plan on printing this explanation in our application.

Northwestern: The best preparation for essays is writing in high school.

USCGA: Speak from the heart; [students should use] something they write, not something they pay someone to write.

Wellesley: There is a book by Sean Covey called *7 Habits of Highly Effective Teens*. Think about who you are and what refuels you as opposed to doing something for college or to get into college.

Sometime in June or July, write an essay. Go online and get the Common Application and try to write a 500-word essay. It's very hard. Don't read other essays. Put what you have written away. Take it out in the fall and reread it. Give yourself time to do the hard work.

What steps do you take to recognize or prevent plagiarism (such as special software)?

Amherst: No prevention; 90 percent of our files are just consistent.

Bates: We're aware of the essays being sold, and we're aware that students buy them, and once in a while we recognize that it's an essay from before. We assume that students are being honest. Bates encourages students to give us a copy of something else that they have written.

Bowdoin: We rely on experience and on judgment. There are also websites we've used.

Claremont McKenna: We ask students to sign something saying that the materials in their application represent their own work. If it comes to light that the essay or a recommendation has been plagiarized, the student would not be admitted.

Middlebury: We try to be very aware of essays that seem eerily familiar and share with the office information about "suspect" essays so we can do our best to monitor the applicant pool collectively.

New College: We do look for inconsistency of style between the writing samples, though at some point you just have to trust the student. We're pretty confident that cheating is rare; a student who is not already a good, solid writer is unlikely to want to join our program in the first place.

Northwestern: We're so specific in the questions we ask, and we change them every year, so we think plagiarism isn't really an issue. We ask our applicants to suggest questions for the following year's essays and those are used in upcoming years.

USCGA: No we don't—you can smell them out.

Wellesley: Avoid plagiarism at all costs. If we see a similar phrase or sentence we go to Yahoo! or Google and do a search. We might also call their high school and ask.

Williams: We don't have anything like that. Our presumption is that students' intentions are honorable—generally the quality of a student's writing is on par with other parts of the application. Rarely do I see writing that transcends the rest of the data given.

Yale: We do cruise those websites. We did find a copied essay this year and we removed that kid's application.

IF YOU HAD THE OPTION OF DOING AWAY WITH ESSAY REQUIREMENTS ALTOGETHER, WOULD YOU?

Amherst: No . . . the more measures you add to the way that you evaluate, the more predicted value you have.

Bowdoin: No, it's very important to the overall application.

Claremont McKenna: Absolutely not! The essays are the best part of the application!

Johns Hopkins: No, we care very much about writing ability. We assess writing directly, through essay submissions, and indirectly, through the SAT II: Writing.

Macalester: No, absolutely not. It's the one chance an applicant has to speak directly to every reader of his or her application. What good would it do to eliminate that?

Middlebury: At this time, no we would not. The essay is still the one opportunity in the admissions process for an admissions officer to hear directly from the student rather than read about her. It can be a very helpful tool in the process. We value the essays so highly that we require two for each applicant.

New College: No way!

Northwestern: Writing is important. We always want to have writing samples.

USCGA: No, it's one of the few ways we can measure writing. We don't require SAT IIs or a graded paper.

Wellesley: No.

Williams: Never. I think the essay is an utterly singular and absolutely invaluable aspect of the overall application picture. It is one of the application's few glimpses past the black-and-white academic forecast, the only chance for an applicant to present themselves in their own words.

DO YOU PREFER TO RECEIVE ONLINE OR PAPER APPLICATIONS?

Amherst: No preference.

Bowdoin: No preference.

Claremont McKenna: Doesn't matter.

Johns Hopkins: Easier to process online; however, no strong preference.

Macalester: Either is fine—no preference. As long as the handwriting is legible and we get the information we seek, there's nothing wrong with a paper application.

Middlebury: We accept both online and paper applications and do not have a preference. We download and print online applications so we can generate an application folder for each applicant.

New College: We have no preference, but it does seem that some of our online applications are not as carefully prepared. Too much like e-mail, maybe. We get about 15 percent of our applications online.

Northwestern: Whichever way students prefer.

USCGA: Paper. All essays are on paper.

Wellesley: It doesn't matter.

Williams: We accept both. Every year we receive a higher number online.

Yale: We probably do prefer to get applications online.

Do you or someone on your staff read every essay that comes to you?

Amherst: Yes, at least twice.

Bates: Yes, every essay is read several times.

Bowdoin: Yes.

Claremont McKenna: Yes.

Macalester: Yes—absolutely!

Middlebury: Every application sent to Middlebury is read, and that includes the essays.

New College: Absolutely.

Northwestern: Yes, more than once. Every application is read twice.

USCGA: At least three people will read every essay. I read every one.

Wellesley: Yes. We read every essay at least three times.

Williams: Yes.

Yale: We read all of every folder . . . every word of every essay.

On average, how many people on your staff review applications? How many essays do you or your staff each read personally? What is the load?

Amherst: Eleven thousand total essays [between] thirteen staff members. We read regionally—i.e. Iowa applicant is read by Iowa admissions officer. . . . A difference of opinion results in a third or fourth read.

Bates: Nine readers [for] 4,100 applications a year. An application will be read by a minimum of three different readers.

Bowdoin: Ten readers and six to eight part-time readers who are former educators or familiar with the college [read] 600 to 1,000 [applications].

Claremont McKenna: Eight [readers], 6,000 [applications]. We require two essays and receive approximately 3,000 apps per year. Each reader reads 800 to 1,000 applications.

Johns Hopkins: Eleven staff members. We read each essay twice. Last year we had a 9,000-student applicant pool.

Macalester: Eight staff members read applications. We require two essays from each applicant. I suppose I read about 2,500 essays during the review period, perhaps more if all committee discussion cases are included. Each application is read by a minimum of two or three readers; some are read by many more.

Middlebury: In a typical year, fourteen to sixteen staff members review applications. Our reading load shifts from year to year based on the number of applications we receive. Each application is read at least twice.

New College: Six—all admissions counselors review applications. [The amount read per person] varies from counselor to counselor—anywhere from about 100 to 340 essays, since each counselor has different responsibilities and "territory" size will vary.

Northwestern: Sixteen full-time and some part-time readers, 1,500 to 2,000 [total applications].

USCGA: Fifty readers volunteer; each read fifty essays. Ten admissions officers read 150 a piece—I do bulk. Every essay gets at least three reads, then they go to me.

Wellesley: We have ten staff members plus faculty and students who read. Every file is read two or three times, then we vote as a committee on each application.

Williams: Ten full time. The workload for an individual admission officer can range from 600 to about 1,000 applications, depending on their other responsibilities. Three adjunct readers; their workload can vary—about 300 applications.

Yale: Our office has about twenty staff members. Every application will be read minimally by one person. And most applications get a second reading. And then there are some that get another one. This year we got over 15,000 applications . . . so that's about 31,000 essays.

How much time do you dedicate to each app?

Amherst: Three to ten minutes on each essay.

Bates: First reading: twenty minutes; second reading: ten minutes; third reading: ten minutes; forty minutes minimum. But [it] could be much more.

Bowdoin: As long as it takes.

Claremont McKenna: Seven to forty-five minutes. It really depends.

Johns Hopkins: Essays can receive anything from one minute to fifteen minutes of attention.

Macalester: I average twenty to thirty minutes per file.

Middlebury: For "first-reads," we typically read twenty-four or twenty-five applications per day for sixteen to eighteen days. Each application requires two essays. Staff usually dedicates a minimum of twenty to twenty-five minutes to each application, but that is a conservative estimate. Most of us take our reading home at night.

New College: Each application gets about half an hour of review and discussion—more in some cases.

Northwestern: We spend ten to fifteen minutes on each, with a recommended length of 500 words.

Wellesley: Each reader devotes approximately fifteen minutes to every application.

Yale: Some of them take about an hour, some of them take six minutes. I'd say a seasoned admissions officer needs to be moving through three applications an hour. We want to use our reading time where it's really valuable. And if it's clear by one reading that this is not going to be someone who's strong enough to get in, then we don't want to waste the time.

How many apps go to committee?

Bates: The first reading is geographic. Any application might get called up by the committee. We probably discuss one-fifth to one-quarter of the applications in committee.

Bowdoin: All applications receive two reads and sometimes up to four.

Claremont McKenna: Approximately one-third of the pool.

Johns Hopkins: After the second read, it's done.

Macalester: Roughly 25 to 35 percent of our applicant pool.

Middlebury: All are reviewed by at least four staff members, most by six or more.

New College: Six hundred or so.

Northwestern: There's no committee. We have over 14,000 applications; the third reader makes the final decision.

USCGA: Eleven hundred to 1,200 go to committee. Five thousand students apply; about 2,500 submit essays, [and] only 1,200 are read. This [the number that are read] is determined by high school and standardized test scores.

Wellesley: Every application is voted on.

What sort of experience do you require of the people who review applications? Are there any particular qualities you look for?

Amherst: Full-time admissions officer.

Bates: Readers are the deans on the admissions staff.

Claremont McKenna: Attention to detail and an understanding of the college.

Middlebury: In general, we look for evidence of critical thinking, disciplined judgment, and articulate expression. All receive specific training.

Northwestern: Our part-time readers tend to be retired high school guidance counselors or doctoral students.

USCGA: Coast Guard officers who are affiliated with the institution and some civilian officers.

Williams: We look for people intimately familiar with the process, the institution, and the age group of applicants. One of our adjunct readers is a former head of school, another is a former college counselor, and another is a recent graduate of Williams.

Is anything on the application really "optional"?

Bates: Submitting scores is truly optional. Bates uses the Common Application [but has a] supplemental form for optional score reporting.

Bowdoin: No . . . .

Claremont McKenna: Yes, information regarding ethnicity and race and languages spoken. For us, SAT IIs are optional.

Macalester: Of course—all the stuff that's labeled "optional." For Macalester, that would include SAT II results, additional submissions—like an art portfolio—additional teacher or coach recommendations, and several questions on the application form.

Middlebury: The SAT I is not required in our process and does not fulfill our testing requirement.

New College: Disclosure of information on race/national origin, religious preference, family background, family finances, other schools under consideration. Interviewing is optional in the application process, although it's encouraged and recommended.

Northwestern: Interviews are not required; one teacher recommendation is enough but send a second teacher recommendation.

USCGA: We have an optional third essay, where students can elaborate on any part of the application.

Wellesley: Race, by law.

Williams: Our peer recommendation is completely optional. Our arts supplement is optional.

How much extra material should students send? How much is too much?

Bates: I always say, more is not better . . . but the applicant has to decide what is enough.

Bowdoin: Extra material ought to be something that adds to the overall application, something we haven't seen yet. It should give a different view of them, not emerge as a normal application. "The thicker the application, the thicker the applicant."

Claremont McKenna: They should not send extra material unless they really feel compelled to do so. There's an old saying, "The thicker the file, the thicker the student." Don't send recommendations from people who don't really know you.

Macalester: They should send only what will reasonably tell us their story. We welcome anything that will add a new dimension and help to inform us about the applicant's values, beliefs, experiences, talents, and aspirations. But they only need to tell us once . . . we don't admit students based on the gross weight of their application files.

Middlebury: Supplementary materials are helpful when they provide information that is otherwise unavailable in the application. Extra recommendations should be truly different from the required letters of reference; supplemental tapes should highlight a talent or time commitment that might be "undersold" by the limits of the application. Students should assess extra materials in terms of quality not quantity. Sometimes less is more.

New College: For writing, not more than one additional sample—or a couple if they're poems. Art portfolios—slides, etc.—are welcome. The primary emphasis of review will be on the required parts of the application, though.

Northwestern: Some will go overboard on the length of an essay. We're happy to receive extra material but not videos or CDs. We have six undergraduate schools, so students may send playbills for drama, editorial clips for the journalism school—but there is no need for extra essays.

USCGA: We get picture books and binders; they show persistence, and it doesn't hurt their chances.

Williams: Good documentation of what is important. I received one student's 1,000-page personal memoir, which was excessive.

Yale: We don't encourage students to send in other writing. But we'll read it.

Can an essay move an application from the "maybe" pile to the "accept" pile? From the "maybe" pile to the "reject" pile?

Bowdoin: Sometimes an essay can do it. A former colleague of mine said, "A great essay could heal the sick but couldn't raise the dead." However, we look at the combined weight of the application.

Claremont McKenna: An essay can swing a vote either way, but other factors in an application come into play as well.

Middlebury: In our process, a compelling essay can keep an applicant in contention, but if the rest of the application falls short, then a great essay will not be enough.

New College: Nothing formulaic here.

USCGA: Essay alone won't do it. We look for more personal contact, a visit to the institution, recommendations.

Williams: An essay alone will not get a student into Williams, no matter how exquisitely it is written. The essay is an important part of the gestalt that is each application. The academic foundation is essential for an application to be viable. Such extras as a strong essay, strong prose support from teachers and peers, and a powerful extracurricular profile are compelling reasons to take one applicant over another equally qualified applicant.

Do you have an overall mission statement that you follow when looking at essays and applications?

Bates: When we read, we are reading to admit. Now that will mean later, when we come into committee, we have temporarily admitted too many people. But our philosophy of reading is a hopeful one. We ultimately this year [2002] admitted 28 percent of our applicants.

Bowdoin: Not really. We look at content and structure. Pretty open after that.

Claremont McKenna: No.

Macalester: No.

Middlebury: Before reading season begins, our director reminds us to keep in mind the College's mission statement that contains specific language about the types of students

Middlebury seeks. There are also other official college publications that make reference to the quality of Middlebury's community and they serve as guide throughout the process as well.

New College: When we're faced with an essay that's iffy, real bottom line is whether the student will be able to write a thesis in the final year. The talent may be a bit raw, but is the potential there?

USCGA: We have an enrollment management formula. Overall we're looking for applicants looking to succeed at the academy.

Williams: I read applications with due humility. I try to keep an open mind and recognize that each application that crosses my desk represents another exceptional young person getting started. I try to bring my full focus and energy to each application even when I've already been reading for six hours and I'm tired.

IF YOU HAVE AN APPLICANT WITH LOWER NUMBERS BUT A GREAT ESSAY, WHAT DO YOU DO?

Bates: If a student hasn't done too well in school but writes a great essay, that student should give us other writing that backs up the essay. We expect a lot from the essay, but one of the reasons that we welcome other writing is all the hype surrounding the essay. Sometimes the essay is not the applicant's best writing because they might write what they believe we want.

Bowdoin: Confirm that [the] essay is not an anomaly. Go to their school and ask about their writing.

Claremont McKenna: It might give the student a slight bump up. Depends on the essays.

Macalester: We read the rest of the application and make a decision based on everything, not on individual parts.

Middlebury: If a student has scores below our averages but rank-in-class and GPA that suggest real academic talent, then a strong essay can be a help to the applicant. If all the academic indicators suggest that a student is not a strong candidate for Middlebury, then even a very strong essay will not result in an admit.

New College: If the student's application is borderline and the writing is excellent, we might well give them the benefit of the doubt and ask the student to interview or submit an extra quarter or semester of grades or other materials. If it is early in the cycle, we will set aside the application and counsel the student to do whatever it takes to present information that will allay our concerns regarding academic success at the college.

Northwestern: We'd have to look at everything. Grades are most important. It's rare that a good essay would overcome bad grades.

USCGA: Numbers are only a small part—and essays are only small part.

Williams: A weak academic record will prohibit an applicant from being admitted, no matter how strong their essay might be.

IF AN ESSAY IS PARTICULARLY BAD, BUT THE STUDENT'S GRADES ARE GREAT, WHAT THEN?

Bates: A student who is a very good student and has taken high-level English courses and has great recommendations as a writer—we have high expectations of that essay; the high numbers with the weak essay: the student has dropped the ball.

The essay itself would never make the decision. An essay can hurt an applicant—if it's rushed, or if it's a copy of something else, if they tried to edit another paper and fit it into the applicant slot, it doesn't work.

Bowdoin: Go back to school or the kid and ask, What should we know?

Claremont McKenna: It might bump the student down. If a student hasn't put time and effort into the essay, we wonder how serious he or she is about us.

Macalester: Then the student may not be admitted.

Middlebury: If an essay is notable for its weakness, then both readers are likely to comment on its shortcomings and factor that into their recommendation to the committee. There are some very bright students who earn great grades but who don't put the care and effort into their applications that we expect. Those applicants don't fare well in our process. Essays can also be an indication of the level of instruction at a particular school. Unfortunately, some students have not been well instructed in terms of grammar and punctuation; we do try to keep a student's educational background in mind.

New College: A badly written essay can certainly tip the scale the wrong way. If a student's application is otherwise strong, we might place the student on our wait list or hold status and ask for another essay. Since this is not done formulaically, it's also possible that we would deny the student outright.

Williams: We turn down many students with great grades and test scores if it seems they are unlikely to contribute to the overall college community. Williams is lucky to have far more qualified applicants than spots in the class.

We make our most difficult decisions among equally academically qualified applicants based on the other criteria in the application. The essay is certainly one of the factors considered, as is the strength and extent of that applicant's extracurricular or community involvement in high school. Scores and grades are most important. The essay won't bring them back. What the essay does is break ties. The most compelling will be admitted.

Yale: There's nothing so stellar about academic credentials that'll convince us to take him without looking at the rest. The transcript is certainly the single most important document. And the recommendations are very important.

You know, we admit students who write flat essays and we reject students who write great essays. At a place like Yale, there just aren't that many kids that are so powerful that we have to take them. At many other institutions, you might not have the privilege of turning down a really strong student based on the tone of an essay. Here, we can do it.

IF YOU DON'T AGREE WITH A STUDENT'S VOICE PHILOSOPHICALLY, IF YOU KNOW THAT YOU DON'T WANT A CERTAIN TYPE OF STUDENT ON CAMPUS, WHAT THEN?

Amherst: Can't do that . . . god awful, politically, you can't do it.

Bates: Writers shouldn't worry about whether we will agree with their point of view; that has nothing to do with it. If it's a good essay, my opinion of the topic does not enter into it *at all*.

Bowdoin: That's a hard one. It depends on what the student writes about or how offensive the content is. Colleges are places where freedom of speech and thought are fiercely and appropriately protected. But I can imagine a circumstance where someone's views are so outrageous or offensive that they shouldn't be part of a college community.

Claremont McKenna: Diversity is something that the college values. If a student argues his or her perspective logically and thoughtfully, that's great. I like the students who aren't in our "mainstream," but it's up to them to decide whether or not the college is right for them if they're admitted.

Macalester: Students generally aren't admitted or denied to colleges based on the opinions they hold unless those opinions are so extreme as to disrupt the campus community. We don't think of our applicants as being "certain types"—instead, they're individuals and we read their applications as such.

Middlebury: The only time a student's "voice" would raise concerns would be if it suggests a personality issue that might pose a threat to other students' well being. If such a concern arose, we would contact the school for further details and discern to what degree, if any, we were over-reading. A student's personal philosophy—his politics, etc.—should not be held against an applicant. To serve as a true marketplace of ideas a college community must be comprised of perspectives that are as varied as the individuals within that community.

New College: No formula here, either. If there's a concern for campus safety, we'll refer it to the dean of students for review.

USCGA: Well, I'm one of the few liberals here. Military academies tend to be right-wing organizations. Students should be open-minded.

Wellesley: Don't try to taunt the admissions people. We don't want outrageous stuff, and we don't want to be taunted or shocked. It is fine, however, if some readers have different political views from the applicant. It is not our job to judge, as long as students are describing their views well, backing up their ideas with examples. We just ask if they have written a good essay. Part of being in college is holding different beliefs.

Williams: A difference of view of topics is great, whether it's personal or political. However, obvious bigotry is a red flag.

Do YOU PREFER TO SEE STUDENTS DECLARE A MAJOR OR APPLY UNDECIDED?

Bates: Most people who apply here are very good students who are undecided about their major. And we kind of encourage that. Liberal arts and sciences colleges have courses that high school students haven't had yet. We'd rather that they make their decision about a major with more complete information.

Bowdoin: Don't really care, so kids shouldn't feel under pressure to have a clear idea of what they want to do academically when they apply.

Claremont McKenna: It really does not matter.

Macalester: It doesn't matter. We like both undecided and committed students on the Macalester campus.

Middlebury: Middlebury is a liberal arts institution. We don't require students to declare a major until the middle of sophomore year. Applicants who have a potential major in mind and indicate that on their application do not have an advantage over students who have yet to narrow down their areas of interest. There is no preference given in the admissions process to either category of student.

New College: No preference.

Wellesley: At Wellesley, students don't have to declare a major until the end of their sophomore year. "Undecided" is the largest major in our applicant pool.

Williams: No preference here. We do keep track of intended major for research purposes, but we find that the majority of students change their mind once they get here.

ARE THERE QUOTAS YOU LOOK TO FILL IN EACH PROGRAM?

(Bowdoin, Claremont McKenna, Macalester, Middlebury, New College, USCGA, Wellesley, and Williams all responded, "No." The other five schools did not respond.)

HOW DO YOU FEEL WHEN YOU SEE THAT A STUDENT WILL BE DEFERRING ADMISSION AFTER ACCEPTANCE?

Amherst: I think it's great, everyone should do it . . . get off the treadmill for a while and do it.

Bates: We ask that they write us a letter outlining their plans. Our experience is, if they have a *good* plan, whatever the plan contains, it's a *good* thing. We allow deferrals for one year. Some students know when they apply that they're going to defer. Others decide in April or May to defer. Fifteen to eighteen people a year defer out or come in.

Bowdoin: It's a great idea, really important for student to get off the train for a while.

Claremont McKenna: That's okay. I'd rather a student be up-front about it.

Johns Hopkins: It's good—it shows a person that thinks for himself. The usual direction of the river is: senior year, during the summer go to the beach, then go to college. We welcome students who defer, who have something else in mind.

Macalester: Deferrals are approved only if the admissions committee feels the student has a good plan for spending the year off in a worthwhile way. Students must write to request deferral after being admitted. When they're approved, I'm happy for them because I know their experience will be a good one.

Middlebury: If a student knows herself well enough to realize that she needs time after high school and before college matriculation, then that is not going to put her at a disadvantage in the process. Most of the time we don't tend to hear about a student's plans to defer until after she has been admitted.

New College: Disappointed, but certainly glad the interest is still there. The only real concern is that it's so easy for "defers" to lose track of the deadlines—for financial aid and scholarship consideration, submitting the housing deposit and so forth.

Northwestern: We have thirty to forty students a year defer admission. We're happy to say yes to that.

USCGA: We don't allow it—unless it's a medical case, broken leg, mono. If a student wants to go to China, fine.

Wellesley: Most students don't tell us they want to defer until after they're accepted. In April, I let them defer for any reason. It's the student's choice, even if they don't know what they're going to do. For your own peace of mind, you should do it after you're admitted just to know that it didn't play a role in the admissions decision. It's a very individual decision.

Williams: Absolutely fine. We usually have twenty students defer each year.

PART 3

THE APPLICANTS

ADAM BERLINSKY-SCHINE

In high school, Adam created and maintained many advanced websites, including some at no charge for nonprofit organizations. He won several school and regional awards for computer science.

Stats

SAT I: 1460 (660 Verbal, 800 Math)

SAT II: 700 Writing, 700 Chemistry, 800 Math IIC

High School GPA: 4.17 weighted

High School: Moses Brown School, Providence, RI

Hometown: Providence, RI

Gender: Male

Race/Ethnicity: Caucasian

Applied To

Cornell University

Please note: Adam did not disclose information about other applications.

Essay

Adam used the following essay in his application to Cornell.

Please write an entry from your own life journal that reports something in "exquisite honesty and accuracy."

Everyone passes that test.

Today was my long awaited driving test. I've driven the course several zillion times flawlessly in preparation for today. I was confident, but also nervous. I was already one of the last people in my class to have a driver's license; if I didn't pass today I'd have to wait another three months until I can take the test again. Worse, I'd have to be on hold at the Department of Motor Vehicles for an hour and a half like last time, when I had to reschedule my appointment because I'd be away at Cornell's summer program on the date I'd originally scheduled. But there was nothing to worry about. It would be an easy and painless ten minutes.

So there I was, sitting in the driver's seat banging my thumbs against the wheel and listening to Dad explain how the secret to success was to make sure my seatbelt was fastened *really* tightly. And red lights mean "stop."

"Sorry," was all I said, as I hit the curb leaving the parking lot where I had been awaiting the inspector. The inspector mumbled something incomprehensible, as I silently panicked. Does that mean I automatically fail? If he had said so, I would have heard it. Maybe he likes me, and is giving me a second chance. After all, he's not too scared to be in the car with me. Maybe...

All my fears were justified when we deviated from the course that I knew so well by turning back into the parking lot that starts and ends the test. Surely, he just wants me to start over and try that turn again. Fat chance. It was only then that the inspector confirmed that hitting a curb is an automatic failure, and that I had failed my driving test.

I couldn't believe it. That was the first test I'd ever failed. All I had to do was drive for ten minutes without screwing up. And I couldn't do it.

Cheerfully reentering the car, Dad was clearly relieved that he wouldn't have to share the road with me for a good three more months. The whole way home I internally yelled at myself for my failure. How could I have hit the curb on the corner that I had successfully completed so many times previously, without *ever* hitting it?

When Laura, the little brat, found out, she commenced running around the room banging into walls to demonstrate precisely how I must have crashed. I can't believe I gave her this ammunition she could use to taunt me. And so I will have to wait another three months and listen to the recording at the Department of Motor Vehicles tell me that my call is important to them and that I should please stay on the line....

See page 304 to find out where this student got in.

ALISON KAUFMANN

Alison was a National Merit Finalist and was inducted into the Cum Laude Society her junior year of high school. She spent part of the summer before her senior year in Croatia working at a camp for children who had been through the wars in the Balkans.

Stats

SAT I: 1590 (800 Verbal, 790 Math)
SAT II: 680 Chemistry, 800 French
High School GPA: 4.0
High School: Marin Academy, San Rafael, CA
Hometown: Berkeley, CA
Gender: Female
Race/Ethnicity: White

Applied To

Amherst College
Brown University
Stanford University
Swarthmore College
Wellesley College
Wesleyan University
Yale University

Essay

The following essay was submitted to each of the seven schools Alison applied to.

Evaluate a significant experience, achievement, risk you have taken, or ethical dilemma you have faced and its impact on you.

Global Children's Organization runs a camp on an island in the Adriatic for children who lived through the Bosnian civil war. Last summer I went to Croatia to be a volunteer counselor there.

The two weeks of camp were over and I was bumping along in a bus full of children en route to Sarajevo when the first glimpses of the horror that had taken place in Bosnia finally began to make the situation real. Until then, I had sympathized with a vague, history-book tragedy. Now I tried desperately to memorize the scratches on the window rather than think of my friends who lived here. I could almost smell burning. The houses crouched with mottled walls, lone chimneys stabbing skyward. This was not, could not be, someone's home.

We drove along the Sarajevo hillsides where the snipers had been and then down through the town. I kept my face toward the window as my friend Fedja pointed out the site of the first massacre, and the second, and the achingly empty hulls of brick and cement where people had once lived. Where were they now? Did they still live? Had they managed to leave or were they, like so many others who walked these streets, trapped in their city as the bombs exploded and the shells rained down?

Fedja's cousin keeps a piece of a bomb in a glass-doored cabinet, the way someone might store a china vase. It was from the time a shell fell into the dining room. When the air cleared, Fedja found his chair studded with scraps of twisted metal where he had been seated only a moment before. I would not touch the piece when they held it toward me. I did not want to touch this death, this confirmation of the horror I would have to acknowledge if I held it in my hand.

I lay in my bed that night in the reconstructed building that had been Fedja's grandmother's home, and I thought of screaming and fear and laughter and silence. I tried to remember to breathe.

At camp I had played with the children, helped them learn to swim, twirled them upside down and sat with them looking toward the sea. I had changed from an outsider who could not understand what was being said to a friend who often found no need for words. I had grown to love the feeling of being needed. I was fed by it, fed by the sense that I was making a difference and fed by the exultation that came from constantly stretching myself.

Now, in Sarajevo, I struggled to accept what had happened to this hill-cupped town. Each conversation brought another wave of denial; each added another layer to what I felt when I heard the phrase "three years under siege." As I listened to the stories, I also realized the significance of what our camp worked to achieve. It gave the children a second chance at a stolen childhood, and it gave me the opportunity to help give this gift. After seeing Sarajevo, there is nothing I would rather give.

At camp and in Sarajevo I was completely independent for the first time. I had come because I wanted to come; I wanted to feel that independence and I wanted to see a change I was helping create. I had raised the money myself. I was there without parents and without anyone I knew. The opportunities to challenge myself were everywhere — in leading activities, in forming friendships with people who knew only three words of English, in conveying to little Nino that he *still* could not swim beyond the rope . . . even though it *had* been three minutes since he last tried. I felt myself bloom in that environment, and no one else's impressions of what was possible or impossible for me could affect that.

I came back to Berkeley with photographs and memories. I have a picture from camp of 11-year-old Amra holding my guitar and pretending to play. I have memories of my three oldest boys presenting me with a seashell they found near the pier, of playing soccer in the hallways, and of singing my kids to sleep. I have the hope and the conviction that I will go back next year.

I also brought back a new level of confidence: a place within me that I have slowly been creating throughout my life and that has finally taken root. I can stand on it now, even jump, perhaps, and stretch my arms to the sky. Each day I am catching more glimpses of what I might reach.

See page 304 to find out where this student got in.

AMANDA JORDAN

Amanda was a two-year volleyball letterman and a three-year track letterman. She was active in the Fellowship of Christian Athletes, Honor Society, and the National Charity League, and was the Senior Class Vice President and Junior Class Secretary.

Stats

SAT I: 1190 (540 Verbal, 650 Math)

High School GPA: 4.68

High School: Humble High School, Humble, TX

Hometown: Humble, TX

Gender: Female

Race/Ethnicity: Caucasian

Applied To

Louisiana State University

Tulane University

United States Air Force Academy

United States Naval Academy

University of Mississippi

University of Texas—Austin

Essay

Amanda used the following essay in her application to the United States Naval Academy, and modified it for the United States Air Force Academy.

In a well-organized essay of 300 to 500 words, please discuss the following: (1) Describe what led to your initial interest in the naval service and how the Naval Academy will help you achieve your long range goals, and (2) Describe a personal experience you have had which you feel has contributed to your own character development and integrity.

Ironically, my initial interest in the naval services was sparked when my brother graduated from West Point. Although I have always been interested in a military career, I realized then that the Army would not provide the best opportunities for me because it prohibits women from serving in its most essential branches. Next, I learned that the naval services allow females to do almost everything! I believe that attending the Naval Academy will best prepare me to achieve my long-range goal of serving America as a military officer. Not only will the Naval Academy train me to accept the challenges that I will certainly face during the next millennium, but also it will help me to accept the responsibilities of leadership.

I feel that my recent experience on the varsity volleyball squad has positively contributed to my character development, and has also proven my integrity. I am proud of my persistence and my ability to remain focused on my goals in spite of personal disappointment I felt during the following ordeal.

I was looking forward to my senior year on the team. I had worked over the summer to improve my skills because I intended to be a key player when the season started. But we got a new coach, and to my dismay, all of the returning varsity players were benched—including me!

Three other former starters quit when the coach informed us that, in his opinion, we were "past history." Seniors would hold down the bench, he explained, because he was going to develop the sophomores and juniors into next year's championship team. I remained on the team anyway, continuing to practice and hoping that the coach would observe my skills land then allow me to play. But I stayed on the bench. After spending several games on the sidelines, I finally confronted him. He agreed to grant me playing time. From that point on, I was a starter and I proved myself to be a real asset to our team.

Truthfully, it would have been easier to quit than it was to sit out while my younger teammates played. But my determination to remain on the team kept me going even though

I felt that the coach had made an unfair decision. I forced myself to work with him, and in the end all of us benefited.

I am convinced that surviving this tough lesson in character development has made me a stronger individual. I did not quit, nor did I seek the easy way out. Instead, I worked my way through the disappointment and embarrassment I felt, and beyond the unfair treatment. Most important, my integrity remains untarnished——I never compromised my principles!

See page 304 to find out where this student got in.

ANDREA SALAS

In high school, Andrea played varsity tennis for four years as team captain, was involved in student government, worked on the yearbook staff, and was a "peer-educator" for the AIDS awareness club.

Stats

SAT I: 1390

SAT II: 730 Chemistry, 730 Math IIC, 760 Writing

High School GPA: 3.8

High School: Santa Monica High School, Santa Monica, CA

Hometown: Santa Monica, CA

Gender: Female

Race/Ethnicity: White and Hispanic

Applied To

Amherst College

Bates College

Bowdoin College

Dartmouth College

Tufts University

University of California—Berkeley

University of California—Los Angeles

University of California—San Diego

University of California—Santa Barbara

University of California—Santa Cruz

Williams College

Essay

Andrea used the following essay in each application listed above. She combined the following two questions from the common application:

Evaluate a significant experience, achievement, risk you have taken, or ethical dilemma you have faced and its impact on you.

Indicate a person who has had a significant influence on you, and describe that influence.

Dear Poppy,

I realize that this letter will not actually be sent to you at Walkley Hill road in Haddam, Connecticut. In fact, it will be sent to the Admissions Office at Dartmouth College. I also know that it has been over two weeks since I received your last letter, and I apologize for not responding sooner. I always have some school-related excuse as to why it has taken me so long to reply, but the truth is, lately it has been hard to write back immediately to my dear grandfather's letters when so much else is pulling my attention away. But once I sit down with pen and paper, I know that thirty minutes later, when I seal the envelope and place it in the mailbox, I will once again be uplifted by feelings of accomplishment and renewed connection to you.

I remember that first letter I sent you ten years ago, thanking you for Christmas money and asking you to "please write back to me, and then I will write back to you, and we can keep a corespondance that way" (that was how I spelled "correspondence" at age six). Those early letters now seem so banal, inevitably beginning with "Dear Poppy, how are you? I am fine." But after a few years, they progressed to "Dear Poppy, I read the most amazing book, *The Count of Monte Cristo*. Have you read it?" I must admit to having told you many commonplace things about myself—my school schedule, the books I am reading, how my sister is doing. But I have also shared with you my most uncommon moments, special moments that seemed removed from time, when I poured out my feelings without concern for what my peers and parents would think. You became the one person with whom I could share feelings back and forth, discussing life's issues, without fear of censure.

When I write to you, I imagine you at your desk reading every word meticulously. Behind you hangs your chalkboard with those Calculus equations that always puzzled me as a child. Now I know that when I next see those equations, I will really understand them! On your desk, a photograph of me, cradled in your arms. When I write to you, I visualize these things and more. Writing to you opens up worlds past and present, yours and mine.

Once I wrote you a letter on a brown paper bag with ripped edges and pretended that I was ship-wrecked, the letter being my only communication with the outside world. In reality, it was only my communication outside my bedroom. There were also the letters written without lifting pen from paper, like the one I wrote when Grandma died. I never worried that I, an adolescent, was trying to console my far wiser grandfather about loss and death. This past August you showed me the folder where you kept all my letters. There at a glance was the Winnie-the-Pooh stationary, the crisp Florentine printed paper, the card of my favorite Alma-Tadema painting at the Getty Museum: the surfaces on which I showed you myself and the depth of my feeling. And all of the letters are addressed to you, Dear Poppy, and signed Love, Andrea, but each is from a different writer at a different moment in her life. Ever changing, yet with you always.

Love,
Andrea

See page 305 to find out where this student got in.

ANDREW COLLINS

Andrew's two most important extracurricular pursuits were his work as editor of The Exonian, *a weekly school newspaper, and piano and composition, for which he was selected to give a major public recital at the end of his senior year. Andrew was a two-year letterman in track, twice served as the sports director of WPEA campus radio, and founded an adjunct student government committee his junior year, which was a forum for student interaction with Student Council representatives. In his junior year, Andrew also won the Sherman W. Hoar award for excellence in American history and the Turner Exonian Award for writing and reporting for the newspaper.*

Stats

SAT I: 1540 (800 Verbal, 740 Math)

SAT II: 800 Writing, 790 Literature, 720 Math IIC, 690 French, 650 Chemistry, 620 Physics

High School GPA: 3.42

High School: Philips Exeter Academy, Exeter, NH

Hometown: Little Rock, AR

Gender: Male

Race/Ethnicity: Caucasian

Applied To

Duke University

Georgetown University

Harvard College

Princeton University

Stanford University

University of California—Berkeley

University of Virginia

Vanderbilt University

Essay

Common Application Question # 1, sent to Harvard, Vanderbilt, and Duke.

Evaluate a significant experience, achievement, or risk that you have taken and its impact on you.

"You'll have a great time. These elderly folks, they're so appreciative when students take the time to perform for them—and they love the music."

Over half of the audience had fallen asleep. Drowsiness had enveloped the remaining residents, who looked bleary-eyed and disoriented in their wheelchairs. One man succumbed to a grotesque yawn, and the sight of his spit-soaked, mangled gums caused me to wince. I had volunteered to play piano at Riverwoods Nursing Home along with some of my classmates, and was next in line to perform. Thinking that this audience would cheerfully applaud anything, I had elected to perform one of my original compositions. The song wasn't perfect, but I figured that an audience full of kindly old grandmothers would offer unqualified praise and perhaps a cookie or two, not criticism. Instead, dozens of eyes were staring right at me through sagging frames of flesh. I sat upright in the hard plastic chair, muscles taut, in a state of total discomfort. Someone in the audience passed gas.

When it was my turn to play, I walked over to the piano and addressed the crowd, as is customary. I said the name of my piece, and then I was interrupted—"Talk louder, boy!"— by a fierce gentleman in the front row. I apologized and tried again, but my efforts were met with jeers from the audience.

"He's just whispering!" one woman shouted with glee. Her friend nodded and whooped in approval, between coughs. No more slumber for these folks—the scene had turned rowdy, and I was stuck in the middle!

Desperate and rattled, I felt I had no choice but to shout at my maximum volume. "MY NAME IS ANDREW COLLINS," I bellowed, "AND I WILL BE PLAYING 'HIGHER GROUND!'" The audience then launched into an in-depth discussion about the origin of my name. One woman said that "Andrew" means "strong" in Hebrew, while another made the absurd claim that it means "falcon" in English. Not waiting to hear how this argument would conclude, I sat down at the piano and tried to play over their cacophonous debate.

It was even worse during the actual performance of the piece. People who heard the song in private usually complimented me heartily, and they encouraged me to play my original music in a performance setting. This crowd, however, was not impressed with the "fancy rock-and-roll" style of my composition. One woman said, loudly enough for me to hear, "I wish he'd play 'Danny Boy.'" Others drifted in and out of sleep as I continued my performance.

At one point, a skinny, pale man in the back of the room punched at the air and yelled, "Shut up!" He engaged in a brief skirmish with a member the nursing home staff, who escorted him out of the room. Finally, I finished my song and walked back to my seat, mentally and physically exhausted.

"Tough crowd," I whispered to one of my fellow performers. The rec room was in total disarray; some people were yelling and many were demanding to be wheeled back to their living quarters. It was hot and the nursing home staff seemed unable to maintain order in the frenetic atmosphere. Sweat was dripping down my face. The next week, and for many weeks afterward, I came back to play at Riverwoods.

See page 305 to find out where this student got in.

ANDREW P. SCHRAG

Andrew grew up in an American household and attended an international school in Tokyo, Japan, before going to boarding school in Connecticut. In high school he was one of four seniors selected by his teachers to be a student representative on the Academic Committee, a committee where teachers, faculty, and the four student representatives review the academic records of other students.

Stats

SAT I: 1330 (610 Verbal, 720 Math)
SAT II: 680 Math IC, 580 Writing, 710 Japanese
High School GPA: ~5.0/6.0
High School: Kent School (college-prep boarding school), Kent, CT
Hometown: San Diego, CA
Gender: Male
Race/Ethnicity: Half Asian (Vietnamese), Half White (German, Italian)

Applied To

Boston University
Brown University
Cornell University
Georgetown University
Lafayette College
Tufts University
University of California—San Diego
University of Southern California

Essay

Andrew used the following essay in each of the above listed applications. (This was the Tufts version.) The essay prompt was to write on a topic of your choice.

Where Do You Want To Go Today?

My Philippine-made *Indiglo Expedition* Timex watch read 2:24 a.m. As I sat at my desk, I looked around my room for the ninety-ninth time in hopes of spotting an object that would spark my imagination to write the essay of my life. On the wall I saw my poster showing Chris Mullin of the Golden State Warriors shooting a jump shot. Although a lefty, Mullin had the perfect shooting form: he had balance, his eyes were on the basket, his elbow was aligned, and he had the finest follow through any basketball player could have—but he did not have anything significant to say regarding my essay. I then looked at the Roswell-Alien poster hanging to the left of Chris Mullin; the alien was gazing straight at me and all I could think about was him slowly mouthing in a deep and evil voice, "We're already here . . .We're everywhere. . ." My eyes then scanned over to Kathy Ireland. She was wearing a skimpy bikini with intricate flower designs on it. Wow. Beautiful. Maybe she has some advice for me. But sure enough she didn't, and only kept on smiling in that oh-so-attractive way.

I was tired and my eyes were dry: they had circled the room for the one-hundredth time, and still, there was nothing. Finally, when almost all hope was lost, my screensaver initiated and the words, "Where do you want to go today? Microsoft . . ." scrolled across the screen in a rainbow of colors. It kept on repeating, "Where do you want to go today? Microsoft . . .Where do you want to go today? Microsoft . . ." While watching these words enter on the right side of my monitor and disappear on the left, my desk lamp suddenly flickered and died out. A gust of air blew through the window and scattered my math homework on the floor. My drawers began shaking. My computer screen clicked on and off. Then, I saw it.

Chris Mullin with his basketball, the Roswell Alien (only his face), and Kathy Ireland in her skimpy bikini were all on my computer screen arguing about something. "Have I gone insane?" I thought. I shook my head and rubbed my eyes, but their voices just kept on getting clearer and clearer.

"No, no, no, that's wrong, he's from Japan!" argued Chris, in a deep and robust voice. "Listen, except for the first six months of his life, he has been living in Japan. He grew up in Japan, learned Japanese, played with Japanese friends, ate Japanese food, celebrated the Japanese holidays, and even climbed Mt. Fuji twice! Trust me, if he thinks like a Japanese person, than he *is* from Japan."

"Japanese, Shmapanese! I completely disagree," squeaked Kathy in her sexy and feminine voice. "I believe Andy is American. He is an American citizen, born in Florida, and raised in an American household. His dad is from Waterloo, Iowa, his first language is English, and he has been to every state except for Alaska. Furthermore, his favorite place to eat at is McDonalds! If that is not American, what is?"

The alien spoke next. Without any expression or movement, he said, "Andy is from Vietnam. What are you humans thinking? His mom is Vietnamese, he has been to Vietnam numerous times, and he even understands the language. His favorite home-cooked meal is Pho (noodle soup) and he is conscious of Vietnamese traditions and holidays. He even told me in his former life form that he wanted to marry a Vietnamese girl. Chief-Alien Rosmickbub also believes Andy is Vietnamese."

As they continued to argue, I whispered to myself, "They are all wrong." Suddenly, everybody fell silent, the arguing stopped, and all three characters on the monitor looked at me in shock. "What was that?" they all blurted back, their voices sounding like an unpracticed acappella group. I was surprised that they heard me, but even more so by my consideration of actually responding to a bunch of animated characters. Nevertheless, I carried on. "I said that all three of you are wrong. I am not from one distinct place or another. I am from all three places—Japan, America, and Vietnam. I can think like a Japanese person, I can think like an American person, and I can think like a Vietnamese person. You could say that I am tri-cultural."

Silence.

Chris, the Roswell Alien, and Kathy all looked at me with facial expressions that displayed amazement, distress, even annoyance. Finally, a response: "How can that be?" said Chris. "No way!" yelped Kathy. "That's simply impossible." uttered the Alien. "That's the way it is, guys. I'm sure you understand."

Thirty seconds passed where they all kept quiet and appeared to be in deep thought. Suddenly, they all blurted out together, "We know *exactly* where you should go to college! Someone with your background should definitely consider going to tuph-unnivs ..." As they said this, my monitor began to flash and fizzle like a television channel with flaky reception. I could barely make out the figures of the characters, let alone their voices. "I should go where? I should go where?" I frantically whispered back, "Please, tell me. I should go where?" I squinted my eyes, searching for any shape or form, or at least some kind of outline of one of them, but my attempts were futile. They were gone.

The screen clicked off and on, and as the monitor became into focus, I saw once again the scrolling marquee, "Where do you want to go today? Microsoft . . . Where do you want to go today? Microsoft . . ." move from right to left across the screen. I looked around my room and saw no disturbance: my window was shut, my math homework was stacked nicely on my desk, the lamp was on, and the posters were still there—still the same. Nothing seemed to have happened.

Peculiar. "Where *do* you want to go today?" I asked myself. Not Microsoft. <u>I want to go to Tufts University.</u>

See page 306 to find out where this student got in.

ANNA HENDERSON

In high school, Anna participated in a variety of sports, including field hockey, basketball, track, and most seriously, rowing. She was also substantially involved in her youth group as a student leader.

Stats

SAT I: 1510 (740 Verbal, 770 Math)

SAT II: 740 Biology, 680 Chemistry, 660 Physics, 760 Writing, 760 Math IIC

High School GPA: ~4.1

High School: John Burroughs High School, Ladue (St. Louis), MO

Hometown: St. Louis, MO

Gender: Female

Race/Ethnicity: Caucasian

Applied To

Carleton College (applied early decision)

Essay

The essay prompt was something like *"What would you say was the most significant moment of your life?"*

I have witnessed a miracle, I think, as the first stream of tears carves a path in the smile lines of my beaming face. Not fifty feet in front of me, my dear friend Andy stands with his head lifted to heaven, acknowledging Jesus Christ as his Savior for the first time. He is beaming, confidently looking towards God's kingdom with a self-assurance I have never before witnessed in him. I realize that I have been exclaiming 'Thank You' over and over in an unconscious prayer to our King - mine and, for the first time, Andy's.

Drawn by the circle of joy surrounding Andy, I stumble over chairs haphazardly pushed aside as others rush to their own friends, and mumble garbled apologies to bruised toes and interrupted reunions. Running now, adrenaline saturates my blood as I come closer to Andy, anxious to see Christ's love pour out of his newborn eyes. Just a few steps from my goal, a trembling hand grabs me with the same intensity I feel, and my nose slams with ecstatic awkwardness into the collarbone of Andy's best friend, Dan.

'I can't believe he did it!' I manage to squeak into Dan's shoulder before my amazed happiness sweeps over me again in a burst of fervent sobs.

Dan gently releases me, his wet face beaming under a mixture of both of our tears. He pushes me encouragingly towards Andy, who stands with his back to me as he receives high-fives and excited squeezes in abundance. Before I reach him, unwarranted worries mar my thoughts. 'Suppose he doesn't mean to share this moment with me? Suppose now that he's a Christian, he doesn't feel attracted to my own fire for Christ because he has the same light in himself? Perhaps since I have been praying for this day for such a long time I have romanticized the whole event and my role in it. Maybe I should step back and let him come to me.' I hesitate, but when he turns around and sees me standing in my happy awkwardness, he opens his arms and I leap into them with a release of joy that nearly topples us into an unsuspecting group behind us. All barriers and feelings of inadequacy at being witness to such pure joy vanish as he includes me in his celebration.

Andy represents the embodiment of all the joy of that night as one of my best friends whom I have watched grow with Christ. Our friendship over the course of the past year has grown from one of playful teasing to one of mutual respect and love as we both grow in our relationship with Christ. His intensely dramatic acceptance of Christ, with one of my favorite praise songs playing in the background and 300 teenagers crying and laughing together in complete abandon, put my emotions in overload. Andy and I make slow progress out of the meeting room that night. I keep him locked in a perpetual hug while he cautiously attempts to avoid my clumsy feet.

Every so often, I pull away from him to study the new peace I now see on his face with giggling fascination. Embarrassed and pleased by all the attention, Andy shakes his head at me and laughs, patiently pulling me back into our four legged odyssey.

As I resume my previous position attached to Andy's hip, I recognize the familiar swing of my cross against my chest. I realize with a fresh surge of tears of the unbreakable bond under which Andy and I have become connected that night. As his best friend Dan later put it, no matter what distance separates us in the coming years, I know that we'll see each other again - in heaven.

See page 306 to find out where this student got in.

ANONYMOUS

At her high school, the applicant was principal violist, sang in an a cappella group, was involved in various Jewish organizations, and was one of the founders of the Women's History Month committee. She won many awards for her poetry and has had writing published in a local weekly newspaper. She hopes to join AmeriCorps.

Stats

SAT I: 1400
SAT II: 770 English, 730 U.S. History, 640 Math IC
High School GPA: 3.9 weighted
High School: Charlottesville High School, Charlottesville, VA
Hometown: Charlottesville, VA
Gender: Female
Race/Ethnicity: White

Applied To

Wesleyan University (applied early decision)

Essay

Common Application Question 5: *Topic of your choice.*

As Soon As I Wake Up

My pillow has blue stars on it. It is the inverse of night; it is a negative of the night time sky. I like to think that when I sleep the stars seep in through my ears and give me sweet blue star dreams; sadly though, I seldom remember them. Every single morning, the first thing I do is try to remember my dreams, and whether they have blue stars or not. Every morning, every single time, they dissipate as I open my eyes. Before I can pin them down long enough to get a glimpse at my subconscious, my dreams are gone. They are fleeting like the dark. Usually I lie in bed, still as death, and argue with my alarm clock about whether morning has broken.

Even more than school, the monster underneath my bed, or the bigger one in my closet, I dread my cold floor. Last year my friend Sarah bought me a pair of yellow chicken slippers to protect my feet from this daily torture. I like them a lot. When I wear baggy pajama pants, the chickens' beak and half of each black eye peer out from under the cloth. The problem is, I need a jolt to wake me up in the morning, and wearing those slippers reminds me of what my mom says when she drinks de-caf: "it just don't cut it." Even though my floor is wooden and very cold, it wakes me up like nothing else. Stepping on my floor is like pulling a Band-Aid off all at once, rather than one painful hair at a time.

This is the point of no return; I've found that last desperate attempts to go back to sleep are futile. But I don't care — I like mornings. I am always greeted by the warm smile of Katie Couric, the bold headlines of The Washington Post, and the hug of my frazzled mom as she juggles coffee and books while rushing out the door. This leaves me sitting in my empty house with chilled orange juice surrounded by sections of news. My mornings are definitely lonely now. After I've devoured the Post I stare at the fruit bowl on the counter next to the compost tub and try to decide whether a nectarine is more like a peach or a plum. When I was little however, mornings were much more riveting.

I think I remember waking up to my mother singing "You are my sunshine", or "Good morning to you, good morning to you," though this memory could easily be fabricated — those rose-tinted glasses playing a trick on me. However, I definitely remember reading in the morning as a kid. I have a picture etched in my memory of sheets of hearts and how I leaned on them that one morning when I read Ramona the Great. Towards the end of the book, Ramona sits in her cellar taking one bite out of each apple, and claims "the first bite is always the best." I remember feeling the same way, wishing that every part of the day could be a morning. The sun would rise continuously, I would perpetually forget my dreams, and from drinking all of that orange juice I would practically live in the bathroom. However, I would settle for having mornings just once a week if they were as magical and dewy as mornings when I was a little kid. Then I was able to enjoy the pause, while now I have to prepare for the events of my typical day.

There really is no typical day, however, though I do have a customary routine. Each day is as individual as the people who inhabit it. And though I never remember my dreams, when I look up at the sun urging me to follow its example and rise, and look down at Sarah's unused yellow slippers, I'm excited by the idea that new events will unfold about which I will dream unremembered dreams, filled in with the bluest of stars.

See page 307 to find out where this student got in.

ANYA MANES

Anya earned the National Merit Scholarship Letter of Commendation. She participated in theater classes and projects and worked with children as a counselor and teacher's assistant throughout her four years of high school. She was active in the Recycling Club, Community Service, Gay/Lesbian Awareness group, and Student Council.

Stats

SAT I: October '96: 1330 (670 Verbal, 660 Math); March '96: 1290 (610 Verbal, 680 Math)

SAT II: 670 Writing, 720 Physics, 690 Chemistry, 670 Math I, 600 Math IIC, 590 American History

High School GPA: 3.14

High School: The Head-Royce School, Oakland, CA

Hometown: Oakland, CA

Gender: Female

Race/Ethnicity: Caucasian

Applied To

Barnard College

Boston University

Claremont McKenna College

Columbia University

Duke University

New York University

University of California—Santa Barbara (College of
    Creative Studies)

Vassar College

Essay

Anya used the following essay in her applications to Barnard, UC-SB's College of Creative Studies, and Duke.

The members of the Committee on Admissions seek to gain an understanding of you as a person. This essay is your opportunity to discuss an idea that matters to you, to write about a person who has influenced you, or to describe an experience that has helped shape who you are. The committee is also interested in how you think and how you express your thoughts. Please use pages 5 and 6 and any additional sheets as necessary.

Window Pain

I have grown up in a middle-upper class family. Nothing much happened; we were robbed once; my parents divorced. The children went to small private schools and well-known summer camps. I have never experienced a fist fight, a drug deal, a gang, a car crash, rape, or murder. We kids never saw a real crisis. As I got older, I made friends with people that were not so sheltered. I learned about drugs, alcohol, sex, violence, rebellion, and all the other emotional and physical hazards that teenagers found themselves involved in. I learned about these things, but I never experienced them. I never found myself in an emergency situation. Three years ago, I experienced my first crisis, and I found out that I could deal with it. I did not freeze up or panic, and I was rather surprised.

My father has been trying to construct an addition to his house for years, all by himself. He is an engineer, and hates to pay more than what he believes something is worth. He has that famous do-it-yourself complex, and today the addition barely has a roof, four or five years after it was started. During those years, many deals came his way. We have a fourteen foot conference table sitting in the garage in the spot were six by six foot windows were supposed to be. The windows were on of the first great bargains to come his way. He saw an ad in the LLNL newspaper and called him. Fifty bucks per window; what a deal. They arranged a day to pick them up.

Sunday, May 15, 1993, was one of the weekends we spent with him. I volunteered to go along to the man's house. We drove over in the jeep and parked on the street. The man greeted us and took us around the side of his house. Stacked up against a wall and under a tarp were double-paned windows taller than I was. They were six by six feet. We had to move them on a dolly through the car port, out to the driveway, and load them onto a trailer. The man had his son and daughter there to help, and the two had brought their families for a day at the grandparent's house. His wife took care of the grandchildren inside. The son and the son-in-law helped hold the windows on the dolly. The daughter and the daughter-in-law stood on the trailer and held the windows up, against a vertical brace. The man had placed two braces on either side of the trailer because it was springy and susceptible to motion.

I stayed and held the windows against the wall. My job was to stand them up and get them ready to be loaded onto the dolly. My father saw the danger that the windows could be upset, and he did not want me under fifteen toppled windows. He had the man run a rope across the windows, retained by hooks set into the wall, so that I could unleash one but hold all the others against the wall. I stood *beside* the windows to hold them up; never in front of them. We had loaded probably about eight or nine of the windows onto the dolly, and the two sons and my father were back with me when we heard a terrific crash. The girls had been in the same danger I was in, but my father had not had their welfare in mind. He felt guilty about that on the way home.

Everyone rushed out to the driveway to find that the windows had toppled over and shattered everywhere. Apparently the grandfather had kicked the wooden braces away from the trailer, thinking that there was enough weight on it to make it stable. The trailer dipped and set the glass off balance. It caught the girls by surprise. The blond got in front of the windows to push them back up, and the brunette was in a position to only pull them back into place.

The momentum and the weight of the glass was too much. The brunette was pulled down on top of the windows. There was a railing on the trailer and the blond girl dove over it, to the best of her ability. She landed on the pavement on her back. The windows hit the rail and shattered over it. The brunette girl had been wearing shorts and she had a long, very deep cut on the inside of her thigh, probably about half way through the muscle. She limped away from the trailer and collapsed on the front steps. I could see her leg. The cut was deep into the flesh, but it was not bleeding at all. It made my stomach turn. The blond girl on the pavement had one leg, her right leg, caught between the railing and the glass. There were shards of glass everywhere, and she had small cuts on her arms from the landing. The skin on her knee cap was completely severed off, and the cartilage of the knee cap was visible.

The man and his tow sons ran out and stopped dead in their tracks. My father had run out behind them and took in the scene in a glance. He did not stop moving. He was the first to the trapped girl and was trying to lift the piles of glass off her ankle when the other three joined him. I followed them out and just stared. I know I would only get in the way of the rescue process. I went to the girl on the steps.

Just then the children came streaming out of the backyard, ages three, four, six, and nine. This was my area and I went to them immediately. I ushered them back into the back yard and tried to answer their questions. Yes, there was a big crash, and their mommies and daddies were trying to clean it. No, you guys can't help, because glass is very sharp and you could hurt yourselves. Yes, your mommies are fine; yes, that was a fire truck going by. The son was in the kitchen, yelling and screaming; kicking the cabinets. "He kicked out the fu— in' support! What kind of idiot would kick out the fu—in' support?! Shi—! I'll kick out his ass!..." The grandmother was trying to calm him down, to shush him so the children would not hear. She gave me a plate of cookies and glasses of milk, and thanked me for watching them. We ate cookies and milk and played hide-and-go-seek. I kept them away from the windows so they would not see the ambulance out front.

Eventually the grandmother took over. I went out side to see the brunette girl with the cut on her thigh climb into the ambulance. The men were shoveling the glass pieces onto the trailer. My father did not want the remaining windows. The grandfather looked sad. The son was still rampaging, but quietly.

We left. Dad asked what had happened to me; he had not seen me take the children to the back. He said I did the right thing and that he was proud of me. I asked about the cuts all over his arms. I asked how the fallen girl was. Was she dead? Oh, no. She had cuts on her leg and ankle, and lost about two teacups-full of blood. She's fine. She was wearing hi-tops and they protected her pretty well.

My younger brother was astonished to hear what had happened while he sat around and played on the computer. It made me think of how much was going on around me that I was oblivious to. I had quite a story to tell when Sarah asked Monday morning, "So, how was your weekend?"

Since then I have handled a few other crises. In the most recent ones, I have played a larger part and the results sometimes depended on me. This was my first, however, and I saw that I could keep my head. It gave me the confidence to deal with the next crisis that came along. I also had a role model; as far as I could see, my father had acted in exactly the right way. His reaction time was instantaneous, and I hope mine has been conditioned to be the same. It was a good experience for me.

See page 307 to find out where this student got in.

AUDREY NATH

*Audrey won first place in the TMTA High School Division Piano
Concerto contest her senior year and placed at the state level each
previous year; she also performed with numerous orchestras. She
was the captain of her high school Academic Challenge B team,
salutatorian of her graduating class, and a National AP Scholar. She
has conducted scientific research every summer since her junior
year of high school for projects dealing with gold-labeling of the
nicotinic acetylcholine receptor and cervical cancer detection using
fluorescence spectroscopy.*

Stats

SAT I: 1550 (760 Verbal, 790 Math)

SAT II: 800 Math IIC, 730 Molecular Biology, 760 Writing,
750 Chemistry, 710 American History

High School GPA: 6.6248/6.0000

High School: Memorial High School, Houston, TX

Hometown: Houston, TX

Gender: Female

Race/Ethnicity: Asian

Applied To

Harvard College

Massachusetts Institute of Technology

Rice University

Essay: Rice

The quality of Rice's academic life and the residential college system is heavily influenced by the unique life experiences and cultural traditions each student brings. What perspective do you feel that you will be able to share with others as a result of your own life experiences and background? Cite a personal experience to illustrate this. Most applicants are able to respond successfully in two to three pages.

I've noticed that if I stare at something and really concentrate on it, I can still see its outline after it is gone; the same goes for focusing on one sound or one word until it lingers in my mind. Four summers ago, as I felt inundated with knowledge and ideas, I centered my mind on my surroundings of art in order to comprehend the volume of artistic concepts. Such was the enrichment I gleaned from studying composition at the American Festival for the Arts during the summer before the 8th grade. The results of this experience are ingrained both in the way I view music and life itself.

On the first day of the music program, I carried myself with a shy and self-conscious demeanor into the composition room where I was initially intimidated by a roomful of people who appeared to be bigger, older, and smarter than I was; little did I know that they would later become a family of mentors to me. Within the first day, Chris, our instructor and sage leader, introduced us to the work of late 20th century composers with a discussion and analysis of pieces by John Corigliano and Tan Dun; before then, I thought classical music ended with Aaron Copland.

Over the course of eight weeks, we would write two pieces to be later performed by faculty, study theory, and analyze orchestral and chamber works. As respite from this arduous study, we would listen to whatever music we deemed "interesting." These pieces would range from Beethoven's last string quartets to Chris' own soundtrack to a Civil War documentary; the dulcet sounds would both inspire us and fill the room for hours. To me, our assignments appeared impossible at the time as I had studied piano seriously for only four years; that training did not give me a fraction of the composition, theory, and literature knowledge that everyone else possessed. However, instead of allowing me to remain a confused spectator during theory lessons and discussions, Chris and the other students would explain the concepts in question. With this guidance and my fears assuaged, I eventually became comfortable enough to complete a complicated voice leading problem on my own or sight-sing in front of this group of encouraging supporters. By the end of the summer, I completed two original pieces and experienced the joy of having my own thoughts played back to me. Overall, I was exposed to a world of art that had previously seemed foreign and intimidating to me.

Even after the summer was over, Chris continued as our mentor and helped us explore our surroundings. We would take trips around town to the living art that is our city. From art festivals and museums to parks and Chris' own neighborhood, our excursions were as enjoyable as they were intriguing. Once, when we visited a special exhibit of photography at the Fine Arts Museum, my friend and I posed as siblings as we proceeded to call Chris "Dad" in order to obtain a family discount. Even though Chris was visibly not more than ten years older than me, and the three of us had about as much ethnic diversity as the Democratic National Convention, our ploy worked swimmingly. Within the museum, our curiosity was piqued by paintings that mimicked picture frames and photographs of doorways. When Chris took us downtown to analyze the architecture of structures and buildings, the city that we thought we knew so well transformed into a forest of sculpted monoliths as the streets we wandered were an odd, one-way maze.

Following my study of composition and our adventures with Chris, the world around me became a different place. Whereas my love for music started as a means for me to grasp onto clarity of thought, it had transformed into a structured passion. No longer was music just a series of soothing sounds. Instead, music became the counterpoint of two dogs barking or the rhythm of lights blinking; music became the movement of life. I realized that there was beauty in every bit of life, from the order within chaos to the chaos itself; it was the relationship between the constantly evolving patterns that grew out of living that was beautiful. Individual relationships and events, as complicated and inexplicable as they may seem, embody beauty when put in perspective of the larger order of life. This idea is modeled by abstract musical concepts that usually seem incomprehensible until they are interpreted in the context of an underlying pattern.

Since the summer when a family of musicians took me in to learn about the world of art and life itself, my perspectives headed in a new direction. I began to see life not as rigid layers within black and white lines; rather, I could relate the complexities of relationships with my surroundings, other people, and myself to a chromatic brushstroke of sound in a Debussy string quartet or an intricate orchestration within a symphony by Berlioz. Similarly, people were no longer simply right or wrong, intelligent or dull, talented or inept; the psychology behind their actions was just as complicated as the thoughts and events that made them. As of this very moment, four years after I studied composition at the American Festival for the Arts, I can still hear the faint resonance of comrades toying with ideas on the piano and singing a tune heard from an orchestra rehearsal; such is the shadow of an experience that filled my mind so long ago.

See page 308 to find out where this student got in.

BENJAMIN SPATZ

Ben spent his high school years acting, directing, and working on design and technical aspects of theater. He received five acting awards from the Massachusetts High School Drama Guild and was a paid employee in the area as a stage manager and a technical crew member. Ben also taught math, theater, and "love theory" to younger students and served on the board of the Project 10 East gay/straight alliance.

Stats

SAT I: 1470 (680 Verbal, 790 Math)
High School GPA: 93
High School: Cambridge Rindge & Latin School, Cambridge, MA
Hometown: Cambridge, MA
Gender & Race/Ethnicity: White male anarchist Jew

Applied To

Amherst College
Brown University
Hampshire College
Sarah Lawrence College
Vassar College
Wesleyan University
Yale University

Essay

Ben incorporated the following essay in his application to each of the above schools. Ben used this essay in response to various open-ended questions.

If I had to do it all again, I'd wear better pants. I simply didn't attract enough attention. When I walked into Harvard Square last September, I had no idea what to expect. With my old ratty crates, my signboard, and my homemade banner, I pranced into the Square, ready to meet my audience. Reaching the appointed spot, I rested my crates on the ground, and, overturning them, dumped the contents onto the brick sidewalk: hats, glasses, masks, and the all-important cape. I hung the banner across the walk, and moved the crates into position. I opened the signboard.

"Friends! Romans! Countrymen!" I began. "Lend me your ears!"

People stopped and stared. They turned their heads towards me and gathered around to see, their eager eyes watching my every move as I recreated the days of Caesar on a couple of crates in the middle of the busy Square. Soon, at least twenty people were watching. As I continued to speak, the crowd grew, and as I moved on to my other monologues - Hamlet, Macbeth, Benedick, Romeo - a great silence overtook the Square. Everyone was watching me. Channel 5 arrived to tape my performance. Anthony Hopkins invited me to lunch. The applause was thunderous.

I wish.

In fact, almost nobody stopped. A couple of people dropped a couple of coins into the hat I'd set out to reap my expected riches. I made three dollars and fifty cents that day, minus a dollar that blew away in the wind. No one stayed through an entire monologue. No one was there for my final bow. And there were never more than three people watching at a time.

I couldn't understand it. What had gone wrong? My performances on stage had always been greeted so warmly! And a friend of mine had juggled in the Square the year before and had ended up making more than twenty bucks a show. Why was it so much more interesting to watch him juggle knives on a unicycle than to watch me wonder, eyes wide, "What light through yonder window breaks?" Was my acting emotionless? Was I not inhabiting the world of my characters? Was I just boring to watch? Or are Shakespearean monologues simply inappropriate for street performance? And would a microphone have helped?

I came home miserable, despite the great efforts of my grandparents, who had watched from a discreet distance, to compliment me into oblivion. After a second performance with similar results, I decided to review my goals. I'd wanted to learn twelve Shakespeare monologues, and that was done. I'd wanted to make some cash, but there seemed little chance of that. I'd wanted an audience - its appreciation, its gaze, and its applause - but I received none of these things.

All I'd really shown was that I had the guts to do it, and the strength to keep on going while the city passed me by. I needed to prove to myself that I had the will to do it a third time, in the face of rejection, so that I could have this experience to remember whenever I doubted my courage in the future. But I couldn't bring myself to play to that cold audience again. So I decided to do it one last time, just for myself. I didn't even fix my broken sign. I psyched myself up into a frenzy, and went into Harvard Square solely for myself.

And I honestly would've done it again, but I lucked out: there, in my spot, was another performer, a magician. I was miraculously saved from a third humiliation. But if I somehow had to do it all again, I'd be sure to wear better pants.

See page 308 to find out where this student got in.

BRANDON MOLINA

Brandon was a four-year letterman in football, wrestling (best finish, third in state), and weightlifting. He was the president of his class junior and senior year and worked as a student body coordinator for the Special Olympics. He was a student representative on the Serious Discipline Committee, whose role is to recommend actions for the administration to take with students who commit serious discipline or honor infractions.

Stats

SAT I: 1420 (690 Verbal, 730 Math)
SAT II: 800 Biology, 720 Writing, 710 Math
High School GPA: 3.67
High School: Berkeley Preparatory School, Tampa, FL
Hometown: Lutz, FL
Gender: Male
Race/Ethnicity: White

Applied To

Columbia University
Elon University
Harvard College
Stanford University

Tulane University

University of Pennsylvania

United States Military Academy

Essay

Brandon used the following essay in his application to Harvard, and a slightly modified version in his applications to Columbia, Elon, Tulane, and West Point. The question is the generic one, something to the effect of *". . . any topic you would like to discuss in 250 words or less."*

The Real Thing

As a seven-year-old, I wrote a personal letter to the president of Coca-Cola, begging for his assistance. Having just returned from a ski trip to Stratton Mountain Vermont, I found my self unable to locate a specific product. At a convenience store on the mountain called "Bear Necessities", my mom bought Coke in eight ounce glass bottles that were reminiscent of those she would buy when she was young (although thicker glass only allowed 6 1/2 oz. of beverage). Whether it was the novelty of the bottles or the nostalgia I knew my mom felt, something made the Coke taste better out of the little glass bottles. I saved the empty container and upon my return home (to Pleasantville, NY at the time), I realized that my local grocery store did not stock these bottles. Neither did the local pharmacy. Neither did the local 7-Eleven nor the one in near-by Chappaqua. In fact, after a day in the White Pages, I realized that the item of my desire was nowhere to be found.

That night at dinner, after telling my parents the story of my day, they suggested that I get some information about the bottles. My mom was a recruiter at the time and furnished me with a telephone number for Coca-Cola. The following day I got a mailing address for the President and CEO, and wrote him a letter. I suppose that not too many seven-year-olds voice their concerns to this man, for I promptly received a response. To my dismay, the letter was an apology. "Unfortunately," it read, "we are unable to provide this product in your region." It began to explain, in very simple terms, that it was not cost effective for Coca-Cola to distribute the product in my densely populated area. His only recourse was to offer me coupons for other Coca-Cola products. For the next two years, I got to sample the bottles on infrequent occasion, whenever we hit the slopes.

My interest in the Coca-Cola Company grew and I began collecting Coke memorabilia, starting with a bank in the shape of a glass Coke bottle, which helped afford later pieces. In sixth grade I was plotting a graph of Coke stock on my America Online account. Also in sixth grade, something great happened: My family moved to our current hometown of Tampa, FL. Here, the eight ounce glass bottles were available in many grocery stores, pharmacies, etcetera. By this time my Coke collection was overtaking my room, and the access to these bottles did not ameliorate the situation. I collected bottles of all ages and editions, some full and some empty.

My collection has meaning that is two-fold. Certainly, a relatively large portion of a seventeen-year life has been devoted to searching, saving, and organizing. However, at a young age, the love that I knew for Coca-Cola taught me lessons about initiative and perseverance that I did not know. Fortunately I learned about these two qualities through a personal interest rather than having to complete an assignment. Of all my Coke products, my Coke-labeled furniture, and my Coke Christmas ornaments, my favorite item is a circa 1920 Coca-Cola glass bottle that was given to me by a friend whose brother found the bottle in a riverbed near Jacksonville, FL. Whenever I look at it, I am reminded of the time when I first began my collection on Stratton Mountain, Vermont.

See page 308 to find out where this student got in.

BRIAN TRACY

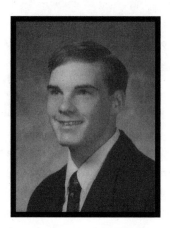

Brian was a four-year letterman in golf, and he qualified for districts in his senior year. He also received the ten-year national award for piano auditions and an altar server award from the Knights of Columbus.

Stats

SAT I: 1380
High School GPA: 4.0/4.0
High School: James M. Coughlin High School, Wilkes-Barre, PA
Hometown: Plains, PA
Gender: Male
Race/Ethnicity: White

Applied To

University of Notre Dame (applied early decision)

Essay

This is the applicant's personal statement, so the question asked him to tell Notre Dame any additional information about him.

"Nowhere else but Notre Dame." These words appear on the front cover of the viewbook, and they immediately bring to mind many images pertaining to the university. This phrase can also be the answer to a myriad of questions about great universities, outstanding athletic programs, and long standing, revered traditions. However, the question that comes to mind when I hear those words is, "Which college do I hope to be attending next year?" I often ask this question of myself whenever I wonder about my future. Friends and family ask me about my dreams for the future as well, because they are eager to know my plans. I believe that it would be a great honor and accomplishment to be able to tell both them and myself, "Nowhere else but Notre Dame."

I consider myself to be an honest, friendly, dedicated, and hardworking person with strong religious beliefs who is eager to help others and to always do what is right. I give great attention to everything I do, and I constantly try to challenge myself. For example, taking college courses during my junior year challenged me and provided an idea of what I would face in college. I also believe that I am a team player. My participation in sports and in groups in school has helped to build and reinforce this characteristic. Besides my commitment to school, I also try to help my community and to be a leader. My experiences in Junior Leadership Wilkes-Barre gave me great opportunities to meet with today's leaders and to become a leader of tomorrow. Junior Leadership also helped me to give back to the community through our service project, a community mural.

I also consider myself to be an enormous Notre Dame fan, not just of the football team, but of the college, too. I'll admit it: I cried the first time I saw *Rudy*. I fell in love with the campus when I visited there a few years ago. There just seemed to be a friendly, warm feeling around campus and on the faces of students I saw. It was during that trip that I first became interested in going to Notre Dame. However, I am not applying simply because I like the university. I did research on the nation's best colleges, and Notre Dame's name kept appearing. I have talked with several alumni, all of whom agree that attending Notre Dame was one of the best things they ever did. In addition, I was greatly impressed with the impressive graduation and employment rates. Finally, because Notre Dame has such strict admission standards, I know that if I am accepted, I will be surrounded by only the best and brightest students in the nation.

I thank Notre Dame for including Section 8 on the application. It does provide a chance to go beyond the transcript and to introduce myself and the kind of person I am. Hopefully, I will be given the chance to become part of a special tradition, one that includes Touchdown Jesus, the Golden Dome, the Grotto, and much more. Where is all of this possible? Nowhere else but Notre Dame.

See page 309 to find out where this student got in.

BROOKE PAUL

*In high school, Brooke was especially involved in speech con-
tests, jazz, marching and concert bands, vocal music, and school
musicals. Outside of school, she was an active member of her local
4-H club, earning several awards and distinctions. Brooke spent her
junior year of high school abroad as an AFS foreign exchange
student in Spain.*

Stats

SAT I: 1220 (590 Verbal, 630 Math)
SAT II: 700 Spanish, 700 Writing, 530 Biology
ACT: 28
High School GPA: 3.94/4.00
High School: Nishna Valley Community School, Hastings, IA
Hometown: Hastings, IA
Gender: Female
Race/Ethnicity: Caucasian

Applied To

Carleton College
Colgate University
Columbia University

Cornell University
Georgetown University
Middlebury College
Northwestern University
Oberlin College

Essay #1

Brooke used the following essay in her applications to Columbia, Cornell, Georgetown, and Middlebury.

Please submit a brief essay that you feel best describes you.

When many people think of an Iowa farm girl, they think of an overall-clad, poop-scooping hick whose favorite entertainment is hog calling. Well, I do wear overalls sometimes, I scoop my 4-H calf's poop, and I saw last year's Iowa State Fair hog calling contest on television.

In many ways, I am the typical, stereotyped farm girl. I know quite a bit about corn, hogs, cows, and tractors. I also know about honesty, a strong work ethic, close family ties, and caring about your neighbor—all strong Midwestern values.

But in many ways, I am not a typical farm girl. I've experienced and done things that most farm kids don't have the opportunity to do.

Over the past years, I've lived with eight foreign exchange students from five continents. Through them, I've experienced the cultures and lifestyles of countries like Thailand and Bolivia. I've learned about the similarities and differences between the United States and their home countries. I've also gained a greater understanding of world politics and social issues.

Last year, I had the opportunity to experience first hand what studying abroad was like. I traveled to Spain where I spent one year immersed in another culture. I was able to learn another language and establish lasting ties with another family.

Through hosting foreign exchange students and traveling abroad, I've realized that the world is a very small place. I've learned the importance of accepting differences and not making judgments.

Another thing that makes me an atypical farm girl is that I've deviated from the norm at my school. I've rearranged my class schedule so that I can take college level courses at the

University of Nebraska and teach Spanish to elementary students as a part-time job. I've focused on getting good grades, and I've worked with teachers to take classes independently. Although sports are "the" thing to do at my school, I wasn't interested in them. Instead, I've concentrated on music and the arts, which I enjoy and plan to make lifetime pursuits.

One of the biggest differences between my friends and myself is that I'm willing to take risks, and I'm not afraid to try new things. My friends are always asking me, "Why?" "Why do you want to study in another country?" "Why do you want to teach Spanish to a bunch of little kids?" "Why do you want to go to college far away from here?" And I think, "Why not?"

Essay #2

Brooke incorporated the following essay into her applications to Carleton, Colgate, Cornell, Middlebury, and Oberlin.

Indicate a person who has had a significant influence on you, and describe that influence.

When I was younger, I never realized how lucky I was. I never thought about what a great family I had or how nice my house was. Getting an allowance was a routine, not a luxury. Having a hot meal on the table was something I just expected.

In the fourth grade, I met a girl who would become my best friend for the next nine years. To me, she was as normal as I was. She stayed over at my house often and came to all my birthday parties. When I asked her when she was having her birthday party, she would always say that she had decided not to have one that year.

A few years later, we started junior high. My best friend and I played basketball together and went to slumber parties. Some days she would come to school crying. I'd console her and she'd tell me her problems. She didn't get along with her stepfather and her mom was never home. I thought this was normal. I thought I didn't get along with my parents and my mom worked a lot outside the home.

It wasn't until high school that it really began to sink in. It finally hit me that there were some big differences between my best friend and me. I had always assumed that everyone enjoyed the same lifestyle that I did. But she didn't. Her mother and stepfather are both alcoholics. She's seen them pass out on their couch, and she's been a passenger when they've driven drunk. Her two younger brothers have grown enough to outweigh her and beat her up.

She's come to school with bruises on her arms and a gash on her hip from the glass ashtray that they hurled at her. She has to lock her bedroom in her own house so her stepbrothers can't steal or vandalize her things. Her parents can't afford to give her an allowance and she makes her own car payments and pays her own insurance. A hot meal is rare at her house because her parents work late hours.

Even though my best friend has had a tough life, she's managed to be a good person. She's gotten pretty good grades and does well in school. She's never been bitter towards her family or situation. Neither of her parents completed high school, yet she has plans to move in with her grandparents and attend college next year. She wants to be a child psychologist.

I've admired her for being so strong and optimistic. Many teenagers with similar lives would be angry and they might give up hope for a better future. Some might become violent and get into trouble, but she's determined to beat the odds.

My best friend told me once that I was lucky and I just didn't know it. Now, I wish I could tell her that I'm lucky for knowing her. I want to tell her how much she's made me thankful for what I have. I want her to know that I admire her for being a fighter, and I want her to know how much I love her. I hope that someday she'll be as lucky as I am.

See page 309 to find out where this student got in.

CAROLINE ANG

Caroline competed on the speech and debate team for three years (winning the state tournament her senior year), the field hockey team for two seasons, and the softball and track teams for one season each. She was the editor-in-chief of her school yearbook her senior year, held various leadership positions in her high school's choir club and Christian club, and worked a part-time job in a coffee shop.

Stats

SAT I: 1500
SAT II: 800 Writing, 800 Literature, 780 Math IIC
ACT: 34
High School GPA: 3.96
High School: Leland High School, San Jose, CA
Hometown: San Jose, CA
Gender: Female
Race/Ethnicity: Chinese American

Applied To

Brown University
University of California—Berkeley
University of California—Los Angeles
University of California—San Diego

Please note: Caroline did not disclose information about other applications.

Essay

The following essay was used in Caroline's applications to each school listed above.

The personal statement is your opportunity to introduce us to you and to educate us about those personal aspects that you determine are vital for us to know. We ask only that whatever you write be honestly written and in your own handwriting.

Personal Statement

I am:

A dreamer who trembles in delight and terror as she considers what happiness and heartache the future may hold.

A humorist who continually expands her repertoire in pursuit of the perfect joke. (Two pretzels walk down the street. One of them was a-salted.)

An athlete who makes up in spirit and hard work what she lacks in talent.

A bookworm who, at 3 a.m., firmly promises that she will read "just one more page" before she sleeps…

A writer who strives to capture on paper the essence of life as she sees it, and who loves to pen short stories and reflective essays.

A daughter who is entering the last stage of the parent-child relationship- friendship with Mom and Dad.

A romantic who tries on her prom dress late at night and waltzes around her bedroom to music unheard by the rest of the world.

A conservative who supports the time honored values on which our forefathers founded this country.

A teacher who carefully plans her Sunday school lesson, but isn't afraid to scrap it last minute to fit the kids' needs at that particular moment.

An aesthete who waits outside her house for that instant when the lavender, fuchsia, orange, gold rays of the descending sun shoot across the sky and man has a glimpse of heaven on earth.

A student who loves learning for learning's sake, not just to pad a college transcript.

A Christian who is continually striving and struggling to follow Jesus' example.

A guitarist who strums and plucks out songs and instrumentals, some that she's written herself.

A connoisseur who celebrates the beauty and diversity of the snack food aisle in supermarkets.

A leader who accepts being a role model with mixed pride and trepidation.

An optimist who can't wait to seize her future and make her dreams of knowledge, writing and love come true.

A sleeper who escapes pressure and reality through a wonderful invention called the snooze button.

A worrier who compensates for general unluckiness through careful planning and anticipation.

A seeker who wants to get to the crux of the purpose of humanity- why we're here and where we're going.

A conversationalist who explores the heavy issues of life in depth, and chats about the lighter ones.

An economist who knows the value of money, now that she's had to work for it.

A skeptic who wants to believe in the innate goodness of man but cannot gloss over the mess he's made of the world thus far.

A sister who inundates her little brother with advice- how to pick outfits, deal with teachers and melt girls' hearts.

A crusader who enthusiastically sets out to conquer the world but gets her cape stuck in the doorway.

A maniac who rides shopping carts at amazing speeds with her best friend in empty parking lots after hours- drunk not on liquor, but on *life*.

An idealist who believes with all her heart that indifference is the worst crime of all… that having passion for what one does makes all the difference…

A complete paradox who is one thing, then another, one extreme, then the total opposite… a bundle of earnest contradictions.

I am:

Caroline Chiu-Ying Ang.

See page 309 to find out where this student got in.

CAROLINE HABBERT

Caroline held many leadership positions in high school. She was president of the Student Senate and was on the yearbook staff and varsity softball team for four years, heading up both operations during her senior year as editor and captain, respectively. Other organizations with which Caroline was involved include the Ohio Math League, Service Club, and her school's Cum Laude and French Honor Societies. Outside of school, she taught and attended religious school for four years, volunteered at a nursing home weekly from middle school onward, and spent the summers bicycling. The summer before her senior year, Caroline cycled across the United States.

Stats

SAT I: 1510 (770 Verbal, 740 Math)
SAT II: 800 Writing, 750 Biology, 750 Math IIC
ACT: 34
High School GPA: 3.98
High School: Seven Hills Upper School, Cincinnati, OH
Hometown: Cincinnati, OH
Gender: Female
Race/Ethnicity: Caucasian

Applied To

Brown University
Stanford University

Yale University
University of Michigan
Washington University in St. Louis

Essay

The following essay was used in Caroline's application to Brown, and was modified for each of the other four applications. There was no formal essay question.

This summer I pushed myself to the limit time and time again. Many times when I thought that I could not go any further, I had to rely on all of my inner strength to pull myself through. This summer I spent eight weeks on a bicycle that carried not only me, but all of my worldly possessions for those eight weeks, from Seattle, Washington to Sea Bright, New Jersey. I moved my legs around in constant circles for seven or eight hours a day, every day, all the way from the Pacific to the Atlantic. And at the end of each day, when I was more tired than I could possibly imagine, I set up my tent, rolled out my sleeping bag, and slept until a "mornin' folks" forced its way into my consciousness and told me that it was time to begin the process anew. We encountered crosswinds so strong that we exerted more effort trying to move in a straight line than trying to move forward; swarms of mosquitoes so thick that standing still for more than ten seconds and maintaining enough blood to function were mutually exclusive; huge trucks heading towards us while passing cars on their side of the road, forcing us to abandon the little strip of shoulder we occupied; and, of course, uphill roads than seemed to take forever to crest at the top of the mountain. Despite all of the setbacks and adverse conditions, I made it across the country under my own power. I will probably never again experience anything so amazing as the feeling I had when we first saw water in New Jersey. Getting there had required me to utilize both emotional and physical elements of myself that had never before been tested. I had never before sat on a bicycle seat for 55 days in a row, nor had I ever faced something I wasn't confident I could do. But I did do it. I called upon all of the tenacity, persistence, and strength that I have, and I made it.

This is not the first physical challenge I have conquered; my photo albums display mementoes from three other long-distance bike trips. Nor is this the first emotional challenge I have faced. Every week, in fact, I am tested in new ways as a volunteer at a nursing home. During my six years there I have worked with countless residents, but one woman has been a constant. Each time I go, I make it a point to stop by Sarah's room to spend some time alone with her. The first I met her, Sarah was the feisty old lady playing Bingo who explained to me that some of the other women occasionally had a hard time finding the right square.

Unfortunately, her spunk did not last much longer. Already 90 when I met her, her health began a slow decline soon after I met her. Most upsetting to me was the fact that her mental facilities were slowly deteriorating. When I first began visiting her, she would challenge my presence on any day other than Sunday. Then, as the days started to blend together, she would realize that it was Sunday when I arrived. Finally, she quit commenting on the days at all. She lost the sparkle that crept into her voice when she talked about her daughter, she stopped telling me about the additions to her photo gallery, and she didn't seem to care about what was going on outside of her room. But she still had enough spirit left to smile every week when I stopped by and ask how I'd been, to listen to me talk about school and my family, the weather and how nice she looked. Until this Sunday, when she didn't recognize me. After I had watched her sleep for a minute, I rubbed her arm and said her name. She slowly opened her eyes and lifted her head off her chest. I waited for the smile and the "Caroline." They didn't come. She closed her eyes and lowered her head again, leaving me squatting by her chair. . .

Watching this transformation has given me my first lesson in the realities of life. Although I am invincible now, I won't always be. Aging is a fatal disease everyone gets if she lives long enough. The nurse I talked to said that she could "go at any time." Time: it is such a relative thing. When I was on my bike this summer, the hour that it took to go twelve miles sometimes seemed like it would never end. The two months that

I was gone seemed to last forever. But I can still remember the day that I met Sarah six years ago as vividly as if it were yesterday. And it doesn't seem fair that Sarah's life, long in terms of human time but short in relation to the world, will soon be a memory too.

See page 310 to find out where this student got in.

CASEY NEWTON

In high school, Casey was a student board member for the Fullerton Joint Union High School District Board of Trustees, editor-in-chief of the student newspaper, captain of the debate team, the lead in the fall play, and a candidate for the International Baccalaureate diploma, which he earned. He also was involved with the California Scholarship Federation and the National Honor Society.

Stats

SAT I: 1370 (800 Verbal, 570 Math)

SAT II: 740 Writing, 710 Literature, 720 American History

High School GPA: 4.3

High School: Sonora High School, La Habra, CA

Hometown: La Habra, CA

Gender: Male

Race/Ethnicity: White

Applied To

Northwestern University (applied early decision)

Essay

What effect has any voluntary research, reading or study, work in the arts, science project, etc., had on your intellectual and personal growth in recent years? Discuss what influence this involvement has had on your academic goals.

Words have always been my sharpest tools. I have used them to make others laugh, to think, to see, and to do. I have seen my keystrokes translated into smiles and laughs on the faces of my readers. I have also had my words trail me like ghosts, reappearing on the faces of angry people, unsettling reminders of a misconstrued comment. My words have taken me to my highest moments, and they have brought me to my knees. Over the past four years, I have had pieces published in several newspapers. The effects of those words have, more than anything else, guided my growth as an individual.

My words have had many positive effects. The words that cemented my fascination with language as a potential career were published February 3, 1995 in the Los Angeles Times. It was a simple editorial piece in a column named "My Turn," in which teens took their turn on a variety of issues. Once the initial euphoria of seeing my name in print subsided, a more lasting feeling of reverence for the power of communicating with millions all at once developed and remains with me. I joined a Teen Panel on the Orange County Register soon after, and wrote articles on a variety of teenager issues. After my yearlong stint there, I joined another Teen Panel for the Register — one that reviewed movies.

My words were on a roll. As co-editor of the school newspaper, I write a popular "Top Ten" column of humorous observations about my school. And in our first issue, item number five on "Good Things About Being Back To School," was this: "We were all starting to miss watching the football team lose." Our football team has a suspect win-loss record, and I made a generalization about that record in an attempt at humor.

The night the paper was distributed, my house was egged. The next day, rabid football players barking thinly veiled threats encouraged me to make a public apology. After a few days, the principal sensed growing conflict and sought resolution. I was brought into a conference room with the principal, my journalism adviser, three football coaches, and two players. I stressed my intent was not malicious, that I supported the football team, that I apologized for offending them. My words were essentially ignored. I was told I had no integrity, and that I was acting out a vague vendetta against the football team. One player accused me of destroying the team's progress.

In that claustrophobic room, the emotions built within me steadily for forty minutes and screamed to come out. I was overwhelmed, ironically, by the power of their words. It is not so much that I regretted making the joke; I do not. Rather, I had been blindsided by the sheer force of communication. The football coaches never understood my comment, and they never understood my explanation. And I will never understand why they gave such power to my words. The meeting ended, and the vitriol of the coaches hung heavy in my mind.

I stumbled into the principal's office.

"Casey," said the principal with sincerity, "you were so brave."

And I cried. For once, there were no words. Reduced to tears in the principal's office, I felt defeated.

But even in defeat, I learned something about words. I have wielded a pen, and I have wielded a sword. The pen is sharper, but it is double-edged. And with careful use, and plenty of practice, my pen will become sharp enough to cut through the most closed of minds.

See page 310 to find out where this student got in.

CHARLES LIGHT

Charles was a varsity tennis player for four years and a team captain for two, playing number-one singles on one of the top teams in Massachusetts. He was also vice president of his high school's National Honor Society, class treasurer, and assistant editor of the yearbook.

Stats

SAT I: 1510 (710 Verbal, 800 Math)
SAT II: 770 Writing, 800 Math IIC, 690 Chemistry
ACT: 33
High School GPA: 4.5 weighted
High School: Tantasqua Regional Public High School, Fiskdale, MA
Hometown: Sturbridge, MA
Gender: Male
Race/Ethnicity: Caucasian

Applied To

Bowdoin College
Cornell University
Dartmouth College
Johns Hopkins University
Massachusetts Institute of Technology
Northeastern University
Swarthmore College

Essay

Charles used the following essay in his application to Dartmouth, Cornell, and MIT.

What was the highlight of your summer?

The highlight of my summer was picking up balls and putting them into my basket. Tennis balls, that is, and thousands of them at that, all of which I put into my teaching basket. As a tennis counselor at Camp Robin Hood in Maine, an international summer camp for the children of the rich and famous, much of my time was indeed devoted to picking up balls and putting them into my basket.

For eight weeks, from the end of June until the end of August, I picked up a lot of balls, and I began to notice that all balls are not the same. I noticed that some balls were Penn while others were Wilson; some were new while others were frayed, and some were of red lettering while others were of black lettering. It seemed that I picked up certain balls daily, ones that I could distinguish by number or color or some stray mark. Other, less recognizable balls, I may have only picked up once over the course of the summer. Some balls that I picked up were right in the middle of the tennis court and easy to scoop into the teaching basket. Other balls tended to drift towards the fences, and I had to procure them from under a fence or from behind a bench. Despite the many different balls (nearly every ball was unique), my ultimate goal was to pick up every ball that I could, and to put them all into my teaching basket.

At Camp Robin Hood, there are over 30 activities for each camper to choose from during his/her eight-week stay. In order to teach these activities at a high level, staff is hired from all over the world. I was unaware of this when I arrived at camp, but over the summer I met all of the different people that I could. I met the third-ranked kick-boxer in Australia, and a Colombian who played tennis at the national level as a junior. I met an Australian vying for a spot on his country's Olympic baseball team, and an American college student on a lacrosse team in the national championship hunt. I met an Australian training to be in the 2000 X-Games (Extreme Games) in the sport of barefoot water-skiing, and a black South African who lived through apartheid. I also met over 100 children on the tennis courts, and I tried (somewhat successfully) to teach them to play tennis and appreciate the game.

Although there were so many people at Camp Robin Hood, I tried as hard as I could to meet all of them. Some of them spoke with an Australian accent and some with an English accent, some were older and some were younger, and some called it "soccer" while others called it "football." Some of the people I met everyday, including the people in my cabin with whom I became good friends. Other people I met only a few times. Despite all of our differences, I tried to meet them all and to learn each one's story.

The highlight of my summer was picking up balls and putting them into my basket. Though some balls were harder to reach than others, I still tried to pick them all up. In the end I learned that the balls were really more similar than different. I also learned that one should try to pick up as many balls as possible, and to put them in one's basket. For each one has its own history, along with a valuable story to tell. And to take all the balls with you in your basket might just make you a better person.

See page 311 to find out where this student got in.

CLAUDIA GOLD

Claudia played piano for eleven years and taught private piano lessons to children. She also helped teach an autistic child to speak, read, and write under the guidance of a psychologist. Claudia was president of the math club her senior year and treasurer as a sophomore. She was active in theatre and drama and took ballet classes for ten years. Claudia attended the Young Scholars Program at Florida State University, where she worked on a research project involving gamma emissions from fused rubidium. She also participated in an exchange program in Spain, which included classes at the University of Salamanca.

Stats

SAT I: 1520 (740 Verbal, 780 Math)
SAT II: 800 Writing, 780 Math IIC, 670 Biology M
ACT: 33
High School GPA: 3.6 unweighted, 4.2 weighted
High School: Spanish River Community High School, Boca Raton, FL
Hometown: Boca Raton, FL
Gender: Female
Race/Ethnicity: Caucasian

Applied To

Brown University
Cornell University
Massachusetts Institute of Technology
New York University
Rice University
University of Chicago
Yale University

Essay

Claudia used the following essay as the main essay in each of her college applications.

Please write something that will help us get to know you better (approximate wording).

It is a statistical fact that about three percent of babies are born breech. It has not been determined, however, whether prenatal upside-downness affects spatial orientation during the rest of the baby's life. But in my case, reversed entry into the world appears responsible for at least one significant subsequent event.

During my twelfth year of life, while attending a performing arts summer camp in New York, talent scouts from Nickelodeon Studios in Orlando arrived on campus to search for kids possessing unusual and entertaining talents. I didn't give it much thought until a bunkmate reminded me of my unique skill: I had developed, after considerable practice, an ability to play piano upside-down. To do so, I would position my back and shoulders on the piano bench and reach up to the keys with crossed forearms. Along with 350 other hopeful campers, I stood in line to show off my talent, aspiring to become the next Nickelodeon television star.

Foolishly, I was ecstatic when I received a phone call from casting agents three months later inviting me to participate in the pilot episode of Figure It Out, a show in which kids with unique talents appear before a panel of so-called celebrities who try to guess the hidden talent through a series of yes/no questions.

Despite dreams of a stylish arrival via Nickelodeon's private jet, my parents packed up the family minivan, and we arrived three hours later in Orlando, Florida.

Upon arriving at the sound stage, I was whisked down a corridor. As I neared a room labeled "Hair and Makeup," what sounded like the tantrum of a spoiled child became louder. When the door opened, I was surprised to see the back of the bleached-blond head of a grown woman, obviously infuriated, surrounded by hair stylists and makeup artists. When she heard me enter, she stopped arguing abruptly and swiveled her chair to greet me with a huge, collagen-enhanced smile.

"Hello, I'm your host Summer Sanders!" she announced a little too cheerfully. "You must be our special guest! I hear you have a special talent. But don't tell anyone. It's a . . . shhhhhhh. . . secret." With that, she grabbed a vat of Vaseline, smeared it across her front teeth, and walked out the door.

With my "specialness" confirmed, I was subjected to a complete makeover. The stylists repeatedly complemented my features yet painted over each of them until they were no longer recognizable as my own. (I still don't understand why I needed a pedicure when I would be wearing sneakers.)

Later, in the coffee room, while searching for any reading material besides Nickelodeon Magazine, I stumbled upon something that solidified the experience as one that would forever change my conception of the world: there, lying next to the sink, was the script for my show! The show, whose essence was spontaneity and suspense, was entirely a sham. Although to the viewers the celebrities' comments appeared cleverly improvised, each word had been carefully crafted, and even the destiny of the player, pre-determined. To my simultaneous horror and glee, amongst the final words of the script were "Claudia wins!"

I learned a lesson that proved to be a guiding principle for my life. My realization that Figure It Out, a seemingly innocent children's show, was nothing more than a derivative, commercialized, and manipulative institution, was the equivalent of many children's realization that the tooth fairy is a myth. As children, we look up to those older than us for the paradigm of how we ought to live our lives. As each facade was unveiled, my perception of the adult world was transformed. Figure It Out has become, for me, a metaphor that has helped me to identify the kind of person I strive not to become — one who is deceptive, hypocritical, and superficial. Thus, it has helped me understand the kind of person I hope to be. It helped me to "figure it out."

See page 311 to find out where this student got in.

CONNIE TAYLOR

Connie was actively involved in math, science, and music activities at her school. She was the principal violist in her school, county, and regional orchestras and was captain of the math team and president of the Black Student Union. Outside of school, Connie held science research internships at the Maryland Psychiatric Research Center, Jefferson Laboratories, and the National Institutes of Health.

Stats

SAT I: 1550 (760 Verbal, 790 Math)

SAT II: 740 Math IIC, 660 Biology M, 670 Writing

High School GPA: 4.46 weighted

High School: Atholton High School, Columbia, MD

Hometown: Laurel, MD

Gender: Female

Race/Ethnicity: African American

Applied To

Boston University

Harvard College

Massachusetts Institute of Technology

University of Chicago

University of Maryland—College Park
Yale University

Essay

Connie used the following essay in her applications to Harvard, Yale, MIT, UMD, and BU.
Indicate a person who has had a significant influence on you, and describe that influence.

While I was cleaning my room the other day, I came across a letter that I received from my friend, Robin. Robin and I both played in the Atholton High School Orchestra two years ago. I first met Robin while I was still in middle school and she was a high school junior. She was the principal violist of the orchestra. I had gone to an Atholton Winter Concert with my sister, and insisted that she introduce me to Robin. From the thirty-second conversation that I had with her, I decided that Robin was everything that I planned to be when I reached high school. She was a hard-working student (3.96 GPA); she was a accomplished violist (best high school violist in Maryland); and most importantly she was one of the nicest people I have ever met.

Originally, Robin had planned to major in biology at the University of Maryland; she later changed to a double major in biology and music. By the time I received her letter, she had decided to major in Viola Performance. I have a sneaking suspicion that is what Robin wanted all along. She had taken steps to turn her dream into a reality, and that is why she continues to inspire me. In her letter, Robin described one of her viola lessons: "Much of the time, [my teacher] will ask me to play two measures at a time and stop me. He will then point out what I should be doing or focusing on at that moment. It is very difficult; I am constantly monitoring my sound, trying to always improve… I can do more… I must do more."

I try to remember Robin's words during my last year in high school and my transition into college. I have an audition for the Maryland All-State Orchestra in less then a month, where I have been a member for the last four years. The best I have ever placed is 18th chair viola. However, I know I can do better. This year, instead of practicing one hour a day, I practice two or three hours a day. I can do more… I must do more… This concept, of course, applies to areas of my life besides music. About the middle of the last school year, I realized that I didn't understand some of the essential topics in my Calculus class. I knew I could do better. I studied harder. I stayed after school for help. I received an A on nearly every test and quiz during the next quarter. For the final, I learned all the things that I had not initially understood and I received one of the highest grades in the class. Again, I proved to myself that I could do better. I have Robin to thank for this.

See page 311 to find out where this student got in.

DANIEL FREEMAN

Dan participated in numerous activities in high school, including four years in student council and class leadership positions. Dan was also very active in the arts through theater, bands, and choir. He served as captain of the regional office of his youth group. Dan was recognized his senior year as a Presidential Scholar, National Merit Scholar, All-State Academic Scholar, and Project Imagine Arts Scholar.

Stats

SAT I: 1590 (790 Verbal, 800 Math)
SAT II: 800 Math IIC, 800 Writing, 790 Biology
ACT: 35
High School GPA: 4.0
High School: North Farmington High School, Farmington Hills, MI
Hometown: Farmington Hills, MI
Gender: Male
Race/Ethnicity: Caucasian (Jewish)

Applied To

Yale University (applied early decision)

Essay

The exact wording of the essay question is not known, but it basically asked applicants to write about an activity that was important to them.

The Conquest

It was a crisp, clear June day in Rocky Mountain National Park, a few miles outside of Estes Park, Colorado. Before me stood an imposing sight: Estes Cone. With a peak at twelve thousand feet above sea level and a base at eight thousand, this mountain would be a challenge for any hiker. I was no hiker; I was an unathletic, awkward 15-year-old boy. Nonetheless, I loaded my pack with salami, pita, and water and set forth.

At first the going was easy. I knew we had to ascend four thousand feet before reaching the peak, and as we passed the fourth of five mile-markers, I questioned whether we had gained more than fifteen hundred. After lunch my trip's supervisor explained the situation. The next mile included almost three thousand feet of vertical gain. We would split into two groups: one would go quickly, the other would be allowed breaks. The fast group would see the top and the slow one would be forced to turn back when they met the others coming down. I decided then that no chunk of rock could conquer me, and so I set forth with the fast group.

The pace was grueling. My muscles screamed out for rest, and I began to regret that I had chosen to audition for the musical instead of trying out for the tennis team. As we pushed forward, the angle of elevation increased from twenty degrees, to thirty, to nearly forty. I fell further and further behind until I was told that I should simply wait for the slow group to catch up and continue with them. I curtly responded that I would be fine and proceeded onward. Pain tore through my legs as I pulled my body weight over each rock. The back of the group flittered in and out of my view, pulling me forward with only dim hopes of success.

Time wore on, and pain faded into numbness. Each foot followed the other in a grim succession. The trees thinned with the increasing altitude, and the peak grew nearer. Suddenly I heard my friend Dan holler down, "Hurry up man, you've just about made it, and we're sick of waiting for you!" My vigor restored, I pushed on quicker than before until I broke through the tree line. A bald, craggy expanse of rock surrounded me. The others were waiting, cameras in a pile, in preparation for a group shot at the summit. In one final act of endurance, I pulled myself over the top to join the others in triumph. My climb was complete.

As I looked down from that peak upon the miniaturized ranger station and the surrounding vistas, I received two things. One would shape my leisure time for the remainder of high school – a love of hiking. Whenever I get the chance, I escape from suburbia and enter the wilds. Since that fateful summer I have hiked in three countries: through the heat of Israel's Judean Desert, over the rocky cliffs of Canada's Lake Superior Provincial Park, and throughout the forests of my native Michigan's many state parks. I now am a hiker. Even more importantly, I was given confidence. Physical limitations and the limitations that others place on me no longer deter me from setting and reaching my goals. Life is my mountain, and no rock-strewn face will keep me from reaching the summit.

See page 312 to find out where this student got in.

DAVID AUERBACH

David was competitive in many areas, competing at the state level in speech and debate, Youth Legislature, and mock trial. He was also active within his high school as editor of the school newspaper for three years, National Honor Society president, a mathematics tutor, and a member of the track and cross-country teams. Outside of school, he did independent genetics research and worked on preserving the ecosystem of a local river.

Stats

SAT I: 1560
ACT: 35
High School GPA: 4.0
High School: Sprague High School, Salem, Oregon
Hometown: Salem, OR
Gender: Male
Race/Ethnicity: Caucasian

Applied To

Carleton College
Dartmouth College
Macalaster College
Willamette University

Essay

The following essay was used in all of David's applications. He explains, "I picked the 'anything you want' option to write my essay because I felt the other questions were too confining."

Cleaning Your Room Can Change Your Life

Recently, during a futile attempt at cleaning my eternally messy room, I tripped over the leg of a chair and fell sprawling to the floor. As I lifted my head, I found that I was at eye level with the very bottom shelf of my bookcase. One book on it caught my eye—a book I had last read in eighth grade. I pulled the book out and began to read....

I read of a world where the written word is forbidden, where books and other printed material have been banned for decades. Without the printed word, intellectual life withers and debate dies. In the absence of debate there are no disagreements. In this dystopia, all are equal because no one excels and mediocrity rules. All are therefore happy. On the surface, the system seems to work.

Enter Guy Montag. Guy is a fireman; that is, his job is burning books. He enjoys his job, for he knows he is making the world a safer and happier place. He is a perfect product of the system...until he meets Clarisse.

Clarisse and her family are misfits. In Guy's hyperaccelerated world, they still enjoy walking. In his world, questions are discouraged, because asking questions is part of the process of discovery. Clarisse is expelled from school for asking questions. She has a natural curiosity about others; in her words, "I just want to figure out who [people] are and what they want and where they're going." Perhaps the most profound question in the book is Clarisse's simple query to Guy: "Are you happy?"

As he ponders this question, Guy realizes the fallacy behind the "equality" he fosters. By destroying books, he forces people (including himself) to give up their individuality and ability for independent thought. They become dependent on the system, expecting everything to be handed to them on a plate.

What did I learn from this book? I learned from the frenetic pace of Guy's world to slow down and take time to enjoy life. I learned from Clarisse's curiosity that there is nothing wrong with asking questions. I have always been an inquisitive person, but since first reading this book, I have become even more inquisitive about the world around me. Finally, I learned the incredible power of knowledge. Knowledge bestows the power to create or destroy. It enables us to judge and to choose. The ability to make decisions is what makes each of us so different and interesting.

For me, reading this book was a life-changing experience. I often pause and ask myself: "What knowledge have you gained today? What power has that knowledge given you? How has it made you different?" One additional difference reading that book made to me was the realization that books and especially their contents need to be protected in order to avoid mediocrity. And thanks to Ray Bradbury, I now know that *Fahrenheit 451* is the temperature at which book paper burns.

See page 312 to find out where this student got in.

DAVID JOSEPH ESTREM

David actively participated in extracurricular activities in high school and held many leadership positions, including editor of the school newspaper, drum major for the marching and pep bands, and trombone section leader for the concert and jazz bands. He was the head of the lighting and sound crew for drama productions and rounded out his activities with running on the cross-country team and participating in group speech competitions.

Stats

SAT: 1340
ACT: 33
High School GPA: 3.963 unweighted
High School: Fairfield High School, Fairfield, IA
Hometown: Brighton, IA
Gender: Male
Race/Ethnicity: Caucasian

Applied To

Embry Riddle Aeronautical University
St. Louis University
United States Air Force Academy
University of North Dakota

Essay

The following three questions were posed in the United States Air Force Academy application:

What first interested you in the Air Force Academy?

Discuss how you feel you will adapt to the military lifestyle of the Air Force Academy.

Discuss a personal value you are proud of and an experience that led to its development.

Applicants were given half a page to respond to each of two questions and almost a full page to respond to the third. David felt that his short essay responses might have been more important in his application.

Discuss how you feel you will adapt to the military life style of the Air Force Academy.

I am not afraid of hard work, high standards and discipline. I have been raised to always work to the best of my ability and to always finish what I set out to do. Since I have the desire to attend the Air Force Academy, I likewise have the will to change my lifestyle to that of the Academy. In addition, I have always been taught to respect authority. My respect for superiors will assist me greatly in adapting to the military lifestyle.

Understanding and agreeing with the reasoning behind the rigor is essential to handle and benefit from it. I realize that the disciplines at the Academy are in place to develop the character, respect and leadership skills that are necessary to prepare its cadets for careers as Air Force officers.

See page 313 to find out where this student got in.

DIANA SCHOFIELD

Diana was a competitive swimmer for ten years and was a four-year letterman and captain of the varsity swim team at Ravenscroft. While on the swim team, she achieved several state honors, including a state record, and was voted MVP twice in a row. Diana played the violin and was concertmistress of the faculty/student orchestra as well as her high school orchestra. She also attended Governor's School for violin and the Spoleto Study Abroad program for orchestra. She was a member of the National Honor Society and was nominated for the Morehead Scholarship.

Stats

SAT I: 1380 (700 Verbal, 680 Math)
SAT II: 660 U.S. History, 680 Spanish, 700 Writing
ACT: 31
High School GPA: 4.23
High School: Ravenscroft, Raleigh, NC
Hometown: Raleigh, NC
Gender: Female
Race/Ethnicity: Caucasian

Applied To

Boston College
Cornell University
Emory University
Georgetown University
Harvard College
Northwestern University
University of North Carolina—Chapel Hill
University of Pennsylvania
Washington University in St. Louis

Essay

Diana used the following essay in her application to each school listed above, with the exception of Georgetown.

Cite a meaningful first experience and explain its impact on you.

I greatly appreciate the concept of taking a *siesta* in the afternoon. I love the fact that the salad comes after the main course, and the cars are all the size of Volkswagen beetles. Olive oil really can accompany any meal. You can't go anywhere without seeing a duomo or a fresco. Punctuality is not a necessity of life. No one in Italy ever seems to be in a rush, because there is no time.

E.M. Forster wrote, "The traveler who has gone to Italy to study the tactile values of Giotto, or the corruption of the Papacy, may return remembering nothing but the blue sky and the men and women who live under it." Such was my experience as I, a student of music, spent a month in Spoleto, Italy this past summer. I originally applied for a spot in the Spoleto Study Abroad program in order to play the violin, study opera, history, and learn Italian. But what I came away with was the influence of the Italian culture, which will follow me wherever I go.

As I lugged my overweight, eighty-pound suitcase (nicknamed "The Big Mama") down a narrow cobblestone alley, I wiped the sweat-smeared makeup from my forehead and worried about what the lack of air conditioning and overwhelming humidity was going to do to me. And no email? Nevertheless, I couldn't wait to start classes, begin rehearsals, and get out into the city. I couldn't seem to get over my American ways of rushing from one activity to another; "exhausted" became my only response to the typical Italian greeting "Come stai?" As I wearily walked to class one morning, I noticed this incredible view overlooking most of Spoleto. I stopped dead in my tracks and studied the fog settling over the tiled roofs of modest stone houses. Laundry lines hung from window to window like vines. This was not the Italy of the Olive Garden and Parmesan cheese commercials. This *was Italy.* Why had I not noticed this magnificent site before? I took a picture, and every time I passed that spot, I paused to study the amazing world below me. My American schedules and routines were discarded, along with my makeup and hairdryer. I slowed down, took many scenic routes, began sampling new flavors of gelato, and trying out my nascent Italian skills on vendors in the piazzas. I could spend literally hours sitting in cafes chatting with friends, and in a very "Lost Generation" style, writing in my journal. Living in Italy for a month is more than eating the food, purchasing postcards, and attempting to decipher the language, it is living the life and the culture. In that month I became an inhabitant of the country, an Italian by my lifestyle and mindset. When I physically returned to the States, my thoughts were in Spoleto, Florence, Siena and in other beautiful cities. As I readjusted to life in Raleigh, North Carolina, I never lost my Italian flair. I discovered that Italy is not only a place, but also a state of mind.

See page 313 to find out where this student got in.

DIANDRA LYN BOBÉ

   In high school, Diandra was editor-in-chief of the school newspaper and attended the 22nd Annual World Affairs Seminar as a representative of her district Rotary Club. She was the founder and organizer of a Habitat for Humanity chapter in her city, was a member of a performance jazz ensemble, and had the lead role in Fame.

Stats

SAT I: 1300 (650 Verbal, 650 Math)
SAT II: 720 Writing, 650 Math IC, 630 Reading
High School GPA: 4.1
High School: Mohave High School, Bullhead City, AZ
Hometown: Bronx, NY
Gender: Female
Race/Ethnicity: Latina

Applied To

ROUND ONE
Columbia University
Duke University
Georgetown University

New York University

Northwestern University (journalism school)

Pomona College

Swarthmore College

Washington University in St. Louis

Yale University

ROUND TWO

Barnard College

Columbia University

Haverford College

New York University

Wesleyan University

Essay

Diandra used the following essay, slightly modified in some applications, as a pre-freshman for Pomona, Washington U. in St. Louis, Swarthmore, and Yale and as a transfer for Wesleyan, Barnard, and Columbia. The wording of the question varied slightly for each school but the premise was *"Tell us about a person/experience that has had an impact on your life."*

Maria

We met Maria when I was 11 years old. A mutual friend introduced her to our family, and, in time, she and her husband became our close friends as well. She was a therapist and enjoyed a thriving, well-respected practice in suburban New York. Her clients were predominantly the upper echelon of society and included several persons of international renown: representatives of the theater, the financial district, government and the like. It was by serendipity that we came to know Maria on a much deeper level.

Maria had a staccato quality to her voice, somewhat reminiscent of Katherine Hepburn. During a party at our house, my father noticed something odd about her eyelid, later stating his suspicion that she had a neuromuscular disease called myasthenia gravis. She agreed to be tested and the diagnosis was confirmed. It had evidently been present 20 years before, when she first noted her voice change, which was attributed to the emotional shock of losing her son to uncontrollable seizures. This came as quite a surprise, as she had consulted a number of physicians over the year and had, up until then, felt entirely well, except for the occasional fatiguing of her voice following long sessions with clients.

Over the next few years her vocal problem worsened and she began experiencing bouts of muscle weakness. My father became her doctor, and, shortly after initiating treatment, she improved. I would frequently accompany him on her house calls.

I remember my first time there. Her home was unassuming: a simple New England-style cottage with none of the usual adornments you'd expect to see in the home of someone who catered to the rich and famous. There were no fancy lighting fixtures, no elegant carpets, and not a single ritzy ornament anywhere. A pleasant aroma filled the room, and I was suddenly overcome by a strange feeling of serenity.

After my conversations with Maria, I understood why she was revered; She was the embodiment of peace. She spoke softly and with a countenance that was warm and embracing. Despite her illness, she was surprisingly upbeat, spending very little time discussing the issues regarding her disease. Instead, she was genuinely interested in what was going on with my family and me. Eventually, I became more interested in her life and what she had experienced. As we spoke, I learned about the path she had chosen. Married to a wealthy industrialist and highly visible in the elite circles of New York City, she began to shun the superficiality of high society and became increasingly disillusioned with her life. The poverty and deplorable living conditions in many of the countries she visited around the world profoundly moved her. She ultimately chose to leave behind her secure affluence to pursue a different value system based on humility and simple truths. Despite several devastating setbacks in her personal life, Marie returned to her education and the age of forty to receive her degree and begin practice.

The fruits of these arduous labors are clear as I observe Maria now. Her keen insight into nature enables her to understand others' feelings, and her sincerity instills a confidence that her suggestions are just and forthright. Many of our discussions center on her belief that life must be lived in truth, with no intent to deceive, either others or oneself. Over time, it has become clear that Maria lives her life true to the tenets she believes, and has been able to counsel others to do likewise.

I have watched Maria now for the last few years as her disease progresses. She remains positive in her outlook and does her best not to let her illness control her. I have learned from her that truth is in not making excuses for what comes along in life, and that nothing should have the power to strip you of your kindness, understanding, and connectedness to the rest of the world. I value my own work in a different way now, because she has shown me that it is in my work that I will come to value myself. I know from Maria that an appreciation of simple values exists in most individuals, and that deep inside we aspire to these values throughout our lives. Sometimes, they become clearer only after we have abandoned them. I remember Maria when my mind drifts off to thoughts of personal gain or self-aggrandizement, because these violate the truths that she has taught me to live my life by.

See page 314 to find out where this student got in.

ELIZABETH KEMNITZER

Elizabeth was on the debate team for four years and was very active in both politics and community service in high school. In addition to participating in school-sponsored clubs, she volunteered for local political campaigns and was active in Girl Scouts. For a Girl Scout project, she started a children's library at a Kansas City homeless shelter.

Stats

SAT I: 1440 (700 Verbal, 740 Math)
SAT II: 750 Math IIC, 700 U.S. History, 670 Writing
ACT: 33
High School GPA: 3.75 unweighted
High School: Blue Valley North High School, Overland Park, KS
Hometown: Leawood, KS
Gender: Female
Race/Ethnicity: White

Applied To

Boston University
Brown University
Johns Hopkins University
University of Chicago
University of Southern California

Essay

Elizabeth used the following essay in her applications to the University of Chicago and Brown University.

University of Chicago: *The Golden Gate Bridge in San Francisco, CA, the Gothic architecture of the University of Chicago, Mardi Gras, the Great Wall of China—all are highly visible landmarks, characteristics, or events that are emblematic of a particular place. In a more subtle way, there are other "landmarks" that are less recognizable but nonetheless suggest a specific place. Perhaps it is the local mall, or spring tulips in your garden, or abandoned warehouses, or an annual Fourth of July parade or October pumpkin festival. Write about a landmark, characteristic, or event that suggests to you a specific place.*

One afternoon, while perusing the racks at a favorite clothing store of mine, I noticed amidst the sequined shirts and novelty hats a counter in the corner of the store labeled "espresso bar." Now why this store wanted innumerable spillable beverages hovering around their clothing was beyond me. At the sight of this symbol of mainstream culture, however, I, like a shell-shocked war veteran in a room full of fire crackers, felt images of wood paneling, specialty drinks, earth-tone carpeting, shelves upon shelves of alphabetically-arranged books, and targeted advertising displays, all of which were representative of the large chain book store where I worked, swarm through my head.

This book store, before employing me in their café, had been, with all of its little unexplored nooks and special interest categorizing, my version of an intellectual paradise. Never did I even consider turning down the opportunity of spending a cloudy Sunday afternoon browsing its many stacks and pouring over its periodicals. My infatuation proved transitory, however, for, as I began working there, the book store gradually came to encompass, not intellectual empowerment, but the conformity present in society, and, as one who had always championed individualism, this did not sit well with me.

I found signs of this conformity in almost every aspect of my job. In fact, the café itself was the embodiment of conformity, for it existed only as a watered-down replica of the true coffee shop. Our café also drew a completely different clientele than genuine coffee shops, as most of our customers, prior to coming to our café, had never tasted real espresso before and would order beverages whose names they couldn't pronounce and whose ingredients they couldn't name, simply because they'd heard them mentioned on

TV, or they would order French vanilla cappuccinos, not realizing that any establishment that does not sell gasoline does not sell a French vanilla cappuccino either. I saw these people as desperately downcast, lacking identity and pitifully attempting to join a seemingly elite culture cunningly created for them by corporate America.

At first, I had naturally placed the blame of this phenomenon on corporate America, maintaining that it was they who were actually marketing and forcing these products and principles down people's throats. Yet as I stood in that clothing store then, staring at that espresso bar, I saw that, although suggestive, corporate America certainly did not demand the attention it received, and upon realizing this, I decided that blaming corporate America merely meant blaming the messenger.

My mind was not settled with this, however, for as soon as I had settled this point, I was led to yet another question which asked why people so readily accept what is placed before them. Are we so starved for identity that instead of forming our own self-concepts, we adopt the corporate trip instead, simply because it comes prepackaged and is easily digestible? This must be so, I reasoned, for not only do most people swallow this tripe, as is evidenced by the café phenomenon itself, but even those who don't swallow it almost always turn instead to a counterculture and conform to it with the belief that by entering a culture that's not the norm, they are not conforming, since conformity, definitive of the norm, could not possibly exist in anything of the alternative. Their actions, however, only further prove the astonishing prevalence of conformity in society.

Suddenly, these thoughts dissipated as my mind was swept back into the present by the insistent whine of milk being steamed, which caused me to yet again scrutinize that espresso bar. And so I looked, expecting to be filled with shock and a sense of betrayal, as I was before, but instead, I felt only a mild complacency. Sure, the espresso bar's characteristic "yuppynish" still reminded me of that chain book store and all the conformity it embodied, but now, it also reminded me of caffe au laits (pronounced "oh lets" by the more provincial), French vanilla cappuccinos, and even plain old Coke, for these are what, ironically enough, I've found to define the search for individual identity.

See page 315 to find out where this student got in.

ELLISON WARD

In high school, Ellison was a Peer Leader and a member of the Cultural Awareness group, as well as a member of the soccer, basketball, and lacrosse teams. She was also extremely interested in Spanish language and culture and did a study abroad program the summer after her sophomore year.

Stats

SAT I: 1570 (780 Verbal, 790 Math)

SAT II: 800 Writing, 770 Math IIC, 740 Physics

High School GPA: Ellison's high school did not calculate GPA, but she had about an A- average throughout high school, and took a total of seven AP courses.

High School: The Nightingale-Bamford School, New York, NY

Hometown: New York, NY

Gender: Female

Race/Ethnicity: White

Applied To

Brown University

College of William & Mary

Connecticut College

Duke University

Johns Hopkins University

Harvard College

Princeton University

Yale University

Essay #1: Common Application Question 1

Ellison used the following essay in her application to Princeton and modified it slightly for her applications to all other schools.

Evaluate a significant experience, achievement, or risk that you have taken and its impact on you.

So I'm sitting on my couch, wrapped in a blanket that I have somehow wrestled from my sister, enthralled by the electrifying activities taking place before me. The movie is *Outbreak*, and our star, Dustin Hoffman, is in the middle of a standoff with his superior officer, Donald Sutherland. Their argument centers on a certain town in California, contaminated with a certain deadly yet suddenly curable virus, and a plane carrying a chemical agent that will wipe out the entire population of the aforementioned town. "No!" my sister shrieks. "Don't drop the bomb!" As the plane veers out over the ocean, the missile flies into the crystal clear waters and creates an immense, mushroom-shaped wave. "All right!" shouts my family, as out of the jubilee rises my tearful cry, "Wait! What about the marine life?!"

All right, so this is an overly dramatic version of the actual events, but the gist is the same. My bizarre attachment to the fictional fish is largely a product of my summer; I worked for eight weeks in the Coral Lab of the New York Aquarium on Coney Island. I'll admit that my interest in the Natural Sciences was pretty general; I thought corals were beautiful, and I had fond memories of childhood trips to the Aquarium every time I visited my aunt and uncle in Virginia. I was thrilled to be working at the lab, but when you came right down to it, one truth remained: I had no idea what I was doing. No amount of ninth grade biology (or tenth grade chemistry or eleventh grade physics, for that matter) could have prepared me for the intricacies of the filtration system in a room full of corals being used for research projects or the manual dexterity required by the micropipeting process. But by the time August rolled around, not only had I mastered the fine art of maintaining a number of different filters and the rather painstaking procedure of micropipeting, but I had figured out what it is that has always drawn me to the sciences. Everyone I met, no matter how grating, overbearing, or bossy he might have been, could be reduced by the mere sight of a tank to an awed silence. And most that I met were not in any way grating, overbearing, or bossy. In fact, they were enthusiastic, dedicated, and friendly to anyone interested in their field to the point of annoyance. And they are just who I want to be.

The funny thing about this whole essay is that I don't even want to be a marine biologist. What I really want to study are the Earth Sciences, but the specifics are not important. I learned this summer what it is to be passionate about what you are doing, to have an unchecked enthusiasm for even the dirtiest aspects of your work. To spend your life in the quest for knowledge that could make the world a better place may sound like a lofty goal, but when it's a real possibility, it's utterly amazing. Like any profession there are twists and turns, opportunities for frustration, disappointment, and conflict, but everyone in that lab knows he is doing something he can be proud of and that might help the world better understand how we can save our planet. Now that I have seen the kind of passion and love with which these people work at their jobs, I would never settle for anything less.

Essays #2-5: Princeton's required essays (all questions are approximations)

What book has had the most effect on you and why? It can be a book you read on your own, in class, or anywhere.

Of all the books that I have read, the one that has affected me the most is <u>Native Son</u> by Richard Wright, which I read for my Harlem Renaissance English elective junior year. Never have I read a book in which the protagonist has such a wildly different sense of the world than the expected norm. Suddenly I was exposed to a way of thinking that was extraordinarily different than my own, and Wright's compelling portrait made it easy for me to understand this startling point of view. Before reading this novel, I had always closed my mind to those who did not agree with my liberal yet stringent morality; I could not (or would not) allow myself to explore a mindset that would allow someone to commit a crime so egregious as murder. <u>Native Son</u> has allowed me to face the fear that comes with venturing into the unknown, and to explore a variety of opinions before settling on one of my own, rather than automatically following that which I feel best fits my profile of convictions. Open-mindedness and the ability to withhold judgement are extremely important qualities in a world where so many cultures and ideals mix, and Richard Wright's novel has helped me to work towards gaining both of these qualities.

Name one thing that you wish you understood better. Explain.

Of the many things that I wish I understood better, the one that I am faced with the most often is my sister. I see her everyday; we attend the same school, share a room, and share our parents. I feel as though I should understand her feelings and be able to identify her moods with ease after thirteen years of living with her, but she remains one of the biggest mysteries in my life. She's talented, intelligent, and undoubtedly the wittiest person I know. Yet she is also picky, stubborn, and prone to outbreaks that I am powerless to stop. Not that I think these outbursts are a sign of some underlying psychological problem; they are hardly that serious. But when I am coming closer and closer to moving out of our room and thus putting a hole in our relationship that may not be refilled, I can't bear to watch our days together wasted on her bad moods. Maybe it is because I am too close to her that I can't see the way my own actions affect her, but I simply do not know how to behave so that I won't set her off. My parents seem to have some idea; they often think that I am trying to aggravate her on purpose. But I want nothing more than to have the harmony (and that truly is how I would describe the situation) that we often live in be permanent. I'm just not sure how to make that happen.

If you could hold any position in government, what would it be, and why?

If I could hold any position in the government, I would be the President. Opportunities such as this do not present themselves very often; it seems only natural to choose the position in which I could effect the most change. Although I have nothing but respect for the principles of our government, there are many aspects of the actual governing of our country that have room for improvement. The corruption, partisan hostility, and sordid scandals that have come to characterize our government are an embarrassment. The most effective way to increase the esteem in which the world and our own people hold the administration is to place in the most visible position someone clearly dedicated to the upkeep of the noble ideals upon which our country was founded. This is where I come in. Although the actual fulfillment of the duties of this office would be by necessity far less idealistic than my diatribe on the Founding Fathers, the government is in dire need of someone who has at least some small sense of the merits of such antiquated conceptions as liberty, freedom, and limited power. If I could, in my stint as President, represent citizens of the United States as the open-minded, intelligent, respectful, and more-interested-in-foreign-affairs-than-the-private-life-of-our-president people that many are convinced we are not, than I would have succeeded in fulfilling one of the most important goals our Presidential candidates should have.

Name one thing that you would do to improve race relations in this country.

The problem of race is one that has plagued our country since its inception, and it is virtually impossible to come up with one or two simple steps to that would lead to its repair. It seems that virtually every solution opens a Pandora's box of new problems, and it is difficult to sort through the insanely numerous opinions, stereotypes, prejudices and points of view that constitute our population. This being said, no real progress can be made without small strides, as controversial and tiny as they may be. The best solution would be a spontaneous dissolution of prejudice and the opening of people's minds; a slightly more realistic solution might be to rearrange the zoning of public schools, and to then promote diversity within those schools. Arranging school districts by neighborhood in many cases results in an uneven balance between different ethnicities, which in turn results in increased hostility and divisiveness. By instead creating magnet schools that draw from a variety of neighborhoods, diversity of race, as well as socioeconomic class, religion, sexuality, and all the other characteristics that make people different, would be increased. Forcing the truly complete integration of the nation's schools may be one of the only ways remaining to break down the barriers separating the vast groups that populate the United States. Although it may create resentment, disagreement, or discomfort at first, it seems a somewhat feasible way of promoting the harmony to which we aspire.

See page 315 to find out where this student got in.

EMILY PETRONE

Emily played varsity soccer for four years in high school and was a member of the Improv Troupe for three years.

Stats

SAT I: 1380 (700 Verbal, 680 Math)

SAT II: 750 Writing, 630 German

ACT: 33

High School GPA: 4.2

High School: Farragut High School, Knoxville, TN

Hometown: Knoxville, TN

Gender: Female

Race/Ethnicity: Caucasian

Applied To

Northwestern University (applied early decision)

Essay

Anatole France once said, "If 50 million people say a foolish thing, it is still a foolish thing." On what subject do you disagree with most people, and why?

A Disparaged Classic

The American Film Institute recently presented their list of the one-hundred greatest films ever made. I strongly disagree with their assessment of one particular film. Sixty-ninth on the list was the classic western Shane, starring the legendary Alan Ladd. I have reviewed most of the movies on the AFI list, and it is clear to me that Shane deserves to be ranked in the top ten. In fact, I would even be so bold as to suggest that Shane is worthy of being named the finest work of cinematic art known to man.

Not only does Shane possess the key elements that distinguidh the so-called "best" films on the AFI list, but it proves superior in areas which these same films are weak. My first quarrel concerns Citizen Kane, lauded to be the greatest film of all time. Unlike Shane, film enthusiasts often praise Citizen Kane for one of its technical innovations, the ceilinged set. However, there is a reason that Shane is not noted for such a thing. Shane cannot be contained in a single room! The acting prowess of Alan Ladd cannot be confined to a ceilinged set in a studio lot! Shane requires an open range, miles upon miles of rugged landscape, to convey his purpose. That fact alone should propel Shane to the top of any greatest films list. Secondly, the vibrant Technicolor of Shane presents a far more visually stimulating picture than the drab black and white of ninth-ranked Schindler's List does. Furthermore, some critics say that Singin' In the Rain offers an excellent example of utilizing song and dance to tell a narrative. I believe that they have overlooked the convivial square-dance scene in Shane, which wonderfully depicts the camaraderie and optimism of the homesteaders. Some critics say that the final scene of Casablanca, when Humphrey Bogart and Claude Reins walk off into the fog, embodied one of the most powerful endings of any film. I wonder if they recall the closing scene of Shane, when Alan Ladd gallantly rides off into the sunset, though severely wounded and perhaps dead. Some critics say that the story of three souls in search of a brain, a heart, and courage in The Wizard of Oz inspires people of all ages. I ask, does Shane not hold all of these qualities from the beginning? These arguments represent just a few of the many I have against the current ranking of Shane on the AFI list.

Essentially, I believe that the American Film Institute has done a grave injustice to Shane, a movie which is a testament to supreme artistic achievement in any medium, most certainly film. The celebrated thespian and heartthrob Alan Ladd once said, "A man's gotta be what he is." For the character Shane, that means a wandering gunfighter with deep-set morals looking for a place to call home. For the movie Shane, that means being ranked nothing less than first on the American Film Institute's list of the one-hundred greatest films ever made.

See page 316 to find out where this student got in.

EMMA FRICKE

Emma was involved in field hockey for four years and was captain of the JV team for two. She was active in student government and was the secretary for two years. She actively participated in volunteer activities with her church and school. She also worked with children through both day-care centers and baby-sitting.

Stats

SAT I: 1220 (640 Verbal, 580 Math)
SAT II: 580 Biology, 550 Chemistry, 600 Math 1C, 620 Writing
High School GPA: 3.35/4.00
High School: Belmont High School, Belmont, MA
Hometown: Belmont, MA
Gender: Female
Race/Ethnicity: White

Applied To

Mount Holyoke College
Smith College
Sweet Briar College
Vanderbilt University
Wellesley College

Essay

Emma used the following essay in each of her applications.

Choose a significant occurrence in your life and discuss why it is has impacted you.

What first comes to mind when the words sing-a-longs, radio shows and art projects are listed together? For my brother and I, these words have a special meaning. For us, they mean to load up our suitcases with every single "important clothing item" and fill our back-packs with tapes, art materials and any other fun items that we deem "necessary" for yet another Road Trip.

For as long as I can remember, my family has been throwing gear into the car and heading off on adventures. My brother and I have always been in charge of packing our own bags and bringing things to keep us entertained. Usually, we don't need many material items. We pool our imaginations to invent games, sing songs, and play bingo. We also do back scratching, head massaging, and feet fighting. The two of us always bond no matter how feisty we have been during the weeks before. Together, we fall into our "road trip mode" of cooperation the second we hit the highways.

I am by no means saying that every road trip we have taken has been perfectly pleasant. Once, my brother, who was three months old at the time, screamed all the way from Texas to Missouri. When I was two and my brother was not yet one we moved from Texas to Massachusetts. On the last leg of the journey in Connecticut, my father came down with the chicken pox. I am told that when I was four on a trip to Alabama, I sang the same song over and over for an hour. At that point I calmly announced, "Let's turn the record over!" And for the next hour I sang a new song. Another time, when I was in eighth grade and I thought hard rock was the coolest. I made my family listen to it all the way from Boston to Florida. My brother and I have also gone through "creative" stages. On our annual road trip to Missouri, we decorated all the windows of our car with beeswax clay. "Hey Mom," we exclaimed, "when it melts on the windows it looks just like stained glass!" Another time we made glitter paintings. We called the glitter "magic dragon dust." When we arrived at our campsite for the night, the mystical "dragon dust" covered our entire bodies, our seats and the floor, (and about 1% of it was on its actual designated spot, the paper.) The dragon dust lingered for years in the car. On a road trip, mechanical difficulties are bound to happen. En-route to Minnesota, our alternator belt fell off along the highway. We exited quickly but couldn't find a gas station anywhere. Luckily, straight-ahead was K-Mart. Rejuvenated with hope, my brother, my best friend and I ran in, asking every sales clerk around if they could find us a new alternator belt for the car. "No" was the answer. Picture us: a family (plus one) sitting on the curb eating carrots at K-Mart next to a smoking and smelly car. We didn't give up, though. Eventually, my dad found a tow-truck service to take him to a gas station so he could buy a new belt. Pretty soon, we were back on the road again singing our hearts out.

As the years have progressed, our Road Trips have changed significantly. Now we have three drivers instead of two and we all can agree on music (well, sort of). My brother has become a professional backseat driver and we can go for longer than one exit without having to stop for a bathroom break. Lately though, my family has begun taking road trips with my father's brother and his family. They have four children ages two, four, seven and nine. Now my brother and I are the designated babysitters instead of the babysittees. They have a van and so my brother and I sit with kids piled on each lap and entertain. Last year, while driving from Alabama to Florida to visit our grandparents, we successively rapped every child's song that we could think of; rap, apparently, is now the cool music of choice, (not hard rock, like I used to think). We also have refined our talent of making up stories "No, I want a scary bunny story, not a funny alligator story," and have learned the gift of patience.

This gift of patience is invaluable. In order to succeed in what I love to do, working with young children; patience is something that I have to draw upon often. When I am ready to throw up my hands in desperation while babysitting or working in the church nursery, I remember how my parents dealt with my brother and me throughout the years of Road Trips. Smiling from this, I roll up my sleeves and whip out some glitter and paper or begin to sing the songs that I remember from my childhood. My parents have taught me that children are a gift and their creativity and outlook on life is something that should never be suppressed or overlooked. Now that I am a senior in high school, I am sad to think that my road trip days with my family are almost finished. Hopefully, college will be one big Road Trip where I will use the important aspects of creativity, compromise and overcoming obstacles. I will always know how to enjoy life even though what is presented to me may not be "magic dragon dust."

See page 316 to find out where this student got in.

ERIC OSBORNE

Eric was actively involved in many areas of student life, working as assistant editor of the yearbook, writing as a columnist for the paper, and serving as a member of the civic-service organization. During his senior year, he was president of the school's Government Club (the school's largest club) through which he served as lieutenant governor at the state model legislature. He lettered in track for three years and in yell-leading for two, winning the "spirit" award his senior year for his dedication and inspiration to the track team.

Stats

SAT I: 1460 (750 Verbal, 710 Math)
SAT II: 800 World History, 800 American History, 790 Writing
ACT: 32
High School GPA: 3.8 unweighted, 4.1 weighted
High School: Memphis University School, Memphis, TN
Hometown: Memphis, TN
Gender: Male
Race/Ethnicity: White

Applied To

Amherst College (applied early decision)

Essay

Evaluate a significant experience, achievement, risk you have taken, or ethical dilemma you have faced and its impact on you.

From a Dunce to Demosthenes

ERX, the word rings clearly in my ears today. In 6th grade some of my peers decided it would be funny to make fun of the lisp that Eric Osborne had. They took my first name and added a lisp sound to the end of it, finally arriving with a new nickname for me, Erx.

As a little kid I had somehow learned to say "S's" incorrectly. Rather than the smooth hissing sound most people make, my "S's" were a saliva-filled slur that lisped sideways from my mouth. In my earliest years my teachers, parents, and friends would try to correct me.

Wanting to please them, I would swallow all the saliva in my mouth and speak slowly, enunciating as clearly as possible. But it never made a difference.

As I grew older the other kids started to make fun of my speech. Every time I opened my mouth, some sneering comment was sure to follow. I was embarrassed by all this and soon preferred keeping quite to being made fun of. I became something of a recluse. Eric Osborne was the shy kid who, for fear of being made fun of, hardly ever spoke. Mute, I became a virtually friendless wanderer.

My parents had opposing views of the situation. My mother was worried about me: she was worried that I never brought friends home, that I never went out to spend the night, that I always seemed sad and depressed. My father had a different view: he was upset that I could never "enunciate clearly." My speech impediment irked my father greatly. For years he corrected me to no avail, and he became more upset with each passing day.

By third grade I had gone through speech therapy, but things had not improved. Afterward I had always looked upon speech therapy as something only young children went through; I did not consider repeating it myself. But by eighth grade things were changing. Although I now had more friends, the teasing was continuing, and I was more aware of my personal image. In addition my father had decided that enough was enough and it was now time to put an end to my impediment. Speech therapy seemed the best course of action. With my guidance counselor's help we found a speech pathologist, and I went back to speech therapy.

It took the pathologist less than ten minutes to diagnose my problem. She told me to move my tongue to the level of my teeth and blow out air. I did, and a correct-sounding "S" reverberated through the room. It was the smoothest feeling that had ever come out of my mouth. A new world of possibility seemed in front of me. For the next year I worked on consciously placing my tongue. I would stand in front of the mirror and practice, pushing against my jaw, moving my tongue, and blowing air. I progressed slowly from the ABC's, to short sentences, and finally to conversation. When talking with my friends I tried to speak correctly, and if I messed up I would correct myself. My friends were amazed at the transformation, but nobody was happier than I when the pathologist pronounced me cured. Fixing my speech problem was an amazing accomplishment that I had never truly expected to achieve, but what amazes me the most is how far I have come since. In ninth grade I joined our school's Government Club and became actively involved in Model UN and the Youth Legislature, conferences involving public speaking and debate. The kid who just a few years before would not talk with anyone, was now giving speeches before groups of a hundred people. Time and again my advisors and my peers would commend me for my speaking (once a fellow delegate even compared my speaking to that of the great orator Cicero). Junior year I won great praise for a campaign speech I had given: dozens of people told me the speech, citing the importance of friendship, had moved them. The speech got me elected Lt. Governor for next year's conference. A month later I was elected President of the Government Club. I had come all the way from being a recluse to being a gifted orator and the leader of our school's largest and most speech-oriented organization.

I consider overcoming my speech impediment to be one of my greatest achievements ever. No longer am I a friendless wanderer, now I am more extroverted and enjoy having many friends. I speak up in class without hesitation and converse freely with strangers. I am even scheduled to give a twenty-minute speech in assembly, something rare for students. Anyone who knew me as a child and could see my outspoken self today would be amazed at my transformation. Correcting my speech impediment was a great achievement that has changed my life...no one calls me ERX anymore.

See page 316 to find out where this student got in.

ERIC WEINGART

Eric was an all-around solid academic candidate. He was a Central Massachusetts all-star in tennis, as well as league all-star for three years, team MVP one year, and team captain for two years. He was heavily involved with every aspect of production in his high school's Educational Television Studio, which operated its own cable channel in town.

Stats

SAT I: 1440 (720 Verbal, 720 Math)
SAT II: 720 Biology, 760 Math IC, 800 Writing
High School GPA: 4.82/5.00
High School: Shrewsbury High School, Shrewsbury, MA
Hometown: Shrewsbury, MA
Gender: Male
Race/Ethnicity: White American

Applied To

Brown University
Bucknell University
Colgate University
College of William & Mary
Duke University
Princeton University
University of North Carolina—Chapel Hill
University of Pennsylvania

Essay: U Penn

Write page 187 of your autobiography.

"goat's breath.

The Barnyard Properties fiasco convinced me I should choose clientele a little more carefully. Sure, the contract paid well, but there's more to being an advertising executive than money. I thought it would be fun to work with that company, but I should have known that potential disasters accompany working with a CEO who consulted his pet yak for financial advice.

I planned to take some time off to recover emotionally, but, as things turned out, my next contract hit me right in the head. Seriously. I was running on the treadmill at the Greenwich Health Club, only a few minutes from my house, as I watched the tennis players practicing on the courts down the stairs from the workout area. It helps me keep my mind off of the fatigue. I looked down just for a second to check my time on the treadmill. When I returned my gaze to the tennis courts, I saw an object whizzing in my direction. Startled, I froze. Unfortunately, the treadmill did not. It carried me backwards and threw me into the wall just as the tennis ball smashed against my head. The wind temporarily knocked out of me, I vaguely recollect watching the player who had hit the errant shot rushing over to check on my condition. After making sure I was all right, the man introduced himself to me. He was none other than Lincoln McLain, president of Eight Nine Tennis Balls, Inc., and he was playtesting a new line of balls. Having been a standout tennis player in high school and college some 20 years ago in the '90's (and still an avid player today), I was familiar with the company. I introduced myself to him.

"I know who you are," McLain responded. "You're with that advertising firm that did the famous ad for the law offices of Tay, Kyorm, Unney, & Runn! I loved that commercial! In fact, we're looking for a new campaign to launch these new tennis balls. How would you like the contract?"

"Are you kidding? I'd love it!" I replied enthusiastically.

I began working with ideas that evening. I came up with several themes, but nothing that really captured me. Let's see, I thought. What would make a brand of tennis balls sell? Finally, it struck me. "The winner always plays with Eight Nine Tennis Balls!" Okay, so maybe not everybody realized that two players in a match must use the same balls, but the slogan was truthful. The winner either used Eight Nine Tennis Balls or the loser didn't. This is why I love my job: I can use creativity while being challenged by limits. The limits, however, are not set in stone. Long ago, I learned to stretch any so-called "limits." One does not know his true abilities until he"

See page 317 to find out where this student got in.

GAURAV P. PATEL

Gaurav graduated summa cum laude as salutatorian of his small, private high school and received several local and national awards, such as the Atlanta Journal Cup Award, the American Academy of Achievement Honor Student award (the top 400 seniors in the nation are chosen annually), Marietta's Teen of the Year, Young Leader of Tomorrow, Furman Scholar, Outstanding Junior Award, and several academic awards in school. Many of his achievements focused on the French language; he was selected to attend the Georgia Governor's Honors Program, received the Oxbridge Academics French Scholarship to attend the Academie de Paris, received the American Association of Teachers of French Travel Award, and placed first in the state and fifth in the nation on the National French Exam.

Stats
SAT I: 1500 (760 Verbal, 740 Math)
SAT II: 740 French with Listening, 760 Writing, 750 Chemistry, 740 Math IIC
High School GPA: 4.4/4.0 weighted
High School: The Walker School, Marietta, GA
Hometown: Smyrna, GA
Gender: Male
Race/Ethnicity: South Asian (Indian American)

Applied To
Dartmouth College
Harvard College
Princeton University
University of Pennsylvania
Yale University

Essay #1
Gaurav used the following essay in his applications to U Penn, Dartmouth, and Princeton.

First experiences can be defining. Cite a first experience that you have had and explain its impact on you.

Here I was in Hemingway's "moveable feast," yet unfortunately I was without a feast of my liking in Paris during OxBridge Academic's L'Académie de Paris on the program's French Language Scholarship and the National French Honor Society's Travel Award. In the world's culinary capital, I, a true francophile who cannot get enough of the French culture, could not find anything to eat. Surely, the croque monsieur or even les escargots tempted the taste buds of the over one-hundred other participants in the program; but my taste buds seemed to cringe at the sight, god forbid the smells, of such foods. However, I somehow survived on les sandwich and by my fascination of France and what else she had to offer.

My classes Littérature française and Medicine at L'Académie unmasked the educational merits that often lie hidden behind façades for the 'traditional' visitors of Paris. Classes began at 9:00 a.m. after a French breakfast and ended at 12:00 p.m., when students traversed the Parisian streets to grab a sandwich and enjoy lunch in the Luxembourg Gardens or in the gardens of the Rodin Museum. Minor classes began at 2:00 p.m., but the city became a teacher's aide, a type of three-dimensional video. Studying literature and fashioning my own poems in a café where Hemingway used to frequent or creating my own literary "salon" at la Mosquée became reality during class. The beauty and the scintillation of the French language came to life even more so for me. I never ceased to be enthralled, for I was finally immersed in the culture, the language, and the tradition of my academic passion in life: French.

The whole city transformed into a massive university; there was always something to learn outside of classes. Attempting to speak French with a native or ordering lunch in French became a unique type of erudition. While studying abroad, I not only received a stable background with lively teachers in my classes, I also began to experience French life — I was a Parisian for one full month (or at least I tried to be).

In Paris, I never had a dull moment. Whether it was a walk to the Eiffel Tower or a short journey to the nearby Versailles or a candle-light stroll in and around Vaux-le-Vicomte, I never tired. Having a cappuccino with my newfound friends at a café as we watched others briskly walking by on the Champs-Elysées or travelling on the Métro became adventures. The French culture offers a city and a country where the joy of life is present all around.

Nevertheless, I had to leave my utopia. On my last stroll around Paris and in the Luxembourg Gardens on the morning of my departure, I came to realize that I had had an extraordinary experience that many will never savor. Learning French amongst les français was a dream that I had finally fulfilled, and it is a something that I crave yet again — without the food if possible.

Essay #2

Gaurav used the following essay in his applications to Harvard and Yale.

For Harvard he responded to Common Application Question 1: *Evaluate a significant experience, achievement, or risk that you have taken and its impact on you.*

Yale provides a blank page and asks applicants to write about themselves.

Every taste of life brings some new knowledge to each person, and thus, experiences are the way we grow, the way we live, and the way we survive in an all too changing world. Each and every unique bite of life fills the human body with suffering, achievement, or satisfaction. Personally, I feel that experiences which content the soul are the most worthwhile. Of my many personal adventures in life, I feel that my experience tutoring a young eighth grader in my sophomore year of high school has given me the feeling of greatest satisfaction.

This young man was of Middle-Eastern origin and was having trouble organizing his thoughts in English; he lacked the motivation necessary to succeed in his class and was, therefore, about to fail. He became overly frustrated and discouraged with himself. His English teacher, my teacher in eighth grade, felt that this student did not believe in himself because English was his second language; his teacher thought that because of my patience, maturity, and agility in working with others I could truly help him. His teacher, moreover, knew that I have the ability to interact in language, for I speak English, French, and Gujarati. And so I began tutoring him. I spent about three hours a week working with his vocabulary and his thought processes in English; I discovered that he had amazing, sophisticated ideas and concepts, but the reason he consistently failed exams and essays was that he could not express his thoughts coherently in English. Nevertheless, after about two months, he not only began to show some improvements, he also gained confidence and enhanced his self-esteem. Furthermore, I feel that he actually started to grasp a larger concept of the English language and its often complicated structure.

Helping others has been a way of life taught to me by my parents ever since I was young. By example, my parents taught me that giving to charity, speaking with one who may be distressed, reading to a youngster, or talking to an aged person enhance the value of the soul, and each awakens a sense of euphoria. Tutoring Parham has truly been one of the greatest experiences in my life, for not only did I aid this intelligent young man in receiving better grades, I feel that I taught him something that he will always remember. Speaking and writing correctly and effectively in English is a necessity in not only the

United States and England but in the entire world; furthermore, I feel that I brought out a new confidence in himself. I realize that this experience may seem somewhat minute to those of others — I could have written about my other awards, but this tutoring taught me something about myself. Helping Parham to learn and to grow buttressed the already strong moral values planted by my parents, and it made a difference in the life of another — the main objective.

See page 317 to find out where this student got in.

GIANNA MARZILLI

Gianna was awarded several Scholastic Art Awards in high school, including a Fine Arts Portfolio award. She was photography editor of her high school newspaper and was very involved in the music department as a pianist, singer, and brass player.

Stats

SAT I: 1460 (770 Verbal, 690 Math)
SAT II: 800 Writing, 770 Literature, 750 Math IC, 650 Math IIC
High School GPA: 4.44
High School: South Kingstown High School, Wakefield, RI
Gender: Female
Race/Ethnicity: Caucasian

Applied To

Amherst College
Brown University
Carleton College
Colby College
Macalester College
Skidmore College
Smith College
Tufts University

Washington University in St. Louis

Wellesley College

Williams College

Essay

Gianna used the following essay in each of her applications.

Common Application Question 3: *Indicate a person who has had a significant influence on you, and describe that influence.*

Within the prison of room 216B, I curled up under a flimsy hospital blanket, flanked by my teary eyed mother and an ever-present nurse. Clenched teeth prevented puddles in my eyes from moistening parched cheeks. How could a body that I'd taken such good care of turn against me so suddenly?

"A classic presentation of insulin dependent diabetes." My soul flung itself against the bars of the bed, attempting to escape the doctor's words. Blood boiled through sugar soaked veins as I envisioned a life dominated by injections, schedules, and restrictions. What right did she have to assign a biological label to something that encompassed so much more than a malfunctioning organ? I resisted the urge to rip out my IV and throw it at her. Instead, I threw myself into the daily struggle of maintaining a quasi-normal metabolic state. Despite my efforts, it became increasingly clear that the human brain was never meant to play pancreas. I became convinced that it was no longer a question of "if" I would succumb such diabetic complications as blindness, kidney failure, and limb amputations, but "when."

Enter Delaine. She had gotten my number through a friend of my mother's, and suggested that I consider an insulin pump, a device that delivers insulin 24 hours a day through a tiny infusion line. I returned her call intending to disregard the advice. I didn't want a constant reminder of my disease clipped to my waistband; I wanted people to leave me alone to contemplate my miserable future.

Fortunately, Delaine ignored my wishes. A diabetic for 16 years and a pump user herself, she had nothing but praise for the little machine. No more schedules, shots, or "diabetic diet." Best of all, the improved control meant a reduced risk for complications. It wasn't a cure, but I was convinced. Delaine was living proof that my diagnosis wasn't a death sentence, and for the first time in months I felt hopeful. A week after I began pumping, we met in person over ice cream sundaes.

"How many carbohydrates are in this creation?" she asked, gesturing grandly toward her dish. I paused, wanting desperately to thank her for everything she'd done for me, to explain that the matted fur of my old teddy bear had finally recovered from the endless nights I'd spent sobbing into his stomach.

I wanted her to know that she had transformed my perception of diabetes so much that I would no longer give it up. I've watched her use her illness to connect with people and offer them encouragement, and I want to help others the same way. Last week, I overheard a woman mention her newly diagnosed husband. I've never been an extrovert; words don't have a particular flair when escaping from my mouth into the ears of strangers. Yet there I stood, offering support and advice to a person in need. She's taught me to enjoy every moment because there are no guarantees; I refuse to have any regrets if this illness becomes stronger than I am. She is a master weaver, creating a blanket of kindness that will warm me forever.

Perhaps I should give her this essay, because I still haven't figured out how to tell her that. How do you make someone understand that she is responsible for turning your life around? As I was about to make an attempt, the waitress approached.

"Is everything . . .all right?"

I tried to recollect my thoughts, but they had conveniently escaped me. Our server must have wondered what was so intriguing about the ice cream that it warranted such intense scrutiny. As I looked down to program 9.3 units of insulin, I laughed. Another thing that I couldn't explain! Only the owner of a translucent blue, back lit, beeping pancreas would analyze the carb content of a double fudge sundae before diving in spoon-first.

See page 317 to find out where this student got in.

HALEY A. CONNOR

Haley attended a classical and Christian high school and was managing editor of the yearbook her junior and senior years. After playing piano for six years, she began playing the harp in her senior year. She also attended the High School Summer Scholars Program at Washington University between her junior and senior years.

Stats

SAT I: 1300 (620 Verbal, 680 Math)
High School GPA: 3.04
High School: Regents School of Austin, Austin, TX
Hometown: Austin, TX
Gender: Female
Race/Ethnicity: White

Applied To

Washington University in St. Louis (applied early decision)

Essay

Washington University in St. Louis wanted each applicant to make up a question and answer it. Haley posed the question, *"Who or what influenced you as a person the most up until now?"*

From the time I was a small child I loved to draw but never had formal instruction on how to draw realistically. Then one summer, while still in my elementary school years, I met a kind-hearted elderly wildlife artist at an art school day camp.

Mr. Hal Irby, an experienced and well-known local artist and teacher, helped me to develop my passion for art. At Laguna Gloria, the art studio where he taught, he was a revered instructor. The art studio requested him to return to teach his beginner's drawing class, long after he had retired and moved to the peace and quiet of the country. Mr. Irby had a unique style of drawing that looked realistic yet he drew only with small dots, no lines at all, even to create shading.

He changed my perspective on art. He made art more enjoyable and interesting. Art has become more than just a pastime for me. Mr. Irby taught me how to draw what I see, something for which I yearned. For me he made art more than just being creative.

Mr. Irby brought books, magazines and his own drawings to class. He asked the students to copy the pictures exactly as we saw them. We were taught to draw what the eye sees, not the image we might have in our mind. He encouraged me and helped me to draw the picture I had in front of me by showing which parts needed improvement and which parts were correctly rendered.

I went back to attend Mr. Irby's class for two additional years after that first camp to get the basics of drawing ingrained fully into my mind. After that first class, I felt more confident and pleased with my own talent and my learned skills. A desire was ignited in me to pursue realistic expression in my art. I intend to improve my skills in the coming years. I may decide in the course of my studies to have my hobby of art become my career because of the fulfillment it gives to me.

See page 318 to find out where this student got in.

HEATHER FIREMAN

In high school, Heather helped found a chapter of the B'nai B'rith Youth Organization and served as chapter president and regional historian. In her freshman year of high school, Heather competed in the International Olympiyeda Science Competition and won a summer trip to Israel to compete in the finals.

Stats

SAT I: 1600
SAT II: 800 Writing, 800 Math IIC, 790 Chemistry
High School GPA: 4.0/4.0
High School: Stratford High School, Houston, TX
Hometown: Houston, TX
Gender: Female
Race/Ethnicity: Caucasian

Applied To

California Institute of Technology
Massachusetts Institute of Technology
Stanford University
University of California—Berkeley

Essay

Heather used the following essay in her applications to Caltech and MIT.

The prompt was to make up a question that is personally relevant to you, state it clearly, and answer it. Heather posed the question, *"What areas are you particularly interested in studying and why? How did your interests develop?"*

Everybody is curious. Some people are more than others. They aren't satisfied with a simple explanation. They must know how and why. They are scientists.

Some people think it's irrelevant how or why the world works just so long as it does. Content not to think too hard, they miss out on the sheer wonder that is the world around them. Scientists, on the other hand, learn something amazing every day.

I first began to think about a future in natural science as a seventh-grader when I started a book called Hyperspace, by physicist Michio Kaku. I was somewhat familiar with science fiction staples like black holes, time travel, parallel universes, and higher dimensions, but only as plot devices on Star Trek. A lot of it was beyond my grasp, since I had never taken a physics class, but I had always been interested in the concepts. To think that real scientists seriously theorized about any of it inspired me to read on.

I turned to The Physics of Star Trek, which considered the possibility (or not) of the many novelties of the show (like the holodeck, warp drive, and matter transporter) actually existing within the confines of the physical world. Physics seemed a wonderful adventure, so naturally I couldn't wait for my first physics course in high school.

I had to survive chemistry first. At my school, chemistry was considered the most difficult subject around. I didn't have much trouble with it, so I enrolled for a second year to prepare for the AP exam. Concurrently, I took physics and a required semester of biochemistry. I wondered at times if I was nuts to do so, but I braved the elements and was fascinated by what chemistry had to offer: a background for interpreting natural happenings and a means to advance scientific understanding in general, a worthwhile pursuit.

The AP in chemistry required not only a wealth of knowledge, but also an abundance of lab work. I grew confident working with the techniques and equipment and always looked forward to working in the lab. Concepts were one thing, but demonstrating them in the lab provided a whole new insight into what made things work and introduced us to many lab techniques and approaches. Investigations into enzyme performance revealed the effects of various influences; countless titrations of solutions perfected our methods; gel electrophoresis and qualitative analysis tested our nerves and concentration. That year, chemistry was my most challenging subject, and it took up a significant portion of my time. But it was also the most rewarding. Suddenly, it seemed like chemistry could be part of my future. Now, it seems a more and more possible path. In the meantime, I am a school science lab assistant. I want to explore chemistry and chemical engineering, physics, and biochemistry before narrowing my choices. I want to work in the laboratory, either on the pure or applied side of science.

In any case, I will never stop being curious. I'm a scientist.

See page 318 to find out where this student got in.

HEATHER HERMANN

Heather received a varsity athletic letter for equestrian team and took part in the All-State Invitational in her senior year. She also conducted organic chemistry research during the summers follow-ing her sophomore and junior years at Michigan State University and Hope College, respectively. Heather was also involved in her high school marching and concert bands, the National Honor Soci-ety, Youth in Government, and several science festivals.

Stats

SAT I: 1340 (630 Verbal, 710 Math)
SAT II: 560 Writing, 710 Math IIC, 720 Chemistry
ACT: 31 (34 Science, 28 English, 28 Writing, 32 Math)
High School GPA: 3.96 unweighted
High School: Spring Lake High School, Spring Lake, MI
Hometown: Spring Lake, MI
Gender: Female
Race/Ethnicity: Caucasian

Applied To

Cornell University
Johns Hopkins University

Michigan State University
Northwestern University
University of Michigan
Yale University

Essay

The following essay was used as the main essay for Cornell and Yale.

Cornell: *Pose a question that you wish that we had asked you and answer it.* **Heather posed the question,** *"Tell about an activity that is particularly meaningful to you."*

Yale: *Please write an essay about an activity of interest that has been particularly meaningful to you.*

Early on a June afternoon, I stood in the arena at Willows Farm. I was about to take my *very first* horse-riding lesson. I was excited, yet incredibly fearful at the same time. I'd never actually ridden a horse by myself. Being led around on one of ponies at the fair didn't count. I tried talking to myself. "What did *I* have to fear? After all, it certainly looked easy." I waited while one of the older girls finished in the arena. I'd never seen such a big horse, and each time as they went around, the horse looked bigger and bigger.

When my lesson was finally ready to start, Aggie, my teacher, brought out a small pony named Kissy. She was so cute and little, I breathed a sigh of relief. I was convinced that I could handle the situation. "No problem," I thought, "I'll be off to the races in no time."

That lesson began with the basics. First I had to learn to put on the bridle and saddle. Then I had to learn to get on and off. That proved to be a challenge, but by the time the lesson finished, I was allowed to "ride" Kissy by walking around in a circle a few times. Sitting there looking down, I knew I was hooked. As John Irving once said, "There is something in bestriding a fine horse that makes a man (or woman) feel more than mortal".

Little did my parents know that one lesson would turn into an obsession. I spent all day out at the barn. I'd probably have stayed the night if my parents had allowed it. I did everything that I could do to learn – I cleaned stalls, walked horses, brushed horses, and fed some twice just to spend a few extra minutes out there. Over the next two years I attended local horse camps and watched others to see if they knew something that I could apply to my riding.

Eventually, I outgrew Kissy and my first trainer. The next step was to move up with the more advanced riders and to Sherry, the next trainer at the barn. Most of the more advanced riders owned their own horses. Switching trainers was the easy part. Convincing my parents to buy me a horse proved to be slightly more difficult.

Aggie talked to them and told them how much I *wanted* a horse. Sherry talked to them, and told them how much I *needed* a horse. Nothing seemed to work. Over the dinner table, the conversation kept coming back to how much money was involved in buying and keeping a horse, but I didn't give up. I kept asking. "A horse" was first on my Christmas list, first on my birthday list, and everything in between.

In the spring, a cute little quarter horse named *Cal* came into the barn. He was there to be sold, hopefully to someone in the barn. He was a good mover and seemed to have a sweet personality. The first time I saw him, I bonded. I *had* to have this horse. There was just one small problem, my parents were still saying no. Aggie seemed to want me to have a horse as much as I wanted it. She even offered to cut my parents a deal on the board. Every time my mother came to pick me up, I was brushing, walking, or doing something for Cal. I'd ask her to hold and talk to him for a few minutes while I got "something ready" before I put him away. I could feel my mother melting. Finally one evening I heard the wonderful words. My parents agreed to purchase Cal. I had *my very own* horse. I was thrilled, and went to work with a brush and comb to make him look as good as he made me feel.

As much as I thought differently, I wasn't quite prepared for the enormous responsibility of actually owning a horse. There was feeding, grooming, daily exercise, and stall cleaning to worry about. Becoming a good hunter-jumper meant spending long hours out at the barn. Getting good grades in school meant putting in long hours for homework. I had to learn to balance both. To get it all done, it was mandatory that I become organized and learn to focus on what I was doing in order to make the most of my time spent.

Riding has also presented a means of learning other valuable lessons. Foremost has been accepting responsibility. Owning Cal has meant that I've had the care of a living, breathing animal that depended on me. I couldn't take a day off, even if I felt that I had something better to do. Dedication to the sport of riding has also been a learned skill. After the hardest fall or a bad day when nothing seemed to go right, I sometimes wanted to quit right on the spot. That was when I had to get myself back on track and do it again until I got it right. Those same lessons have carried over to school. If I've gotten less than a perfect grade on something or have found something difficult to understand, I've learned that I can't just throw in the towel or blame it on the teacher. My education has become my responsibility, and I have had to go back and try twice as hard to prove to myself that *I can do it*.

In my ten years of riding and competing, I have never grown tired of it. I still have my little horse. We have competed and won at many horse shows, and we've grown to love and trust each other. My trainer often referred to him as my best friend, and I've come to think of him that way too. Sometimes it is fun to lie in bed at night and look at the ribbons hanging on my wall. I know that every day that passes now brings me closer to the "someday" when it will come to an end. When it does, I will have the memories of the great times I've had and the lessons that I've learned, but most of all, I will have the memory of a little horse with a big heart named Cal.

See page 319 to find out where this student got in.

JAMES ROBERT COOLEY

In high school, James's greatest achievement in speed skating was making the Short Track Speed Skating Junior National Team. He was an Eagle Scout and was a pole-vaulter for varsity track. James was also the president and first chair of his high school jazz band and leader of a quintet outside of school.

Stats

SAT I: 1210 (570 Verbal, 640 Math)
SAT II: 660 Math IC, 560 Physics, 540 Biology
ACT: 24
Class average: 89.261
High School: Saratoga Springs High School, Saratoga Springs, NY
Hometown: Greenfield Center, NY
Gender: Male
Race/Ethnicity: Caucasian

Applied To

American University
SUNY College at Fredonia
United States Coast Guard Academy
United States Military Academy
United States Naval Academy
University of Hartford
University of Miami

Essay #1

James used the following essay in his application to the USCGA.

Why are you interested in attending the Academy and pursuing a career in the Coast Guard?

I wish to attend the United States Coast Guard Academy so that I can pursue a career in the United States Coast Guard in a leadership role, partaking in peacetime missions for my country. At the Academy I would receive the best education possible while studying engineering, my special interest. This would provide me with limitless future opportunities. Such a career is both challenging and demanding, be it rescue, law enforcement, or maritime protection. I have always loved the water and would love to keep it as clean and safe as possible. At seventeen, I have already proven to be reliable, dedicated, adventurous, educated, motivated and fit, in order to pursue such a career.

I have a particular interest in maintaining and surpassing the physical fitness level I have achieved. I would be able both to do this and to continue playing the saxophone at the Academy. The Coast Guard Academy is a unique place where character is built, while obtaining the finest education and training for an adventurous life. It is my desire to serve my country, as I have represented my country in speedskating competition.

Essay #2

Describe a personal accomplishment or experience that uniquely illustrates your character, commitment, and capability, helping us to recognize your potential as a successful Coast Guard officer.

The accomplishment that best shows my character, commitment, and capability is achieving a Category 1 status in Short Track Speedskating.

In the most recent skating season, 1997-1998, I had one goal: to achieve Category 1 status, which means I would be one of the top six Junior skaters in the country and earn the right to wear the USA uniform. An extreme amount of dedication, drive, and focus on my part was necessary to accomplish this. My day would begin with 5:30 AM workouts with Olympians and end with late night ice practices. My coach knew what we had to do as he had trained Olympians before. I was joining them, as well as taking a full course load in my junior year in high school and pursuing my musical commitments.

I soon saw much improvement in my strength, endurance, and speed. When the Junior Trial Competition arrived, I was physically and mentally ready. Along with the physical training came intense mental training so that focusing was possible during the stressful times. I proved to be capable of achieving the goal that I had set for myself by being committed to the task at hand.

My accomplishments boosted my confidence immensely. This was due in part to my beating skaters that previously had been faster than I, and also because I had set a difficult goal and was successful in achieving it. All the components of that skating season: tending to proper nutrition, goal setting, regimentation, physical conditioning, as well as school obligations, enhanced my character and led me to realize that I can achieve whatever I set out to do.

See page 319 to find out where this student got in.

JAMES SAMUEL FLETCHER

Sam was involved in a wide variety of sports, including tennis, swimming, baseball, and cross-country in high school. He participated in the music program as well, singing in the chamber choir and playing trumpet. He also received the DAR Award and was president of the Latin Club.

Stats

ACT: 34
High School GPA: 10.855/11.000
High School: Cape Central High School, Cape Girardeau, MO
Hometown: Cape Girardeau, MO
Gender: Male
Race/Ethnicity: American (white)

Applied To

Hillsdale College
Samford University
United States Naval Academy

Essay

Sam used the following essay in his application to the United States Naval Academy.

In a well-organized essay of 300-500 words, please discuss the following: (1) Describe what led to your initial interest in the naval service and how the Naval Academy will help you achieve your long range goals, and (2) Describe a personal experience you have had which you feel has contributed to you own character development and integrity.

I was privileged to visit the Naval Academy for the first time through the Summer Seminar, although I remember previously passing through Annapolis on a family vacation to D. C. On that occasion, I was particularly impressed with the picturesque beauty and the plethora of sailboats. Upon returning for the Seminar, Annapolis was as gorgeous as I remembered, and I had greater appreciation for the sailing because of lessons that I took in Maine last summer.

It was my Latin teacher who introduced me to the ideas, purpose, and heritage of the Naval Academy. I discovered immediately what a unique place it was, and this impression was justified again and again as I learned more about it from other sources. As I received input from individuals about what being in the Navy was like, I thought life in the service sounded like a fascinating adventure.

I especially like two things about the Navy. The first would be the environment. I may be something of a romantic, but I love stories of courage, bravery, and honor, from the *Iliad* to the movie *Braveheart*. These tales stir an emotion in my soul which I see developed and encouraged at the Academy. In a culture that exhibits a total lack of morals, and seems not even to know what "honor" is, I feel the Academy is perhaps one of the few places left where these ideals are cherished as being vitally important.

So many of us have forgotten the sacrifice that our fathers endured so that we could have what we have today. Out of the fifty-six brave men who signed the Declaration of Independence, five were captured by the British and tortured; twelve had homes sacked, looted, or burned; two lost their sons; one had two sons captured; nine died in the war from wounds or other hardships. These were men who not only exemplified courage and honor, but who left an incredibly awesome responsibility to us. John Adams speaks to us with these words: "Posterity—you will never know how much it has cost my generation to preserve your freedom. I hope that you make good use of it." What a challenge for us to live up to!

The second thing about the Navy that I especially admire is what it does to people. It literally changes people. Changes in attitudes and a closeness of relationships with others was even evident from the short *week* at the Seminar.

A personal experience that contributed to my character development and integrity would be "totaling" my mom's brand new Nissan Altima. This was a result of recklessness and rebellion on my part. Being so dangerously close to death greatly terrified me. As a result, I realized the need to respect rules and authority, and how my actions have consequences which I must live up to. This mistake led to my getting a part-time job to pay for a car and insurance. Working at Steak & Shake as a waiter has been a tremendous character-building experience

See page 319 to find out where this student got in.

JAMES GREGORY

James served as student body treasurer his senior year and was a two-year letterman in basketball, as well as being the team captain. He was a National Merit Scholarship winner and was named to the Academic All-State Team his senior year for basketball.

Stats

SAT I: 1540

SAT II: 800 Math IIC, 780 Spanish, 800 Writing

High School GPA: 5.13/6.00

High School: Walter Hines Page High School, Greensboro, NC

Hometown: Greensboro, NC

Gender: Male

Race/Ethnicity: White

Applied To

Duke University

Harvard College (applied early action)

Princeton University

University of North Carolina

Yale University

Essay

James used the following essay in his applications to Duke and Harvard, and modified it for Princeton. He also used it in his National Merit Scholarship application.

Write about a matter of importance to you on any topic. If you have written a personal essay for another purpose—even an essay for another college—that you believe represents you, your writing, and your thinking particularly well, feel free to submit it.

To really understand who I am, remember your childhood. Remember the pleasure that eating a great big peanut butter and jelly sandwich delivered? How it seemed to just slide down your throat and ease into your stomach? That sandwich is the result of the perfect combination of ingredients, all working together to create a satisfying experience. If any one ingredient were missing, the whole sandwich would fall apart. In fact, I would argue that the world is very much like one large PB&J, filled with many different ingredients. People can be classified according to their personality and similarity to these ingredients. I am like the chunky peanut butter. Although I may not be as showy as the jelly or as visible as the bread, I am the heart of the sandwich. I am essential to the sandwich's success. I work behind the scenes, holding it all together, keeping all the ingredients organized and focused on their task. I lead through example, but I am flexible. I am able to work with any kind of jelly. I am slightly shy, so I do not need to be the center of attention; I am content in leading without recognition. However, you always know I am there. You taste all my chunks, all the little quirks that set me apart from the rest. Whether it is my dry sense of humor, my volunteer work at a summer day camp for my kids, or my fervent school spirit, each unique piece guarantees that your experience will not be mundane and bland. With every bite you take, you taste more of me: my excellent grades, my size 15 feet, and my dedication to Student Council. I am more fun than creamy peanut butter; you never know what to expect, but you know that it is going to be good. However, my most important attribute is my willingness to sacrifice to help others. I have unselfishly stepped aside on the basketball court to let the team as a whole shine, and I enthusiastically devote time to service projects through Junior Civitans that help the community. This desire to help is ingrained in my personality, and drives my plan to become a physician and continue my service to others. I refuse to give up before I attain this dream; I have the persistence of the little glob of peanut butter that sticks to the roof of your mouth. No matter how many times you smack you mouth, I will not go away. This drive has enabled me achieve academic success, success that I will continue into my higher education, and into my life. I am fun, I am good for you, and I am more than the sum of my pieces. I am the chunky peanut butter.

See page 320 to find out where this student got in.

JAMIE MANOS

Jamie was a very active, well-rounded student in high school. She played soccer and ran track for four years and actively pursued her passion for music by performing in a number of instrumental ensembles, allowing her to travel across the country and receive national recognition for festival performances.

Stats

SAT I: 1280

SAT II: 710 Writing, 680 Math IC, 660 Biology E

High School GPA: 95.7/100

High School: Old Town High School, Old Town, ME

Hometown: Old Town, ME

Gender: Female

Ethnicity: Caucasian

Applied To

Cornell University (applied early decision)

Essay

Write about 3 objects that will give the admissions office insight to who you are.

The Jigsaw

Jigsaw puzzles are challenges that test one's ingenuity. They are composed of a number of pieces, each piece separated from and unique to the others. It is the job of the puzzle solver to examine the many pieces of the puzzle and find correlation between them, using these relationships to mold the seemingly unrelated mass into a finite object, a beautiful picture. I have always enjoyed assuming the role of a puzzle solver. Even as early as the age of three, I would spend my spare moments piecing together puzzles, always eager to see the diverse, colorful masterpieces they formed. As I grew older, I was able to apply my puzzle solving skills to life and began to view the world I lived in as a collage of puzzles. It became apparent to me that the people in this world are each a separate puzzle in the collage of life; they look similar when viewed from afar, but upon close examination it is apparent that each puzzle is unique; each is composed of separate sets of experiences and personality traits. I, too, am a puzzle in life's collage. My experiences have molded me into who I am. The many facets of my life and personality can be portrayed by the three types of pieces that compose a jigsaw puzzle: the rounded, filling pieces, the corner pieces, and the edge pieces.

The edge portions of a jigsaw puzzle are generally the first pieces that the puzzle solver tries to work. Once the solver has connected the edges, he has a strong foundation from which to build. This foundation leads the puzzle solver to the puzzle's solution as I lead others. The foundation of a puzzle is rigid, strong, and unwaveringly straight in much the same way as I am disciplined, strong, and honest. These qualities allow us both to be effective in leading others to success.

Success is not always easy to come by, however. The foundation of a puzzle would not be complete without one very important type of piece, the corner piece. The corner piece, which is not always easy to find, is a key piece to the jigsaw. It shapes the puzzle, bends a straight line. Like the jigsaw puzzle I have been shaped by many turning points. One corner piece of my life occurred during my sixth grade year when my band director saw much talent in a very young flautist. He recognized my alacrity in learning and started me out on the trombone, the basics of which I had mastered in a few weeks. Within a month I had been placed in the top jazz band and was introduced to the art of jazz, a form which has offered me a variety of opportunities and experiences.

The most important source of variety in the jigsaw is provided by the middle, filling pieces. Each piece is different in size, shape, and color, but fits together with all of the others to fill the framework, to portray an image with essence, to solve the mystery of the unfinished puzzle. My mind is like a collection of fillers; it is able to analyze situations and provide solutions from a variety of different angles, depending on which pieces are put together. It is only by viewing the problem from all angles simultaneously that I am able to generate the final picture, portray the puzzle in its entirety.

Solving the jigsaw is not an easy task. It takes much hard work and dedication on the solver's behalf, even when he is getting to know himself, deciphering his own puzzle. I, as the middle piece, the corner piece, and the edge piece, provide many representative components of my whole puzzle. The many facets of my personality and my life experiences converge to make the puzzle that is me. However, mine is a puzzle that is not yet complete. As I grow and undergo new experiences, I discover new facets to my personality. My life is a unique, unfinished puzzle to which all of the pieces have yet to be found.

See page 320 to find out where this student got in.

JASON FREIDENFELDS

Jason was a leader in music, business, theater, and academics in high school. He won statewide trombone awards in jazz and classical, performed magic shows as a business, held leads in dramas and musicals, and won top awards for his achievements in writing and science.

Stats

SAT I: 1520 (780 Verbal, 740 Math)

SAT II: 800 Biology, 800 Writing, 800 Mathematics, 800 Physics, 790 French

High School GPA: 4.7/4.0 (includes honors credit)

High School: Madison High School, Madison, NJ

Hometown: Madison, NJ

Gender: Male

Race/Ethnicity: Caucasian

Applied To

Cornell University

Harvard College

Princeton University

University of Pennsylvania

Yale University

Essay #1

Jason used the following essay in his applications to Harvard and Yale. The question that prompted the following essays was something to the effect of *"Describe an experience that has shaped the way you have grown personally and intellectually."*

They Got Me Too

I sat in the middle of the third row at the closing ceremony for the 1995 NJ Governor's School of the Arts — a fittingly mediocre seat, considering my mood at the time. Everyone around me seemed to have bonded in friendship over the past month. The dancer in front of me sobbing into her friend's shoulder must have had a spiritual experience. But here I was, in the very center, unable to share the nostalgic vibes. Why wasn't I as emotional as the rest of them?

An experience was finished that I had dreamt of since fourth grade, when my sister attended the School for dance. I remembered her description of a great magic trick in the student "Coffeehouse" of her Governor's School that had piqued my interest so long before. I suddenly felt much older. I now sat on the other side of the fence, looking back. I had practiced hard on trombone, auditioned, been selected, and performed my own magic trick in the Coffehouse. My dream had come true, and passed. As director Jack McCullough was saying in his speech, I was now a Governor's School alumnus. Where did that leave me? Stranded.

Words failed me for good-byes to my friends. I only felt a strong impulse to leave the building before my friends could see how unmoved I was. Avoiding eye contact, I strode back to my family and urged them to leave with me. My mother, noticing something unfulfilled in my expression, asked, "Are you sure?"

Taking one last survey of the auditorium, I spotted Dr. William Silvester, the director of the Wind Ensemble (the group in which I had played trombone) on the stage. He was a giant man, so tall his body bowed outwards around the center like an exaggerated Greek column. Everyone liked "Doc." When the candy machine next to the rehearsal room had swallowed someone's money one day, he tilted and shook the entire half-ton unit until the candy came free. This was a man to whom I could say a heartfelt good-bye. When I got to Dr. Silvester, he pulled my handshake into a bearhug. With that hug, my flak jacket of *machismo* ripped open.

The bridge of my nose stung as my eyelids overflowed with tears. Here was the man to whom I had given more respect in a month than I have most people in seventeen years. The bond that had developed between us as I focused all my energy on him in rehearsals, glowed brilliantly. Memories of his intensity matching my own, during the climax of *Esprit de Corps*, flashed through my eyes as I hugged him back. I had played the notes that he could not reach from his conductor's stand. In return, he had become the grandfather that I never knew; he was my mentor — my *sensei*.

Ashamed of my tears, I left without a word and sneaked to a bathroom to dry my face. New tears mixed with water from the tap as I tried to douse my eyes. In my mind I relived the rush of crushing out a low Ab in *Symphonic Metamorphasis* as Dr. Silvester pantomimed the note — jaw dropped, head lowered, eyes intense, and hand poised upward as if crushing a bowling ball. I recalled matching his grand vision of *Armenian Dances* with my sound. I could not erase the tears from such an intense experience, so I wore them as a badge of honor instead.

Outside in the auditorium, a fellow scholar said, "They got you too, huh?" She was right, and it's a good thing they *did* "get me." I might have just done some magic tricks, met some cool friends, played trombone in a good band, and left Governor's School in a hurry, my macho exterior unruffled by the experience. Instead, my reluctant tears revealed to me how powerful a bond I had formed with Dr. Silvester through the music.

Essay #2

Jason used the following essay in his applications to Cornell and Princeton.

Mr. Magic

"The profession of magician . . . is as difficult as music, as deep as poetry, [and] as ingenious as stage-craft . . ." William Bolitho. *Twelve Against the Gods*, "Cagliostro and Seraphina," 1930.

Long before magic was my "profession," I loved it. Magic was one of my favorite childhood hobbies because I found it technically fascinating, intellectually stimulating, and psychologically revealing (of myself and of the audience). Now, when I perform magic shows for children, my deep-rooted enthusiasm uplifts my audiences. I began billing myself as "Mr. Magic" four years ago, when I started appearing at kids' birthday parties and community events. As I developed and refined the elements of a successful magic business by performing over 70 shows, I learned about advertising strategies, professional relationships, business courtesy, and financial responsibility. But there is more to "Mr. Magic" than just business. I also find great personal satisfaction in being a role model. Because I am still a "kid" myself, not an intimidating adult authority figure, kids can easily imagine putting themselves in my place.

I have many fond memories of satisfying shows. I once performed for a group of fifth graders visiting Madison from Newark. Many of these children had never seen any sort of live performance, never mind a magic show. They were one of the most appreciative audiences I have ever had — they gasped when the magic happened, laughed when I made jokes, and cheered when their friends helped in a trick. I loved that show and those kids, even though I knew I would never see them again. One of them, a wide-eyed, soft-spoken boy, asked me if he could keep the red sponge rabbit that had magically appeared in his hand during the show. He was inspired by my show, and wanted to take something tangible from it.

I now wish I had given him the rabbit. But I believe he received something even more valuable — inspiration. I like to think he is now sitting in his room practicing magic tricks with a bedpost for an audience, as I did when I was his age. Or perhaps his inspiration took some other direction — music, or sports, or writing, or whatever. But regardless, I am deeply moved to know that I might be his source of inspiration. Children living in such an oppressive environment as inner-city Newark urgently need role models. So do the rest of us. Therefore, I strive to be a role model as well as an entertainer in all my performances.

In my magic career, I have experienced an exciting taste of entrepreneurship. At the same time, I am thrilled to see by the expressions on children's faces that I may have sparked their inner drive and passion. That double satisfaction is why I love the "business" of being Mr. Magic.

See page 320 to find out where this student got in.

JESSICA LAU

Jessica was elected class president, Student Council vice president and secretary, and National Honor Society president in her small suburban high school. She won four varsity letters on Dayton's soccer and track and field teams, and also played JV softball. Jessica wrote for the school paper, competed on the Quiz Bowl team and in the Science League, appeared in four school musicals, and was an active Key Club, Volunteer Club, and FBLA member. Outside of school, Jessica volunteered at her church, the Lions Eye Bank of New Jersey, SAGE eldercare agency, and the local hospital. Jessica also was selected for the New Jersey Governor's School in the Sciences, the U.S. Senate Youth Program (New Jersey delegate), and the Rensselaer Polytechnic Medal for Math and Science.

Stats

SAT I: 1580 (790 Verbal, 790 Math)

SAT II: 800 Writing, 780 Math IIC, 770 Math IC, 760 Chemistry, 700 Literature

High School GPA: 4.38/4.50

High School: Jonathan Dayton High School, Springfield, NJ

Hometown: Springfield, NJ

Gender: Female

Race/Ethnicity: Asian American

Applied To

Brown University

Dartmouth College

Harvard College

Pennsylvania State University

Princeton University

Rutgers University

Tufts University

University of Pennsylvania

University of Michigan

University of Virginia

Essay

Jessica used the following essay in her applications to Harvard, Tufts, Dartmouth, and UVA, and modified it for Princeton (cut it in half lengthwise).

Common Application: *Indicate a person who has had a significant influence on you, and describe that influence.*

I had the best seat in the classroom. Second row from the front, fifth seat back—not the most facilitating position for a slightly near-sighted freshman to learn world history from. No matter. In my mind, the Bantu and the Bushmen played second fiddle to a boy named Brian.

To me, Brian was the paragon of human existence. I, on the other hand, remained quietly, passively, and uninterestingly in the background, stifled by shyness, and getting out of high school not much more than good test scores and As on my report cards. I was part of the furniture, and "Unobtrusive" was my middle name. Brian was the oil to my vinegar. His strength of character (combined with his extremely good looks) lit up any room he entered and touched all those lucky enough to be graced by his presence. His self-confidence, persuasive abilities, unending capabilities, and almost childlike enthusiasm for everything literally put me in awe. I recognized in him not only qualities I desired in my potential boyfriend, but also everything I'd always wanted for myself.

My excessive adoration drove me to ridiculous lengths. I went about meeting my goal of becoming his girlfriend strategically. The closer to him I got, I figured, the easier the catch. Therefore, when soccer season started, and Brian joined the team, I decided to give the sport a try myself. Brian chose computer science as his elective, so I did as well. When he auditioned for the school play, I followed suit. Like a lemming, I blindly trailed his footsteps, wherever they led.

Alas, my efforts failed, and my beloved soon found a love of his own. It was a sad day in my life. However, all was not lost. I was left with all the new activities, the residue of my unsuccessful pursuit. To my surprise, I realized that they were more than meaningless, leftover obligations; they had acquired personal significance and importance to me. Before soccer, I had never played on a sports team, and my eyes were opened to the benefits of the comradery and cohesiveness of a team, and even to the physical benefits of aerobic activity. I discovered my hidden talent in computer programming, and I proceeded to take all of the classes my school offered. I loved the thrill of becoming a new person (even if only a townsperson or chorus member) on the stage, and I fed my interest by making play auditions an annual event.

From there, I started taking my own initiatives. I had forgotten my timidity; I gained the confidence to go out and do things by myself and for myself. I joined the softball team and volunteered for the Key Club. I raised my hand in class and took an active role at school. I fearlessly and enthusiastically tackled everything in my path. This change in me benefited not only my school career, but everything I did, from the first impressions I make on new friends to my mood in general.

One late spring day in history class, our teacher, Miss Duke, opened the class for student council nominations. Sure, I was now involved in the school, but I was no leader. I promptly shut my ears and diverted my attention. A few minutes later, in the midst of my daydream, I heard my name. Its source? None other than He Himself; Brian. Did I accept the nomination? I forgot my hesitancy, delivered a somewhat shocked and disbelieving nod, wrote a speech, and before I knew it, became class president.

This single event completed the transformation in me. My role as a participant developed into that of a leader. I learned the thrill of spearheading a project. I realized the excitement of making things happen. Best of all, I discovered the reward of inspiring other people, showing them what was shown to me.

Following a boy around was not the proudest moment of my life, but in doing so, I grew a lot as a person. As my eyes were opened to the benefits of simple school activities, I gained self-confidence, an open mind, and an ambition that has defined who I am and where I am going.

See page 321 to find out where this student got in.

JESSIE SEYMOUR

Jessie was a four-year letter winner and senior captain in field hockey, four-year academic letter winner, and senior captain of the track and field team. She was president of the National Honor Society, four-year member and senior president of the chorus, and was the recipient of many academic awards, which include being a National Merit Scholarship Program Commended Student.

Stats

SAT I: 1370 (730 Verbal, 640 Math)
SAT II: 740 Writing, 620 Math IC, 710 Literature
High School GPA: 94.96/100
High School: Central High School, Corinth, ME
Hometown: Kenduskeag, ME
Gender: Female
Race/Ethnicity: Caucasian

Applied To

Cornell University
Dartmouth College
Middlebury College
University of Maine

Essay

Jessie included the following essay in each of her applications. The essay was written for the Common Application on a topic of the applicant's choice, to be kept under one page.

To say that my summer at Gould Academy was an eye-opening experience would be the understatement of a lifetime. It's more like for four whole weeks I didn't even blink. I signed up for a summer of intense learning, intense play, and the chance to get away from my flat, eastern Maine home and live in my beloved Western Maine lakes and mountains. At least this is what I told my friends at home, who couldn't begin to comprehend why someone would WANT to go to Summer School for FUN. Summer and school are two words that clash in the ears of the average 14-year-old, but to me it was the opportunity of a lifetime. To quiet my friends' disapproval, I told them it was kind of like summer camp with classes and went happily on my way.

I arrived with big expectations. Meeting my dormmates on the first night there was the first indication that my expectations weren't big enough. My roommate was a girl from Eastern Maine with a background similar to mine, so we understood each other. The rest of our floor, however, we met with awe and appreciation. Maine is not a state noted for its racial or cultural diversity, yet here we were surrounded by several girls from the Dominican Republic, a girl from Spain, one from France who was of Asian descent with an American name (she alone was diverse enough for several people), and lots of girls from Western Maine, New Hampshire, and the rest of the U.S., all of different social classes and carrying with them their fascinating life stories. We were all incredibly different, but we all had one thing in common: we were nuts enough to want to go to school during the summer.

The novelty of the situation didn't end with the many faces of different colors. The class I took was an immersion in Creative Writing, which also included interpretation of literature and cultural analysis. Eight students sat around one enormous table and we read, wrote about, discussed, and interpreted literature and the world around us on a level that none of us had ever been on before. On my first paper I got a B on what would have been a definite A+ at my home school. The class was drastically different from anything I'd ever experienced. Like taking up a new sport, it hurt at first. Gradually, though, the playing field became familiar territory and I got grades like any I had ever achieved. In every English class I'd ever had, teachers were too concerned about where kids put their commas to worry about seeking deeper meaning. At first I was skeptical about what I was supposed to be learning. I didn't think that E.B. White's "Once More to the Lake" was about something other than a man who takes his son to the spot where he spent his summers as a kid, or understand the truth behind pop culture. It took awhile, but my young, sparkly-eyed teacher finally convinced me that there was meaning behind the words. It was quite a revelation.

The teachers, the students, and the energy at Summer School forced my mind to contort itself into new positions that it had never been in before. I was used to effortless A's. While that fueled my self-esteem, it wasn't satisfying. If I could get A's with no effort, what could I do *with* effort? At summer school, I learned more about my potential than anything else. At my regular school, I was a big fish in a small pond, but by doing well at summer school, I realized that I could be a big fish in a big pond too. After summer school, my whole outlook on life was different. Like in "Once More to the Lake," there was *meaning* behind everything. I saw the world and my future in a broader perspective. Suddenly I saw that there *are* people who care about learning, and they *are* interesting. It *is* possible to bask in the pleasures of life and challenge yourself intellectually *at the same time*. That is what I learned in Summer School. This is also what I seek in college.

See page 321 to find out where this student got in.

JOSEPH A. RAGO

In high school, Joe was an editor of his high school newspaper and president of the Honor Society, and he was also involved in independent scientific research.

Stats

SAT I: 1470 (780 Verbal, 690 Math)

SAT II: 700 Chemistry, 800 Writing, 680 Math IC, 690 Math IIC

High School GPA: 3.9/4.0

High School: Falmouth High School, Falmouth, MA

Hometown: Falmouth, MA

Gender: Male

Race/Ethnicity: Caucasian

Applied To

Brown University (applied early action)

Dartmouth College

Princeton University

Yale University

Essay

Joseph used the following essay in each of the applications listed above.

Write on a topic of your choice.

At the last minute, I was snatched from the clutches a southern upbringing.

When I was quite young, my family moved from a small town in Northern Virginia to Falmouth, Massachusetts, a small town on Cape Cod. While it is impossible to empirically test my hypothesis, I have come to believe that this relocation has been one of the major influences in my life. College-bound students often write of the significant people or the important events in their life that have been formative in their intellectual development. In the same vein as these other factors, the flinty character of Cape Cod has shaped my personal growth and evolution.

Jutting thirty-five miles into the Atlantic, many parts of Cape Cod were isolated for years from mainland America. But this rustic area is the same one where some of the first Americans persevered in an uncertain world for the sake of principle. And though their Puritan faith is no longer the Cape's dominant religion, its ethic of common sense and hard work, its demands for a life of independence and clarity, and its aesthetic of simplicity and harmony have genuinely affected the character of Cape Codders.

These attributes have sustained the region both through times of confidence and times of urgency. At the beginning of the eighteenth century, the golden whaling industry, the foundation for success, began to falter and decline. The Cape surrendered the easy reliability of prosperity and lapsed into a recession. But within a few years, a Cape Cod resident developed a method for extracting salt from seawater on a massive scale. By mid-century, the region was exporting 35,000 bushels of salt annually, and the economy rebounded. The Cape is a land where necessity is met by resourcefulness. Whether it is harvesting cranberries or netting cod, people have always ably used their intellect and ingenuity to earn their livelihood.

Now, things have changed. The Cape does not depend on whaling or salt, but largely on tourism. Sightseers, like the barbarian horde descending on the Roman empire, overrun Cape Cod each summer. The popular image of the place, nursed by a bustling vacation industry, is the one found by these wayfarers: catered, served, and enjoyed. But the Cape less traveled is where the deeper truths, with an explorer's inspiration, can be discovered. It is where the scotch pines murmur and the soil unfurls a chorale linking residents to all things past and present. It is where the thundering ocean communicates possibility and optimism. It is where lonely, crumbling stone walls, denoting a faded hierarchy, stretch off into the woods obscured beyond sight. In the isolation, the qualities of reverence and veneration for community and continuity are conveyed. The Cape has rooted residents to the past, advocating a respect for history and an admiration for natural beauty.

Cape Cod is rapidly succumbing to the incessant pounding of the Atlantic Ocean. One foot of ephemeral coastline is washed away each year; on the outermost shore, the sacrifice is three times that. Although these changes are swift in geological time, they pale in comparison to the changes induced by human development. We look at a world that has taken far longer than a single lifetime to create, an environment whose fragile and ineffable beauty is swiftly evaporating. The pace of geologic changes, measurable in human time scales, reminds us that all life is fleeting. Yet if this realization is elegiac, it is also rousing. The Cape tells us to live life fully - to let no moment pass by unappreciated, to enjoy what we have, and to find the august world delightful to live in.

There is a fine line between ego and egotism. And all areas of the country can find some kind of pride in their distinctive cultural flavors and tales of history. But I am thankful that the lessons I have culled from my community have come from Cape Cod. The wisdom found there will stay with me throughout the course of my life.

See page 322 to find out where this student got in.

JULIA HYPATIA ORTH

Julia was self-taught (homeschooled) for seven years. She won awards for woven work and in dog agility. She also received a National Merit Scholarship.

Stats

SAT I: 1390 (750 Verbal, 640 Math)
SAT II: 750 Biology, 730 Writing, 660 Math IIC
ACT: 32
High School GPA: 3.915
High School: Clonlara High School (home program), Ann Arbor, MI
Hometown: Cedar Hill, MO
Gender: Female
Race/Ethnicity: Caucasian

Applied To

New College of Florida
Southampton College of Long Island University
University of California—Santa Cruz

Essay

Julia used the following essay in her application to New College of Florida. The New College asked for four different one-page essays, and she included her favorite.

Recommend a book to us and tell why you are recommending it.

Many books have touched my life and changed my perspectives, and choosing a single one to recommend seems not difficult so much as unfair to all the others. Jim Nollman's

Spiritual Ecology has been the source of a great deal of enthusiasm, frustration, and irritation for me. Grace Llewellyn's *The Teenage Liberation Handbook* set me free. Even a few well-written textbooks, like Hopkins's *Ka Lei Ha'aheo: Beginning Hawaiian* and Haviland's *Cultural Anthropology* have inspired me to learn about worlds of knowledge I hadn't even been aware of before. That's not to mention the works of new and classical fiction (*Nineteen Eighty-Four*, *Portrait of Jennie*, *The Catcher in the Rye*, and *Dandelion Wine* being particular favorites) that I spent summer afternoons devouring in full. Yet . . . a book recommendation should be more than personal fancy, something that one feels compelled to share particularly with the recommendee(s). As I am quite unfamiliar with you, I wish to come up with something of fairly general interest as well as something that excites me. To my surprise, a particular book has presented itself to me for just such a purpose. I recommend *The Lorax*, by Dr. Seuss.

I can't in good conscience recommend it and be done with it though. This journey to "the far end of town where the Grickle-grass grows" with its environmental message might seem a touch moralistic or naive, out of context. Besides, Dr. Seuss wrote poetry, and it is poetry meant to be read aloud. I recommend that you do just that. I recommend that you check this book out of a library and take it outside. Stand on a hill-top or by the edge of a forest or in the middle of a park, perhaps under whatever local vegetation resembles Truffula Trees. Don't go alone. Bring your best friend or your younger brother or your cat or whatever neighborhood children are willing to listen. Dr. Seuss wrote *stories*, and stories are meant to be told to people. Chant the story with your best story voices to whomever will listen, and I can all but guarantee that bits of rhyme will lodge themselves in your head like the choruses of popular songs. Whatever you do, don't forget to look at the pictures.

The story itself is told by and about the Once-ler, the well-meaning antihero who chops down trees for his business. He means no harm, but undoubtedly causes much—a familiar situation indeed. (In the famous words of Walt Kelly's Pogo: "We have met the enemy, and not only may he be ours, he may be us.") The Lorax, defender of the trees, also does not follow any sticky-sweet good-guy stereotypes. He's ". . . shortish. And oldish. And brownish. And mossy", and speaks with a voice that is "sharpish and bossy." Finding himself entirely at odds with the Once-ler and his business, all the Lorax can do is shout out warnings and remonstrations at the top of his lungs. The perception gap between the two is tragicomically familiar, and leads exactly where one might expect. We would do well to learn not only from the Lorax's message, but also from the failure of his method of communication to result in anything but opposition.

It's food for thought, but don't get your thinker too excited. This is, after all, a children's story. It is my hope in recommending it that it will at worst provide you with a pleasant addition to your day, spent under the sun with a friend or two and a book that is, in the end, a great deal of fun . . . and that at best, it will provide you with inspiration—to plant a tree, to create and share your own artistic or literary worlds (a skill at which Dr. Seuss was adept), to spend more time outside, or more time reading to young friends, or perhaps even "only" to remember to not take even the most serious subjects *too* deadly seriously (again a bittersweet Kelly-quote comes to mind: "Don't take life too serious...it ain't nohow permanent."). Enjoy!

See page 322 to find out where this student got in.

JULIE YAU-YEE TAM

Julie was a three-time state spelling champion and two-time state opera bronze medalist, and she also won medals in other academic subjects. She trained at the nationally renowned Houston Ballet Academy for nine years and finished the pre-professional program. Fluent in three languages (English, Spanish, and Mandarin and Cantonese Chinese), Julie attended Chinese language school until she graduated with honors in twelfth grade. Julie also held offices in school clubs and community service organizations.

Stats

SAT I: 1410 (660 Verbal, 750 Math)

SAT II: 700 Chinese, 740 Math IC, 680 Writing, 680 Biology, 690 Spanish

High School GPA: 4.314/ 4.000

High School: Second Baptist Upper School, Houston, TX

Hometown: Houston, TX

Gender: Female

Race/Ethnicity: Asian American

Applied To

Rice University (applied early decision)

Essay

The quality of Rice's academic life and the residential college system is heavily influenced by the unique life experiences and cultural traditions each student brings. What perspective do you feel that you will be able to share with others as a result of your own life experiences and background? Cite a personal experience to illustrate this. Most applicants are able to respond successfully in two to three pages.

Friday, September 11, 1998

Cebu City, Philippines

As I stare into my mirror, I see a face long and tired, worn out by distance, by time, and by too many things happening all too fast. The trip here was not easy. It took 27 hours in flight and airport waits – from Houston to Los Angeles, to Hong Kong, then finally to Cebu City, Philippines.

I was awestruck when my mother and I arrived here Tuesday morning and were taken directly from the airport to the funeral home. As I passed through the doors, I found myself in an atmosphere I had never before experienced. In the Philippines, funeral homes are like hotels. There are living quarters behind the grand hall, which is a large room with a sitting area where visitors can view the casket. Somber guards scrutinized me as I entered the grand hall, where my maternal grandfather, a former Taiwan senator and adviser of Head of State Chiang Kai Shek, lay in state. Although I am Chinese, to them, I looked different, walked differently, and even acted differently. I *was* different. As I entered the grand hall, I saw the banners, each four characters long and painted in traditional Chinese calligraphy, that extolled my grandfather's virtues. Flowers of every description, from governmental agencies, banks, schools, churches, and other organizations from all over the country and abroad, lined the walls. Newspaper articles, newsletters, and other notices announced the passing of my grandfather and listed the names of those who had given memorial contributions in his memory.

As I gazed into the casket, which was covered by a piece of glass because my grandfather's body was to lie there for over a week to be viewed by people from near and far, I saw how his face was hardened like clay. His loving spirit, his vivid smile, and his caring eyes had left his countenance, but not my memory. However, I still felt all these parts of him through the people and institutions he had touched so profoundly. At that moment I also realized how much he would be missed by them.

I slowly drew away from the casket and retired into the living quarters. A few guards carried our luggage into the back room, and several servants were at our attendance. Having someone constantly asking to serve me in any way possible was new for me.

During the next few days, I began to feel the discomfort of being continually in the spotlight, due to the attention I had received because of my grandfather's passing. Every time I wanted to refill my water bottle, I would have to don formal clothing, put on my uncomfortable high-heeled shoes, and fix my hair perfectly before leaving my room. At one point I took a chance and ran out in my pajamas and slippers. Unfortunately, my aunt saw me and upbraided me, saying that I "must look perfectly proper at all times in the event anyone important arrives." I found that being thirsty was easier.

Nightly memorial services at the funeral home had begun before our arrival and continued during our visit. On the first evening, my uncle, my aunt, my mother, and I thanked all who had come and received condolences. From both prominent and ordinary, I heard how my grandfather had treated all people with equal consideration. Humility and high office came in the same "package" for him.

We were up early the second morning to go to Cebu Eastern College, where my grandfather was Director for 32 years, for another ceremonial tribute to him. I told the students how my grandfather had inspired me. Because my grandfather was also a lover of music, I sang a song in his honor. Although most of the students had never met my grandfather personally (because he had retired at age 82 and died at age 91), they were definitely affected by his work in improving school facilities, erecting new buildings, increasing student population, and making Cebu Eastern College a premier force in secondary education in the Philippines. Their respect and admiration touched me deeply. At the end of the tribute, every student and faculty member individually offered words of sympathy.

My grandfather was cremated on the day of his state funeral. This morning our family and a few close friends used chopsticks to pick out his bones from the ashes. It hit me that, when I die I will just be, quite frankly, a pile of bones. Therefore, if my physical body is of little importance, then I need to cherish every day because what I contribute to society will be significant. Just as we took Grandpa's urn through the halls of Cebu Eastern College and the Lieh Fu Chen Building, named in his honor, I want to die knowing that someone will remember me for changing the world positively.

Now as I sit here in front of the mirror in "my" room, getting ready to leave Cebu City for home, I am thinking: Should I be feeling nostalgic for home? Do I miss being at school after a week in a far away land? I cannot say that I want to leave all this behind. Although most of the people here I have never seen or have only seen once or twice, they are almost like family to me. I can relate to them so well because of the language and cultural ties and our common regard for my grandfather. The Chinese, of course, emphasize the importance of family and respect for the elders, so this plays a role too.

I know my grandfather would be so happy to see me carry on his legacy of values. When he named me Yau Yee (幼 慈), he gave me more than a name. He gave me personality, meaning, and a heritage. I am reminded of my duty every day. My Chinese teacher has always said that I am one of the few who come to learn Chinese willingly – not forced by my parents – and that I have an authentic Chinese accent and realize the importance of learning the language of my ancestors. Reading some of the books my grandfather wrote has truly inspired me to pursue a political career to improve education and humanitarian values.

Now that my grandfather is gone, I will no longer have an immediate need for returning here. However, just as my mother has brought me here and to Taiwan to see the countries my grandfather influenced, I want to bring my children back through the halls my grandfather walked. If my grandchildren admire and remember me as I do my grandfather, then I know I will have continued his legacy, and my life will have been a success.

See page 322 to find out where this student got in.

KAREN A. LEE

In high school, Karen received a full diploma in the International Baccalaureate program and was a two-year "A" student on the Academic Decathlon team. She played the violin in the school's top orchestra, co-edited the literary magazine, was the secretary/treasurer of the French National Honor Society, and was a member of National Honor Society and Mu Alpha Theta (Math Club). Outside of school, she studied piano and Mandarin Chinese.

Stats

SAT I: 1600

SAT II: 800 Writing, 800 Math IIC, 780 Chinese with Listening, 690 Physics

ACT: 34

High School GPA: 5.4561

High School: Garland High School, Garland, TX

Hometown: Garland, TX

Gender: Female

Race/Ethnicity: Asian

Applied To

Duke University

Johns Hopkins University

Rice University
Southern Methodist University
Stanford University

Essay

Karen used the following essay in her applications to Stanford University.

How has the place in which you live influenced the person you are? Define "place" any way that you like . . . as a context, a country, a city, a community, a house, a point in time.

The Land Down Here

When it rains, the inhabitants where I live are the last to know. Welcome to Short People Land. At an early height of four feet eleven inches, I thought I had solidly established residence in the People of Average Height Land. Nonetheless, as I noticed myself moving toward the front of class pictures over the years and I remained four feet eleven inches on my twelfth birthday, I obtained Short Person status. While my personality has its roots in my childhood Average Height Land, becoming and remaining short has greatly influenced the person I am now.

Because I have not reached adulthood, human thought can naturally mistake me for someone younger. For instance, due to the limited size of our school's gymnasium, ninth-grade students are barred from peprallies. When I tried to attend my first one as a sophomore, students behind me shouted, "Freshman! Go back to class!" I never forget that this confusion will not end with graduation. Employers and coworkers may view me as immature and inexperienced based solely on my height. Keeping this possibility in mind, I consistently put forth extra effort to exceed expectations until perfectionism became automatic. My physics teacher handed back my second lab report of the year with a comment that my lab reports bordered on overkill. I hoped to transform my height into an asset, a trait to make me and my meticulous care stand out in others' memories. My work is by no means flawless, but living in Short People Land encourages my industrious attempts to prove that height and ability are not directly related.

On the other hand, being petite has always brought me the warmth of human compan-ionship. As a short child, I had advantages in certain games, and my playmates welcomed the challenge of playing against me. In hide-and-seek, I would be the only one to fit under a table in the back of a closet under a staircase. I was one of the last people left in limbo. Many of these early diversions gave birth to long-standing friendships. When the stress mounts, we still rely on each other for commiseration. On another occasion, my Short Person citizenship helped me bridge the freshman-senior gap. When the seniors in the International Baccalaureate program at my school formed a club to tutor underclassmen, those who arrived for tutoring were too intimidated to ask for help. I joined a group of ninth-grade girls and casually discussed their biology lab with them. Until ten minutes into the discussion, they had thought I was just another freshman, but by that time, we had overcome their fear, and they gladly accepted me as their official biology tutor. I cannot describe my gratification when one of my protégées stopped me excitedly in the hall, "I made a B on my biology test! Thank you so much!"

While I accept my height with open arms, I recognize all the small annoyances packaged with it. For several years before I turned sixteen, I feared not being able to drive. I had difficulty seeing over the steering wheel and reaching the accelerator with my foot at the same time. In large tour groups at the art museum, I end up memorizing the back of patrons' shirts rather than enjoying the masterpieces. Window blinds are adjusted so that glaring sunlight just misses everyone's eyes but mine. Remembering my own frustrations, I developed a sympathy for others' aggravations and a sensitivity to others' needs. I can empathize with lefties trying to use a right-handed mouse or pale people who sunburn easily, both of whom, like me, suffer simply because of a physical characteristic. I remember to adjust the music stand in orchestra so that my stand partner can also read the music. At a pre-college summer program at Southern Methodist

University, my apparent intuition for helping others earned me the nickname "Mother." People came to me for first aid, pocket change, or advice. Probably my limited caretaking talents did not quite deserve my honorable nickname, but I always did my best to help and always felt content that they appreciated my efforts. Despite their inconveniences, irritations of the vertically challenged mostly disappear before one of Short People Land's finest fruits, a sense of humor. Even I can laugh when someone quips, "You're so short you could pole vault with a toothpick." Knowing I would not take offense, my history teacher used me as an example for situations in which trying as hard as possible may still fail. He asked me to jump and touch the ceiling. I actually came within six inches, but I joined the class in laughing at the ridiculousness of his demand.

My residency in Short People Land has shaped my capacity for diligence, camaraderie, empathy, and laughter. Thanks to my height, I have nearly everything required to attack the ordeals of life and still maintain sanity. Neither have I lost respect for the people up there, so please do not hesitate to bend down. I'll meet you in the Land Down Here.

See page 323 to find out where this student got in.

KATHARINE ANNE THOMAS

Katharine was a four-year varsity tennis player, the number-two player her junior and senior years, and co-MVP her senior year. During her final year of high school she took two 200-level English courses at Franklin and Marshall College. In addition to community volunteer work during the scholastic year, she participated in a UNESCO month-long volunteer program teaching English abroad in Poland during the summers of her sophomore and junior years. She was a winner of several Scholastic Writing Awards and won a first-place Gold Key in the Short-Short Story category her freshman year.

Stats

SAT I: 1390 (740 Verbal, 650 Math)

SAT II: 750 Writing, 680 Math IC, 620 Math IIC, 660 French, 710 Literature

High School GPA: 4.152

High School: Lancaster Catholic High School, Lancaster, PA

Hometown: Lancaster, PA

Gender: Female

Race/Ethnicity: White/Caucasian

Applied To

Essay

Katharine used the following essay in each of her applications.

Common Application Question 5: *Topic of your choice.*

My first real college writing assignment: five neat pages of argument and examples, insightful prose in black type and white space where my professor could write little words of praise. I replayed a little daydream I had developed of him reading the paper, pausing and nodding at the particularly insightful points, scribbling excitedly in the margins and finally closing it with a satisfied sigh. The reason I was looking forward to getting my work back was not that I truly believed it was a work of genius. My sleep-deprived, bleary-eyed misery refused to let me be a fan of my work. At that point I was cursing the uncountable nights of rubbing my temples in the unforgiving glow of the computer screen I had spent on it. Instead, my prediction was based on precedent (not to mention each aching bone's demand for restitution). Teacher's responses to my work had always been positive, and I grew increasingly confident about my ability. But in the process, my purpose in writing shifted from self expression as it should be in its purest form and instead to gaining recognition.

Upon reading the paper, my professor suggested that I take a second look at it. His comments clarified ideas that had always been beyond my grasp. So many of my papers with similarly obscured errors had gone without being criticized, but, strangely enough, no red-inked "Fantastic!" was nearly as gratifying as having my own vague sense of flaw verified. While other teachers' compliments had been flattering, what I appreciated more than anything, and what I would require to become any better in my craft, was a healthy dose of criticism. I realized that being selective enough in choosing my words would ensure that my ideas would never be misunderstood.

Envisioning the images that words have the power to create restored my passion for writing. What had made me love writing initially was the gloriously specific nature of words that enables them to provoke the exact response we intended them to and convey the most complex of emotions more so than any other outlet. Had I meant that Catholicism pervaded Irish tradition or was the religion embedded within culture? Did Joyce's Stephen Dedalus stray from the church or lose his faith? If there hadn't been a deadline I could have worked on that paper for weeks, editing day and night and probably still not being fully satisfied. I was at fault for having the haughtiness that led me to believe that I manipulated words, when in fact the opposite is true. Their role as the messenger of thought demands reverence. Words are for me what shapes and colors are for artists, what notes and beats are for musicians. But the medium by which we choose to express ourselves has little bearing; it need only fulfill its purpose. I gained from this experience a realization that I cannot be above laws that govern mankind's communication. The ability of words to touch one's core is timeless and beyond our grasp.

See page 323 to find out where this student got in.

KATHLEEN ANN MIRANDA

During high school, Kathleen was editor of the school newspaper and was a member of the varsity swim team for two years. She maintained a 4.0 GPA while working part-time for four years.

Stats

SAT I: 1450 (740 Verbal, 710 Math)

SAT II: 660 Writing, 630 Chemistry, 750 American History, 710 Math IIC

High School GPA: 4.0

High School: Our Lady of Mercy Academy, Syosset, NY

Hometown: East Norwich, NY

Gender: Female

Race/Ethnicity: Left blank on all applications

Applied To

Princeton University

University of Notre Dame

Essays #1-4: Princeton

Describe an event that changed or impacted your life in a special way.

I only remember crying once; it was when I first saw him and before they let my relatives into the room. He looked so strange and different. Standing there staring at my dad, I could not believe it had happened. My worst nightmare had come true.

Although my dad did not die until October 3, 1995 my challenge began six months earlier. It was then that Dad got really sick and had to go to the hospital for blood transfusions and chemotherapy. It was a strange time for me. I was afraid that I might get Dad sick; the cancer had lowered his immune system incredibly. Everyday during school I waited for an announcement calling me to the Principal's office to be told Dad was dead. Luckily it did not happen as I envisioned. Instead after a night long vigil Dad died at 6:04 a.m.; I was only a few yards away.

Dad's death taught me very quickly that grieving is not a process, it is a way of living. Some people thought I was cold because I never seemed to cry. These remarks did not really bother me. I knew that only family support and internal strength could see me through this ordeal.

Shocked at what happened for some time afterwards I was engulfed by a strange numbness. Each day I completed the tasks I had done in the past, but I found it difficult to realize that Dad was not home to answer obscure trivia questions, teach me something new in mathematics, or face me in a good argument.

After some months I realized that the only way to overcome the challenge placed before me was to resume life with my usual dedication. Although my father was gone and my dream to be first in my class had ended, I knew what to do.

My job, school, and family became my main concentrations. By focusing on them I learned to succeed under anxiety and that the fastest method for curing depression was hard work. As my grades rose so did my spirits. Soon after I noticed life was getting easier for all my family. Leaning on one another for support is the quickest way to the top.

If you were given the time and resources to develop one particular skill, or talent, or area of expertise, what would you choose to pursue and why?

Bounce, spring, splish, splash! I lift my hands up to salute the judges after completing another great dive. It sounds wonderful, but too bad this scene only happens in my imagination. No matter where I see a diving board I can picture myself either practicing each dive to perfection or looking at my score during a competition. Unfortunately, I have never fulfilled my dream to dive.

A water rat all my life, I always hoped for a chance to learn how to dive. Perhaps because I am disciplined in schoolwork I hoped to try my work habits on a physical activity. I think the desire to excel in something that requires concentration, skill and strength is what really attracts me to diving. Add this to the romantic side of being able to perform maneuvers few others can complete plus the already vivid imagination of a ten year old and I was hooked on diving.

Quickly mastering the forward dive, I managed to impress my family with a decent back dive. However, my exhibition of talent ended there. Previously I had found friends who could share their tricks, but now I was on my own. Countless red lobster backs and few successful dives told me I was at a dead end. My outlandish dream of being the first self taught Olympic diver had died. This funeral, however, did not stop me from trying to dive, no matter how unsuccessfully. Perhaps my birthday wish will come true, and someday I will learn to jackknife or somersault perfectly.

Describe how you make a moral decision.

Moral decisions are usually most difficult to make. They often involve friends and family, the tug-o-war between right and wrong is often a hard battle to fight and win.

As I grow older, I have found, to my dismay, these battles are more common and more difficult. Unlike some repetitive events, which get easier with time, the process of making moral decisions never lessens. I have found that the only way to make these decisions less difficult is to prioritize my concerns. The first issue I look at is danger; can a poor decision place those I am with or me in a harmful situation? Could I hurt someone or be hurt by my actions? My second concern is selfish, but since I must live with myself for all eternity, it is essential. I cannot make a decision of which I will be ashamed. My third concern regards my family. Since they have always been present for me I try to do the same for them. My parents have always been my confidantes, and I could not be happy if I did something to tarnish the faith and trust they have in me.

If I were a lucky person then moral decisions would be easy to make. I would go along with my friends, cause no one harm, be proud of my decision, and receive the approval of my family. However, because I am human this rarely happens and I am forced to sacrifice one or more pleasures for the better decision.

In what ways can you image yourself growing and changing as a result of spending the next four years in college?

Every new struggle and challenge changes a person. It breeds character and strength and prepares the individual for the next obstacle in the game of life. I feel college is one such challenge.

Warnings from teachers, parents and friends have taught me that college will not be an easy road to follow. Common sense and the application process have convinced me. This is one reason I wish to go to college. I love hard work; easy tests and methods have always bored me. A 100% on a simple quiz is not nearly as satisfying as 97% on a demanding calculus test.

I hope and expect college will be a challenge demanding all my strengths and teaching me to conquer my weaknesses. If this is true I can envision myself growing in wisdom and understanding. I believe the diversity of my future classmates will help me become a more understanding, compassionate person, who can recognize the good in others and can respect, if not agree with, their opinions. Simultaneously class work will help me attain true knowledge and teach me the skills essential to thrive in a fast paced society.

Essay #5: Notre Dame

Write about being a hero for a day.

Beep, BEEP, BEEP! The blaring sound of the alarm clock awoke me from the comfort of my dreams. With deft hand I rolled over and slapped the sleep button. "Ahh, ten more minutes of sleep. Then I'll have to find the answer to that homework question: What is a hero?" With the blankets snug around me I drifted off into the land of dreamers. A hazy picture of what appeared to be a kitchen loomed before me.....

Charlie the chef arrived on time today. As he began unpacking the meats and bread just dropped off by the delivery man he glanced at his watch, 5:30 am. With a sigh he looked around. Charlie enjoyed these brief hours when most of the town was still asleep or groggily heading to the bathroom for a morning shower. It was peaceful and quiet. Charlie used the time to think and relax as he began to prepare the daily selection of food. With skilled hands he started slicing the bread to make the sandwiches. With a few strokes of the knife a selection of tasty sandwiches adorned the counter top, ready to be purchased by the earliest customers. With these simple snacks finished Charlie was ready to make the heroes.

The recipe for one of his specialty heroes is the following. Start with a six inch loaf Italian bread. This is just the right size for one hungry person. Choosing only the finest meats Charlie pieced me together with the care and skill of a surgeon. Along with the typical meats found in an Italian hero he added some ham for flavor and humor. A mild provolone added a simple taste that blends well with my other flavors. It gave me the desire to be simple and to help others. Before closing me up Charlie added the perfect touch of mustard, filling me with a zest for life. After he finished, Charlie surveyed me with pride, chuckling to himself, "Here is a hero fit for a king." That honest praise caused the red in my tomatoes to shine more brightly as I glowed with pride. I was an important hero, worthy of only a king. Today would certainly be a good one.

As Charlie hummed to himself, I was wrapped up and tossed on a dark shelf. A little ruffled from the landing I settled down, smoothed my wrappings, and awaited for the king to arrive. In a short time the lights were flicked on and Charlie opened the store for business. At first I was overwhelmed by the noise and bright lights but, with time, I became used to my new surroundings and warily looked around. To my left was a chicken sandwich. The poor fellow was afraid of his own shadow. "Hah!" I thought to myself, "He is not worthy of a king. Why, he is hardly even a hero." To my right was a rueben sandwich; she was a friendly hero and always eager to talk. Quite simple though, made of only one type of meat, but she had the quaintest Irish brogue. Since Colleen, that was the rueben's name, had been on the shelve longer than I had she was filled with useful knowledge. Colleen explained how a person picks a hero out and gives Charlie some paper and metal in exchange it. Then Charlie wraps the hero in paper and gives him away to the person. This was so interesting to me; I had so many questions. "What is a person? What happens after the person takes you?" I asked Colleen excitedly. She kindly answered my questions. A person, she explained, is similar to Charlie, only they stand on the other side of the counter and can leave by the door. They come in all different shapes and sizes, sort of like heroes, no two are exactly the same. I nodded in amazement. Shaking her head, Colleen admitted that she did not really know what happened after Charlie gave a hero away. All she knew was a hero never came back. It was rumored, she told me, that a sandwich only becomes a real hero after a person takes him away. Now I could not wait for a person to pick me. I wanted to become a real hero and save the king.

I was thinking this as Charlie's hand reached into the shelf. "Pick me, pick me," I prayed, but nothing happened. When I looked over to my right Colleen was gone. Her place was taken by a ham sandwich, Frank. Unfortunately, Frank believed himself to be funny and was constantly telling terrible jokes. During the rest of the day all of the sandwiches around me left to become heroes and I sat and waited. "The king just is not ready for me," I thought optimistically.

Then late in the day a mother with two small children came in the deli. I soon felt Charlie's hand on me. "Wait, you are making a mistake," I shouted hopelessly, "A king will buy me, not two kids." Charlie did not seem to hear my pleas; he wrapped me in white paper and handed me to the mother. I was devastated; I would never be a real hero. How could two dirty kids be able to take me, one who is fit for a king. I sighed in despair. With my salami heart heavy with sorrow I was carried out of the deli.

When my paper was unwrapped again I was on the counter of another kitchen. This one was much smaller than the deli's. The mother was standing over me with a knife. She quickly cut me in two and handed me to the little children. "Thanks Mommy. I am so hungry," exclaimed one child. "Yeah, this is cool! I've never had a hero before," chimed the other. With that they quickly devoured me. As they ate me I realized I

was a hero. I was sacrificing my small meat filled body for the pleasure of two small hungry kids. Surely this was just as great as being eaten by a king who has hero sandwiches twice a week. I felt proud. Settling back, I was ready to accept my fate. The mouth opened and BEEP, BEEP, BEEP!!

I jumped out of bed and rushed to get dressed. It seemed like a day since I first pressed the sleep button. Yawning and stretching, I noticed a scent of salami on me. Shrugging I decided it must have been something I ate. As I washed my face the answer to a question for homework came to me. The question was, "what is a hero?" A hero, I decide, was someone who could sacrifice his life of happiness for that of another. Relieved that I had finally thought of a good answer, I ran out to the bus. Once safely one board I checked what was for lunch. It was an Italian hero. Careful that no one was looking, I bent over the sandwich and whispered, "Thanks."

See page 324 to find out where this student got in.

KATRINA ERIN FLETCHER

In high school, Katrina was an officer in the National Honor Society and the French Honor Society, as well as a peer mentor and a member of the soccer team—first as a manager, then as a player.

Stats

SAT I: 1400 (720 Verbal, 680 Math)

SAT II: 610 Math IC, 670 English Writing, 710 Literature

High School GPA: 3.99

High School: Greensburg Central Catholic High School, Greensburg, PA

Hometown: Greensburg, PA

Gender: Female

Race/Ethnicity: Caucasian

Applied To

Amherst College

Bowdoin College

Colby College

Dartmouth College

Middlebury College

Wesleyan University

Williams College

Essay

Katrina used the following essay in her application to every school she applied to.

Evaluate a significant experience or achievement that has special meaning to you.

To most, a car accident would not be a positive experience, rather it would be a harrowing ordeal better forgotten. My crash came on a frigid Saturday morning in January. The air had an especially cold sting as I scampered from the house to the Jeep parked in the driveway. I was anticipating my weekly morning riding lesson as I fired up the engine. With the defrost on and the hot air blasting, I began the long drive to the stables.

The roads were glazed with a thin coating of ice, not enough to worry me, but enough to make me cautious. Not far from home, I hit a particularly icy spot. The rear of the Jeep swerved from side to side, as if unsure of where to go. I frantically tried to regain control of the car, but only succeeded in making the situation worse. Unbelievably, I saw the landscape whirl around me. Across the opposite lane I skidded. Feeling a sickening tilt, I realized the Jeep was going to roll over. I covered my head with my arms, in a feeble attempt to protect myself. Then the crash of breaking glass and crunching metal pierced the air. Suddenly it was over; amazingly I was still right side up. The vehicle's roll had been intercepted by an enormous tree—the only one on the road. Instead of tumbling down the steep embankment on the other side of the road, I had whacked into the only tree remotely nearby. As a result, the entire passenger side roof was caved in, the windshield was smashed, and I was absolutely quivering with fear.

My parents rescued me, and in all truth, were more frightened than I was. This experience definitely left me thinking. If someone would have been coming from the opposite direction, it could have been a fatal accident. If there would have been a passenger, they would have perished from the impact of the tree on the roof. If there wouldn't have been a tree, I could have been just another roll-over statistic. How had I happened to locate the only tree on the road? Why had I been so lucky? Was it mere luck, or maybe divine providence at work? For me, the answer was that I was meant to survive. It wasn't the plan for me to perish, not then. There must be some things left on earth that only I can do. From this experience I received a new appreciation for life. I have a purpose in life, there's a reason I'm here. I needed to realize that there is much for me to do before I go. It might have taken a pretty big jolt to remind me that I have a lot of life left to live. But I got the message, and I plan on making good use of it.

See page 324 to find out where this student got in.

KENDALL MORRELLY-BOTT

Kendall was a four-year varsity women's epee fencer and was captain and county champion her senior year. She performed research at Cold Spring Harbor National Laboratories on neural plasticity for two years, entered in the Intel and Neuroscience Prize competitions, and earned Honors at the Long Island Science Congress. Kendall has played flute since fourth grade, and throughout high school she played in wind ensemble, orchestral winds, marching band, concert band, and pit orchestra for school musicals. During her senior year, Kendall was in charge of leading 160 musicians as the drum major of the marching band.

Stats

SAT I: 1420 (750 Verbal, 670 Math)
SAT II: 720 Writing, 760 Biology, 690 Math IC, 710 Literature
High School GPA: 95.886
High School: Huntington High School, Huntington, NY
Hometown: Huntington, NY
Gender: Female
Race/Ethnicity: Caucasian

Applied To

Cornell University (applied early decision)

Essay

"A stone, a leaf, an unfound door." —from **Look Homeward, Angel** *by Thomas Wolfe. Write about three objects that would give the admissions selection committee insight into who you are.*

A Weeble, a spork, a piece of sandpaper. These three objects can represent tenacity, balance, truth and, to some degree, a sense of humor (depending on whose opinion you ask). How do you get such virtues from a child's toy, a utensil from Taco Bell, and a banal object you can pick up at any hardware store? Simply put, ignore what they are, and contemplate what they could be, as if you had never seen these objects before and never known their purposes.

A Weeble is unquestionably a very resilient, persistent, and dependable figure. You know the jingle: "Weebles wobble but they don't fall down." With their stable, weighted bases, you can knock these little fellows down and they will always pop back up, regardless of how much teetering they do. It's interesting...my other toys have long been packed away, but stuffed in my desk drawer is a blue and white Weeble, wearing a sailor hat. I never thought much about the reason I kept him around, until now. I suppose I related more to him, than to my Barbie doll.

While at Drum Major Academy, this past summer, the speaker, George Parks, warned: "The drum major never shows any sign of discomfort, in front of the band." If the drum major stumbles, the entire band may falter. I am so proud of the Huntington Blue Devil Band, that I will not allow them to be anything less than the champions they are. I may waver at times, maybe even wobble a bit, but I always get back on my feet and continue on, determined to be my best.

A Spork is quite a formidable object, when you consider it in a more abstract sense. It is a novel, ingenious, and creative balance between two utensils, a spoon and a fork, in a ying-yang parallel. I try to have that same sort of harmony and duality in my life. My interests are largely divided among academics and research, a passion for the flute and a dedication to fencing.

I revel in the fact that I have an analytical, serious, and logical side, tempered by a creative playful spirit. My neuroscience research, at the Cold Spring Harbor Laboratory, has shown me the importance of being sporkian. When results do not support my hypothesis, I find that a different, sometimes unconventional approach, can reveal a new perspective to my research.

Fencing is as much a psychological game, as it is a physical sport. It requires sweat exuding concentration and control over every muscle. Still, you must trust your natural reflexes and instincts to be spontaneous. The winner of the match is the one who can cunningly lull the opponent into dropping guard. With feline agility, the touch is taken. It is when this balance is attained, that I feel most exhilarated.

The sandpaper was not chosen for its mere abrasive quality, but for its ability to smooth the rough edges and get down to the essence of the matter. I try to hold to the idea of less being more, a direct echo of Occams Razor: "Entities ought not to be multiplied, except from necessity." Anything superfluous is polished with 660 grit until only the fine grain of the problem is revealed. In my research, a tremendous amount of data is collected and quantitatively analyzed. I must sort through it all and uncover the relevant, the truth and disregard the unessential.

On a personal level, this ability, to expose the central issue, has resulted in late night phone calls, from friends in conflict. I don't pretend, to have all the answers, maybe not any, but at least I can help them to focus.

These objects represent the quintessence of who I am. They are more revealing, honest, and amusing than any common griffin or lion could be, reflecting a kind, earnest, and gamesome spirit. In life, people won't remember you for your prowess in calculus, but they will remember you for the kind of person you are, and that is what matters most.

See page 325 to find out where this student got in.

KIM HAMMERSMITH

A dancer since age four, Kim was a four-year member of her high school's Dance Ensemble and Cheerleading Squad as well as the Math League, Civitans service club, and yearbook staff. A top-ten graduate and member of several honor societies, she devoted her time outside of school, dance, and cheerleading to tutoring an autistic teenager for her last three high school years.

Stats

SAT I: 1390 (590 Verbal, 800 Math)
SAT II: 760 Math, 710 Writing
High School GPA: 4.565
High School: Walter M. Williams High School (public), Burlington, NC
Hometown: Burlington, NC
Gender: Female
Race/Ethnicity: White
Please note: Kim had an alumni interview at Duke and sent in a supplemental arts video showcasing her talent in dance. Kim did not send in any "extra credit" optional materials to Johns Hopkins.

Applied To

Duke University

Johns Hopkins University

North Carolina State University

University of North Carolina—Chapel Hill

Essay

Kim used the following essay in each of her applications.

Write about a matter of importance to you on any topic. If you have written a personal essay for another purpose—even an essay for another college—that you believe represents you, your writing, and your thinking particularly well, feel free to submit it.

The distinct smell of fresh leather from my brand new ballet slippers excited me. It seemed as if the summer months had gone by so slowly, as I had been anticipating this very day. There I was, at the actual Eloise Glass Dance Studio, in my itchy tights, bright pink legwarmers, and my Mary Lou Retton leotard (it resembled an American flag and it actually had her signature in the corner). My extremely long, brown hair was secure in a side ponytail. My freckles seemed to be darker than ever because of the summer, my bangs had been recently trimmed, and, boy, was I ready to take my very first dance lesson. I was not even the slightest bit frightened by staying with those strange old ladies in dance skirts for an hour or so—most of the other little dancers were clinging to their mommies tightly, but not me. My mother walked me in, and I gave her the OK to leave us (my personalized dance bag and I) on our own. Finally, I was officially a big girl. Ever since I had known what dance was, I had dreamed of growing up to be a ballerina. I had no idea what it took; I just wanted to be able to wear a big fluffy tutu and dance on my toes with a big, strong, cute guy. Walking into that small, one-room studio, in a residential section of Burlington, I did not bother to picture my future realistically. I was only four-and-a-half then (going on five), and simply dreaming, or rather letting my life appear as a dream, and just sitting back and watching it happen, amazed. What I did not know at that one magical moment was that dancing would affect my life forever, and that I was only at the beginning. It would leave a lasting impression with me that would help me gain discipline, responsibility, self-confidence, and independence.

As each year of my dance career progressed, my weekly schedule became more and more packed with dance lessons: ballet, jazz, tap, acrobatics, lyrical, you name it. The dance studio was my second home, and my teachers were my second mothers. They encouraged me to pursue everything I could accomplish within the short time span of a life. I learned who I was from dancing, through my classmates and teachers.

Because I have had to balance schoolwork, cheerleading, extracurricular activities, and work, along with dance, I have gained independence along with the skills to manage my time wisely. Dance has given me structure; it is the backbone of my life. I have been given the talent to express myself through movement, and I have had something to work hard at for the last twelve years. Through thick and thin, I have stuck with it. I have remained dedicated to dance because I know now that if for some reason I would have had to quit, my life would have fallen apart.

Through performing so frequently, and in front of so many people, I have acquired confidence that I can use in my everyday life, not just when the spotlight is on me and people are in the audience. I am able to carry myself well and interact with a variety of people because of my self-confidence. I have gained many skills throughout all of my dance training, all of my studios, all of my teachers, and all of my fellow dancers, and everything related to dance has contributed to my confidence. Dance has not only left me with more physical strength, but greater mental agility, as well. Although commitment to college may require a compromise with my dancing, dance will continue to provide discipline and structure for me.

Because I have learned so much from my dance lessons, performances, and teachers, I hope that my peers might take note of the strengths that are now part of me, which I have directly acquired from dance. I hope that they will find that passion that will make them work harder and longer, as I have. I want people to realize that I am not the same person today that I would have turned into without the intense involvement in dance that I have maintained. I prioritize my responsibilities well, manage my time wisely, balance my activities, keep my commitments, and practice until I reach my goals. Unknowingly, on that magical first day at the dance studio, that four-and-a-half year old certainly began a lifetime journey with that first dance lesson.

See page 325 to find out where this student got in.

KIMBERLY RITTBERG

Kim was the president of Student Government and won National Spanish Contest Award (AATSP). She was a three-sport varsity athlete and received all-conference and Unsung Hero awards for lacrosse her junior and senior years. Kim also had an art portfolio, which she presented to the admissions committee.

Stats

SAT I: 1350
SAT II: 740 Writing, 690 Spanish
High School GPA: 96/100
High School: Plainview Old-Bethpage JFK High School, Plainview, NY
Hometown: Plainview, NY
Gender: Female
Race/ Ethnicity: White

Applied To

University of Pennsylvania (applied early decision)

Essay

Write page 219 of your autobiography.

I begin to eat my soggy Corn Flakes, and I try to swallow; it feels like there is a rock in my throat. I feel my forehead; it's warm. A glance at my soft, cozy pillow makes me debate remaining in bed all day or going to school. Mrs. Smith's face pops into my mind, and I suddenly find myself in the car on the way to school. Second period rolls around – time for Spanish class.

Even half a hallway away from her classroom, I can hear the shrill voice and thick Brooklyn accent of Mrs. Smith. I greet Mrs. Smith in Spanish and approach her from above. Despite the fact that she wears two inch heels and I am about average height, I tower over her little body. Her clothing size multiplied by three does not even equal mine. But, what Mrs. Smith lacks in size, she more than makes up for in influence, enthusiasm and intensity.

Because Mrs. Smith was my teacher for the past two years, two periods a day in one year, I thought I would be ecstatic to escape her penetrating voice and bizarre jokes about her ex-husband. Yet, I feel a bit sentimental about leaving her as the end of eleventh grade approaches. I was sure that I was invisible in my ninth grade Spanish class with a different teacher. I received no special treatment; I didn't really receive any treatment. The teacher neither complimented me, nor belittled me. When I reached Mrs. Smith's room in tenth grade, I felt distinctive. My cheeks warmed and turned a light shade of crimson when Mrs. Smith praised me. I felt all twenty-eight pairs of students' eyes staring at me. The praise embarrassed me immensely, but it also made me feel extraordinary. It evoked the feeling I had in second grade when after spelling the word "ambrosia" correctly the teacher gave me a sticker. Well, Mrs. Smith always knew just how to give that sticker, not only to me, but to every student.

Part cheerleader, part comedian, part raconteur, Mrs. Smith always tries to get students more involved in class. The strongest image I have of Mrs. Smith is that of the cheerleader. Mrs. Smith always finds one good quality in every student. Even the boy who sits in the back of the class who barely understands one sentence of Spanish receives some form of praise. Now that I am a tutor of Spanish for younger students, I am able to find something positive in every student of mine. My students may not have an amazing command of the language, but I am able to encourage them by complimenting their accent or grammar.

In tenth grade, Mrs. Smith coerced me into taking a second foreign language, French. It was not relevant to her that I had to sacrifice art class, my first love, and my only free period (and my second love), lunch. All that mattered to her was that I enjoyed language and had a talent. That year I had her class for two periods each day: Spanish and French. We grew close. Mrs. Smith often inquired about my Student Government activities. She also joshingly asked me if I was swapping clothes with her grandfather, or was living in the wrong decade, referring to my vintage clothing. I enjoyed French, and continued the course as a junior. I did very well in French class, and I must thanks Mrs. Smith. I know that I would have said "au revoir" to anyone else who attempted to make me take another foreign language. But, I am very glad I did. What I learned from Mrs. Smith is that if I enjoy something, whether it is art, foreign language, or Student Government, I should continue with it. Taking a course in French also confirmed my tentative feeling that I love foreign language, and that I will continue studying it throughout college.

I participated in two Spanish poetry performance contests. After many hours of memorization, I was assured by Mrs. Smith that I would carry home a gold medal. When I left empty-handed, she said, "Kimbuhly, you wuh rawbbed." She made me feel like my ordinary participation certificate was a first prize trophy. She told me to shrug off the disappointment. I followed her advice, and success followed defeat – I won several National Spanish Contest awards. Her attitude about losing instilled in me a sense of perseverance.

Now, a look at Mrs. Smith brings a new picture to my mind. No longer do I simply see a woman with a thick Brooklyn accent and shrill voice; I see someone who encouraged and guided me and taught me that sacrifice is necessary for success. I see someone who showed me that in order to succeed, one must experience failure and learn from it. I see a special person who made every student feel like a somebody, including me.

See page 325 to find out where this student got in.

KIMEN FIELD

Kimen played on her high school's volleyball and softball teams. She was a member of a community philanthropic group and volunteered over 400 hours of service. She is also a lifetime Girl Scout and earned her Gold Award. Kimen worked each summer during high school gaining valuable experience working with technology.

Stats

SAT I: 1530 (730 Verbal, 800 Math)
SAT II: 740 Writing, 720 Math IIC, 690 Chemistry
High School GPA: 4.2
High School: Irvine High School, Irvine, CA
Hometown: Irvine, CA
Gender: Female
Race/ Ethnicity: White

Applied To

California Polytechnic State University—San Luis Obispo
Rice University
Stanford University
University of California—Los Angeles
University of California—San Diego

Essay

Kimen used the following essay in her applications to Stanford and Rice.

How has the place in which you live influenced the person you are? Define "place" any way that you like . . . as a context, a country, a city, a community, a house, a point in time.

Each December a Christmas tree and Menorah share my family room and dreidels and Santa Clauses are juxtaposed on the coffee table. Each spring my family displays Easter decorations and prepares for the Seder. Such is the dichotomy of my family's religion: a division that has caused me much confusion and inward contemplation over recent years. When I was younger, I attended Sunday school at a local synagogue, but it was a duty and never a pleasure. I did not enjoy my time there and thus lost interest in Jewish philosophy. My friends and my mom's family exposed me to Christianity, yet its doctrines never captivated me. After long consideration of Judaism and Christianity I now realize that I am an atheist. I am also a secular humanist—a moral person trusting in human rights, education, and intelligence, not God, to propel us into the next millenium.

My family always promotes morality and integrity with a relative absence of spirituality, yet my mom occasionally remarks, "I have brought you up without religion, and I regret it." My parents wish for me to be religious, and I can feel my mom encouraging Christianity while my dad insists on Judaism. When my dad discovered I had been exploring atheism, he brought me books about Judaism to let me "give it a shot," but I do not think I ever could have. I lead a secular life and cannot find a reason to begin believing in an elusive God. Perhaps I am too scientific to comprehend the spiritual necessity of religion, but with billions believing, I understandably fear that I am missing out on a meaningful part of the human experience. While my family and childhood molded my theological beliefs, these same beliefs heavily impact and alter my family relationships. Hitler murdered my dad's family because they were Jews, and when I see my grandmother, the lone survivor, I feel like a traitor; I am not continuing the faith that my family died to protect. Christmas is my favorite holiday, and although we celebrate on a secular level, I feel hypocritical celebrating it when I do not believe in the religion. However, if I share my true feelings I fear I will be excluded from the family traditions I cherish. Throwing away a family's heritage might seem impossible, but with the candid words "I don't believe in God" so much of my family life might disappear.

I have come to understand the hardships of being an atheist and staying true to that title. Before a volleyball match last season, my teammates wanted to have a group prayer, and I said I felt uncomfortable. The looks that flashed back at me made me want to run off the court, but I stayed strong, and was relieved that they accepted my choice and moved on. This small incident foreshadows my future as I deal with the alienation that this declaration undoubtedly entails.

My overall childhood lacked religious upbringing, and I have shed my religious façade. The familial tension that resulted has led me to a balance between my religious beliefs and my family traditions. Having conquered this "crisis" at a relatively young age, I realize that I am more confident, strong, and honest. I can defend my beliefs (or non-beliefs) and I have truly discovered my convictions about the enormous spiritual cloud that hangs over us. I have had intensely uncomfortable discussions with my family about religion, but I am confident that choosing to be sincere about my lack of faith is the right choice. Being true to myself has proven to be a challenge, but a rewarding one. As a member of a philosophical minority, I have felt the effects of discrimination, yet I know I will persevere and become a stronger person from my assertion.

See page 326 to find out where this student got in.

KRISTI DERRICK

Kristi received several awards for volunteer recognition and for individual and group musical performances in band competitions. She was leader of her school's band and participated in the math club as president and treasurer, the physics club, and the school-based Big Brothers Big Sisters program. Outside of school, Kristi volunteered 2,000 hours at a local hospital and worked twenty hours per week.

Stats

SAT I: 1370
SAT II: 620 Math IC, 740 Writing, 610 American History
ACT: 30
High School GPA: 3.84/4.00
High School: Central High School, Omaha, NE
Hometown: Omaha, NE
Gender: Female
Race/Ethnicity: White

Applied To

Johns Hopkins University
Swarthmore College
University of Rochester

Essay: Johns Hopkins

"The house of the soul," "a musical instrument," and "machine" are three examples of the many metaphors that are often employed to describe the human body. Write an essay in which you examine how the use of the metaphors affects the ways in which we study human life, see our bodies, take care of ourselves and others, or define health. Be sure to include and explain your own metaphor for the human body.

Sometimes, a situation cannot be accurately described using literal phrases. A metaphor makes it abstract and easier for some people to understand. Several metaphors for the human body have worked their way into mainstream vocabulary; in their own ways, each of these serve to better educate different people about the "machine," "house of soul" or "toasted marshmallow."

The first two of the aforementioned metaphors are complementary. "The machine" accurately describes the innate precision of the human body's vast amount of functions, including the timely pumping of the heart to the lightning-quick messenger from the brain to all other parts. On the other hand, "house of soul" correctly implies that the body is a unit with its own path to follow, with individual emotions to accompany it. To combine the physical and emotional aspects of the human body, I have created the metaphor of a toasted marshmallow. When toasted, the outside of a marshmallow becomes hard and changes pigment while the inside remains soft and gooey, much like the inside of the human body. Most people I know would describe themselves emotionally as tough on the outside but a "softie" on the inside. Children find this concept cool, adolescents think it weird and adults believe it to be overly simplistic. Yet, in coming to these conclusions, these people must have contemplated the body and its comparison to a toasted marshmallow. Thus, even if people disagree with my metaphor, they are forced to clarify their personal ideas of the human body. Knowing this, they can begin to understand the complexity of human life.

See page 326 to find out where this student got in.

KRISTIN SHANTZ

Kristin was valedictorian of her high school class and a National Merit Finalist. She competed in piano and voice, winning first place at the California State Talent Competition in each division during her junior year of high school. She was granted the Arthritis Foundation Summer Science Research Fellowship the summer following her junior year, allowing her the opportunity to do ten weeks of research at Stanford University in the Department of Immunology.

Stats

SAT I: 1520 (740 Verbal, 780 Math)
SAT II: 760 Writing, 790 Math IIC, 690 Chemistry
High School GPA: 4.0 unweighted
High School: Valley Christian High School, San Jose, CA
Hometown: San Jose, CA
Gender: Female
Race/Ethnicity: Caucasian

Applied To

California Institute of Technology
Claremont McKenna College
Harvard College
Pepperdine University
Princeton University
Stanford University
University of California—Berkeley

University of California—Los Angeles
University of California—San Diego

Essay

The following essay was used in Kristin's application to Caltech.

What event or events have shaped your life?

It was the most agonizing moment of my life. I hesitantly climbed the three stairs that led up to the seemingly enormous piano and slowly approached the bench. As I sat down, my tiny hands shook and my face flushed with fear, but somehow I managed to get through my little song…and then the moment was over. Everyone clapped, and I sat down with my mom to watch the rest of the recital. As I listened to numerous other students play song after song, each progressively more difficult than the previous one, I began to feel more and more insignificant. My short, simple little song seemed worthless in comparison to the other amazing pieces performed with style. The experience was a bit too much for me, a mere five-year old, to handle, and I began to cry…and cry. But I kept practicing.

I have played the piano for twelve years. I have practiced for over three thousand hours. I have performed at least fifty times. But each performance is still pure agony. Each moment of performing is painful, as an intense fear of making a mistake or forgetting my song overwhelms my entire being. I fear utter and complete embarrassment more than anything in the world. And it has happened…I have made mistakes that seem to echo throughout the room, and I have forgotten notes so entirely that I am forced to start the song over. But I have kept practicing.

Some may wonder why I keep persevering through the pain, through the sheer agony of performing. I tolerate the trauma, because after my very first experience performing, I realized that success would only be achieved with hard work. Now, when I perform, the moment when it is over is the greatest feeling in the entire world. There is no moment like the one right after the final chord is struck, when the audience wildly applauds my beautiful ballads or spicy Spanish arrangements. As I take my deep bow, and the people clap, I realize that all my practice is worthwhile. No feeling is greater than the feeling after a successful performance. And at the very moment when the 1st place trophy was handed to me during my most recent competition, I knew that I had achieved my goal.

Piano performance has taught me so much that has truly molded and changed my mental perspective on life. When I was young, I used to think that I would be able to coast through life, and in the end, life's problems and challenges would work themselves out. After my first recital, however, I learned that just as the great, after-performance feeling must be preceded by pure torture, all great successes in life must be preceded by hard work and many struggles. I've realized that if I want to make a difference in this world, and make a contribution to society, I'm going to have to give it some elbow grease. But I don't mind…I'm ready for the challenge.

See page 327 to find out where this student got in.

LAUREN FONTEIN

Lauren was a member of her high school Madrigal choir and Concert Choir and sang in Nevada All-State Choir for two years. She was also involved in several musical theater productions both at her high school and with the Nevada Opera Theater. She lettered in varsity track and was a National Merit Scholar.

Stats

SAT I: 1550 (750 Verbal, 800 Math)
SAT II: 680 Writing, 720 Math 1C, 760 American History
High School GPA: 4.65 weighted, 3.95 unweighted
High School: Durango High School, Las Vegas, NV
Hometown: Las Vegas, NV
Gender: Female
Race/Ethnicity: Caucasian

Applied To

Dartmouth College
Harvard College
Princeton University
University of Nevada—Reno

Essay

Lauren used the following essay in her applications to Dartmouth and Harvard.

Explain something or someone that has had an impact on your life.

A Day's Work

I twist the multicolored curls on my head, as my permanent smile melts on my face. Two eager parents approach with their 11 month old son, requesting a blue teddy bear. At the sight of me the baby burst into tears, wailing uncontrollably. I don't blame him. I'd be scared of me too – insanely colored frizzball on my head, candy apple nose, a face that exaggerates elation. I sympathetically hand the bear to the apologetic parents.

Two boys compliment my shoes. Who wouldn't? They're about a foot and a half long, red and white polka dotted. They clash perfectly with my outfit. I make the first boy a hat which adds a couple of feet to his height as he laughingly puts it on. (My fingers pull, twist and knot, callused from the constant pressure of powdered rubber - more dogs, hats, flowers, hearts, teddy bears, swords.)

A man with beat-up sandals and a baseball cap asks for a monkey on a palm tree. I oblige. He chuckles and tips me a couple dollars. I watch him walk over to his wife who smiles as she lovingly accepts the piece of balloon art. As long as I keep smiling everyone is happy. A toddler with blonde pigtails hugs me and I forget my fatigue. I have fun making these kids happy. I have fun getting hugs and dancing to the background music while an ambitious nine year old brainstorms about his selection. By the end of the day my hands are chapped – a testament to my hard work, which to me is more of an accomplishment. I can't remember how many balloons I've made or all the children I've seen that day. But each one has affected me and has made my inside match my oddly happy exterior. I wave goodbye and take a mental picture of the day. On the way home other drivers do a double take. They laugh. I can't help laughing with them.

See page 327 to find out where this student got in.

LILLIAN DIAZ-PRZYBYL

Lillian was an honors student and lettered for four years in varsity swimming. She also played saxophone for her high school's award-winning jazz ensemble, jazz combo, and wind symphony.

Stats

SAT I: 1520 (750 Verbal, 770 Math)

SAT II: 800 Biology, 740 Spanish, 720 World History, 800 English Literature, 740 Chemistry

High School GPA: 4.46 weighted

High School: Lexington High School, Lexington, MA

Hometown: Lexington, MA

Gender: Female

Race/Ethnicity: One-Half Polish, One-Quarter Cuban—she usually defines herself as Hispanic

Applied To

Williams College (applied early decision)

Essay

The following essay was written in response to the free response question on the Common Application.

I am a stargazer. Something about the sky, especially at night, intrigues me. The stars represent both science and poetry, two things I love. I remember one Christmas when I was little and I received a big, black telescope and a little blue dress with tiny silver stars on it. Both gifts made me want to explore, to make a difference in the world, discover a new solar system or maybe even track down far away signals from a little life form in a different blue dress looking back at me across the light years.

I grew older and out of the blue dress, but I couldn't outgrow the telescope or my love for the sky. The few times a year when we would bring it out to look at Saturn's rings, a distant nebula, or a double star, were always exciting times for me. I was fascinated by books about the sky and what was going on in it. There was so much wonder and mystery out there, only barely perceptible to the naked eye, which unfolded itself for the curious mind with a few lenses stuck on the ends of a tube. Stars change over time, and like humans, eventually grow old and die. Their mortality made them all the more beautiful to me, because in the gas jets of a supernova and glowing clouds of dust, new stars and solar systems are born. I read everything I could get my hands on, and even as I turned more to fiction than science, the way authors used the stars as metaphors for purity, distance, hope, or humanity itself captivated me.

However, in addition to the thrill exploring the heavens, astronomy involves a lot of sitting alone in the dark, waiting for stars to come up, skies to clear, instruments to function, or just for lightning to strike. Literature can be equally lonely, involving long searches through library stacks for references and literary criticism, and hours upon hours of reading and writing in isolation. There is adventure and joy to be found, it just takes time and patience.

Where in my life do I find companionship, then? Well, pretty much everywhere else: at school, at home, at swim team spirit parties, at jazz ensemble rehearsals. (Now that is one thing I love that is not at all lonely!) One of my favorite quotes is from Carl Sagan's novel, Contact; "For small creatures such as we the vastness is bearable only through love." I want to go to a college where I can find a community that will respect my interests and whose interests I will respect, where I can work with people who are interesting and challenging. I want to go to a college where I can find friendship and love to fill in the vastness (which really isn't so bad- everyone needs their space, after all). In short, I want to go to Williams College, for literature, astronomy, and love.

See page 328 to find out where this student got in.

LINDSAY CLAIBORN

Lindsay was involved in junior varsity soccer and varsity gymnastics. She was section leader in marching band and band council president. She was a National Merit Finalist and member of the National Honor Society for two years. During her senior year, she participated in an internship program at NBC Studios.

Stats

SAT I: 1530 (750 Verbal, 780 Math)

SAT II: 690 Writing, 750 Math II, 700 Chemistry

High School GPA: 3.6 weighted

High School: Thomas Jefferson High School for Science and Technology, Alexandria, VA

Hometown: Vienna, VA

Gender: Female

Race/Ethnicity: Caucasian

Applied To

Claremont McKenna College

College of William & Mary

Emory University

Pomona College

Stanford University

Yale University

University of Southern California

University of Southern California School of Cinema-Television

Essay

Lindsay sent the following essay, with slight modifications, to each of the schools to which she applied. The question was different for each school, but the essay fit all requirements. She initially wrote the essay for Stanford; their question asked the applicant to send a photograph and describe the meaning behind it.

"Can I hear a B flat please?" Our band director directs his question to the brass. "Now the woodwinds…" Then I hear it—the unmistakable squeal of four piccolos, skidding across the entire ensemble. I cringe and step out of line to look at my piccolo section. They look back with apologetic stares and one of them rummages for a tuner. These four girls are my responsibility. They must have their music memorized and their marching exact. They are a product of the time I have invested every year, from June to November, since 9th grade. We are part of a giant family that spends countless hours playing connect-the-dots on a football field. We are the marching band. We are each dots that move in unique patterns across a grassy game board. Each summer, June begins with individuals marching to unique patterns. In July, tempos start to coincide with one another, if only for a split second. In August, many tempos become one, blending all differences and creating a new cadence. From September to November we perfect our uniform tempo.

As my name thunders across the loud speaker amid the other leadership, I look no different than anyone else, one drop in a sea of uniforms. But my section knows that I am a darker dot, a bigger drop, like the checker piece that has reached the other side of the board and is coming back "kinged". I am the section leader. Leadership takes time to establish and more time to perfect. I have yet to perfect mine but our daily practices challenge what I know.

Thinking back to my freshman year, my section leader was a model of perfection. She seemed to know everything and everyone, and I felt privileged to be part of her section. Now I wonder if the freshmen feel the same way about me. They have yet to learn that my "perfection" comes from little more than experience, maturity, and dedication.

It is 10 minutes to show time. Anxiety runs high as the freshmen experience the rush of competitive performance. It's the last few seconds I will have to instill words of confidence in the minds of my flutes and piccolos. "Good luck, march your best." *Tap…Tap…* The solitary snare drum beats a solid tempo. Each drop adheres to another, collecting and combining. We are a mass; I am part of the sea again. We flood the dark alleys to the stadium. *Tap…Tap…* We are all united into one common goal; uniformity. *Tap…Tap…* We all appear exactly the same yet travel our specific paths. But that is impossible; to appear exactly the same is wearisome. Our own individualities create diversity, even when conformity is crucial. *Tap…Tap…* It's our turn; we may take the field in competition, in uniformity, in individuality. I locate my starting spot, dot #1. Downbeat, now my personal tempo is gone I must stay in step. Right, Left, Right. Where do I go next? Dot #2 . . . aha, four steps to the right. I am still traveling my personal path; my section follows me. They depend on every step I commit to. Left, Right, Left. I am alone in my directional movements but part of a whole picture. Dot #3, 4 steps diagonally left. Right, Left, Right. As the figures on the field ebb and flow with the musical tides, my individuality

shifts with the demands of the performance. The show ends, and the drum tap resumes. *Tap...*
Tap... Reality is beaten back into our heads, reminding us of what we have just accomplished.
We are unified in an endeavor to entertain and impress.

As I stand on the field at the end of my final performance, my individuality comes back, my
own rhythm returns. But a shred of the band's past unity remains. The bonds that we have formed
do not split but stretch and evolve. Those of us who have led leave something behind for the next
class and take with us the experiences of a lifetime.

See page 328 to find out where this student got in.

LISA BLUMSACK

Lisa was the Florida Junior Classical League Recording secretary her junior year and president her senior year, and she received gold medals on the National Latin Exam four years in a row. She also earned a total of ten varsity letters in swimming, cross-country, and track and field and received All-Big-Bend honors in swimming and track and field. She studied piano throughout middle and high school and qualified for All-State Chorus six years in a row (including the Sight-Reading Choir, the ninety best sight-singers in the state, her junior and senior years).

Stats

SAT I: 1420 (630 Verbal, 790 Math)
SAT II: 800 Writing, 800 Latin, 760 Math IC
High School GPA: 4.0 unweighted at time of Amherst application;
    3.98 unweighted final high school GPA
High School: Florida State University School, Tallahassee, FL
Hometown: Tallahassee, FL
Gender: Female
Race/Ethnicity: Caucasian

Applied To

Amherst College
Harvard College

University of Florida
University of Virginia

Essay

The following essay was used in Lisa's applications to Amherst and Harvard.

Evaluate a significant experience, achievement, risk you have taken, or ethical dilemma you have faced and its impact on you.

I will never forget the words, "It's hot! It's hot! It's hot in here! There must be a Floridian in the atmosphere!" Along with the other 42 delegates of the Florida Junior Classical League (FJCL), I screamed these words over and over again at the top of my lungs in the summer of 1997. Maybe if we were loud enough, spirited enough, enthusiastic enough, then the entrance of our state's delegation into the Fargodome at the National Latin Forum would catch the attention of the other state delegations, and, more importantly, the spirit award judges. Although all our screaming and cheering didn't capture a national spirit award for our delegation that year, I was anything but disappointed— on the North Dakota State University campus in Fargo, in the middle of nowhere, I had just had the week of my life.

Why would over 1300 Latin students from across the country spend a week in filthy dorms with no air conditioning, secluded from the rest of their known world, only to enter Latin competitions? I soon discovered the answer. In the Florida delegation were people with whom I usually didn't associate because they were from rival schools competing at the Regional and State levels. But, at National Latin Forum, individual schools were no longer pitted against each other, and the antagonistic atmosphere dissolved. Intermingled with written tests and the speech contests, solely for the purpose of fun, socializing, and state spirit were dances, spirit assemblies, and even games of basketball and volleyball. It was clear there that the love of Latin was the bond shared by all of us, not the reason for our gathering.

Once I realized that there is more to Latin than academics, I was inspired to become more involved with the FJCL, so that other Latin students could have the same wonderful experience I had had. The following year, I ran successfully for the office of FJCL Recording Secretary, and I am currently FJCL President. I have attended National Latin Forum every year since 1997, and when it was held in my home city this past summer, the FJCL did win a spirit award for the first time in five years. By taking an active role in FJCL and attending National Latin Fora, I have acquired a new appreciation for learning, for fellowship, and for spirit.

See page 328 to find out where this student got in.

MARIA INEZ VELAZQUEZ

Maria was editor-in-chief of her high school's award-winning literary magazine, a participant in the Alpha Kappa Alpha Partnership in Math and Science Program, and president of her school's Amnesty International chapter.

Stats

SAT I: 1400

SAT II: 800 Writing

ACT: 32

High School GPA: ~4.16

High School: Springfield High School of Science and Technology, Springfield, MA

Hometown: Springfield, MA

Gender: Female

Race/Ethnicity: Black Hispanic

Applied To

Connecticut College

Elms College

Smith College

Trinity College

Yale University

University of Massachusetts—Amherst

Xavier University of Louisiana

Essay

Maria used the following essay in each of her applications.

Please describe an experience of great personal importance to you.

In Search of Solitude

It is hard to come home again. I'm finding that out now. Over the summer I was stripped away, like an onion, a gradual pruning of all but the essentials. I became purified. I spent the summer as far away from home as I could get: two weeks in New Mexico as a Student Challenge Award Recipient, contemplating unknown constellations; four weeks as a scholarship student at Xavier University in New Orleans.

Leaving home was the scariest part. I have made myself malleable; I am the good student, the understanding friend, the dutiful daughter. I have always defined myself in terms of others: the ways they understood me was the way I was. It is so easy to do that. It is an easing of the mind, a process of surrender, a fading to oblivion, a surrender that kept me from thinking too hard about my self.

After building myself up from a heap of other people's thoughts and dreams, how shocking, then, to emerge into the stark fluorescent lights of an airport, to enter its crass brilliance, and discover I had no self, no one to define me. My plane ride to this new and foreign land of Albuquerque, New Mexico was my first solitary journey, my first layover, my first disembarking; I got off the plane in a cold panic, lost. I frantically tried to disappear once again, to hide from the harsh light. Huddled between the shelves of an airport bookstore I examined myself and found that I was empty. There was nothing there to see. Finally, the passage of time and the glare of the cashier ripped me from the grip of Nullity. Prompted by her look, I grabbed the cheapest, nearest book I could find. The book's weight in my hand was vaguely comforting.

In New Mexico, my book and I are left alone again. I spend the hot, noon bright days letting the glory of bone-white sidewalks burn away my pretensions towards identity. I play lightly with my voice, letting it flit and gravel-throat its way through stories and normal conversation. I experiment with the movement of my body, the inclination of my look. I discover I can be profound. I become outrageous, controversial, glinting glitter-bright fingernails every which way.

Two weeks later, my book and I leave New Mexico. I have memorized its cover: *The Hanged Man* by Francesca Lia Block. We travel onwards to New Orleans; its weight in my hands is again an anchor to reality.

In New Orleans, I am seduced by sepia, absorbed into a heaving mass of hued skin; I gladly lose myself in the balm of sweetly scented hair and cocoa butter. Here, again, I play with my identity. I leave my hair unrelaxed and wear it out. I learn to flash my eyes out, a coquette, and link arms with two girls I have befriended, we three ignoring the catcalls and hoots that track us down the street.

In New Mexico, I discovered the desert night. I let its silence fill me and transform me, until I was at once ethereal, eternal, serene. In New Orleans, I learn to be strong: I am the one the dorm girls come to at night when the black sky has descended and someone has ordered pick-up chicken; I am the one known for being unafraid. By now, I have let my nails grow out, long and blunt, colored them a crimson red – looking at them, I feel taloned and fierce, teeth blackened and filed to a point, like some old Mayan war story. I let my walk mime assertive strides.

It is hard to come home again, to once again surrender to the community of family, friends, and peers, whose chafing needs and desires chafe and brush against the skin with a subtle, bitter susurrus. It is hard to return to school, to the daily routine: I feel sometimes as though the person who claimed mountains is no longer there. But I try to remember this: the human soul is like a deck of tarot cards, and the mind is the dealer. Each card flipped is a facet of the potential self, each card a piece of a new person to be.

"Some of the faces will be mine. I will be the Hanged Man, the Queen of Cups. I will be Strength with her lions."

— *The Hanged Man*, by Francesca Lia Block

See page 329 to find out where this student got in.

MEGHAN BUTLER

In high school, Meghan was very active in the drama club as well as choral groups such as the Chorale and elite Chamber Singers. She was also very active in volunteer activities.

Stats

SAT I: 1380 (740 Verbal, 640 Math)

SAT II: 800 Writing, 640 French, 580 Math I

High School GPA: N/A. Top 12% of class, ranked 29 out of 225.

High School: Wakefield High School, Wakefield, MA

Hometown: Wakefield, MA

Gender: Female

Race/Ethnicity: Caucasian

Applied To

Boston College

Catholic University of America

Colby College

Fairfield University

Providence College

University of Notre Dame

Essay

The following essay was used in Meghan's applications to BC, Fairfield U, and Providence. It was the Common Application topic of the applicant's choice.

My Worst Habit

"You must break her of this habit."

My mother stared at these words before her in disbelief. It was September of first grade, and I had already brought home a note from the teacher. According to this note, I had been distracting the other students in my class by constantly humming and singing to myself. My teacher believed that this habit, if not stopped immediately, would prove "problematic in my future school years." She asked my parents to please help me overcome this "problem."

Looking over the note once more, my mother smiled. She explained to me that my teacher would like it if I was a bit quieter in class, but she encouraged me to continue my singing. What was wrong with humming, after all? I had always loved to sing. My mother saw that I had a keen sense of pitch and a true feeling for music.

"Who knows?" she commented to my father that night. "Maybe she has a real talent."

Over the years, I never stopped singing. However, I stopped myself from humming in school fairly quickly, after my classmates scolded me enough times. I joined every chorus that was available to me, and was active in the local children's drama group. Every year, I also religiously attended the Wakefield High School drama club's spring musicals. My greatest dream was to someday have the lead in one of these prestigious productions, to sing my heart out on a stage in front of hundreds of people.

When I entered high school, singing truly became my greatest passion. I took private voice lessons, joined the chorale, and as a sophomore was accepted into the distinguished Chamber Singers. Slowly but surely, my voice grew and matured. I received small solos in concerts and a supporting role in the spring musical as a sophomore. However, I never dared to dream that my achievements in voice would go any further than this.

As February of my junior year in high school drew near, I prepared for auditions for that year's spring musical, Li'l Abner. I wondered who might receive the lead role of Daisy Mae; this usually went to a senior, and I was curious as to who that might be. Predictions flew through the music hall in whispers. No one was quite sure of the perfect Daisy. However, on the day that the cast list was posted, I learned with disbelief that no senior, but I, Meghan Butler, was cast as the lead!

The next three months would prove to be very difficult. I struggled to learn over one hundred and fifty lines and more than four solos and duets. At times, I felt like giving up. However, my voice always comforted me; I sang to myself when I grew frustrated, and forgot my problems for a little while.

Opening night for Li'l Abner finally arrived, with much apprehension on my part. Had my first grade teacher been right after all? Did I really possess any talent, or was my mother wrong? My hands shook as I stood in the wings, waiting for my entrance. Would I succeed? I walked onto the stage with an anxiety that nearly overpowered my excitement.

Luckily, my fears were all for naught. The play was met with instant success. The next day, I received more compliments on my voice than ever before in my entire life. Some of the same classmates who had been bothered by my humming ten years ago came up to me in school and made a point of congratulating me on my success.

Almost before I knew it, the third and last show of Li'l Abner arrived. As I went through the motions of the play, I tried to remind myself to cherish every moment. I attempted to bring back the dreams I possessed as a small child when I had sat and watched the high school plays. However, some questions continued to plague me. Was all the work and effort of these years worth it? What had I accomplished, after all?

After the show, I walked out into the lobby. My friends were already outside waiting for me to come with them to the cast party that night. I slowly walked through the nearly deserted hallway until I came upon a little girl. I noticed that she was dancing and, upon closer observation, humming one of the songs from the play.

"Mommy, mommy!" she called to the woman beside her. "Listen to me! I can sing like Daisy Mae!"

Her mother only smiled. "That's great, honey. Maybe someday you'll be up on that stage!"

The little girl only laughed, and began to sing once again. As they walked out the door, I realized that my efforts had indeed been worth it, if for nothing else than the fact that I had lived out my childhood dream. Some people never have the chance to do this in their entire lives, and I had realized my own dream while I was still in high school. I knew that my voice had taken me there, one step at a time. Looking once behind me, I left the building with a smile. "I'll never break that habit," I whispered, and ran outside to meet my friends, humming all the way.

See page 329 to find out where this student got in.

MELISSA HENLEY

Melissa was on the varsity tennis team and was a member of the National Honor Society for two years. She worked a part-time job (about twenty to twenty-five hours a week) during her junior and senior years and took part in a local tennis academy senior year.

Stats

SAT I: 1400 (690 Verbal, 710 Math)

SAT II: 670 Writing, 740 Math IC, 690 Math IIC, 640 American History,
650 Chemistry

High School GPA: 4.0

High School: McMinnville High School, McMinnville, OR

Hometown: McMinnville, OR

Gender: Female

Race/Ethnicity: Caucasian

Applied To

Dartmouth College

Lewis and Clark College

Linfield College

Stanford University

Essay

Melissa used the following essay in her applications to Dartmouth, Stanford, and Linfield College. The essay question was something along the lines of *"Use this space to tell us anything else about you that you feel we should know."*

Although it may be difficult to tell, I hate talking about myself. I feel arrogant and self-centered and boastful when I go on and on about what I've done and what I want to do. And since I've had to answer the question "Tell us about yourself" on every other application, whether it's for a college or a scholarship, I've decided not to tell you about myself, but to tell you about my apple tree.

I grew up in the country, in a neighborhood where there were only three girls my age, but about ten boys two or more years older than I, one of whom was my obnoxious older brother. With this excess of torture, torment, and testosterone, I was often forced to find places where I could escape the plague of cootie-infested boys. Unfortunately, being both younger and a "girl", I could find no place the boys couldn't go. And so my mother, being the wonderful and patient woman she was, granted me sole access to our apple tree.

Before I continue, I feel I should describe my apple tree to provide you with a mental image as you read on. It's a young tree, no older than I am and so it's rather small, just a bit shorter than our old one-story house. It looks it's best in the summer, as most trees do, when it's laden with the greenest and sourest apples imaginable and it's covered with little white blossoms. With all the apples weighing them down, its branches would scratch the ground and form a curtain between the outside world and itself.

My apple tree first gave me respite from the harassment even before I was big enough to actually climb it. I spent days sitting at the base of the tree, writing the oh-so-juicy diary entries of a 7-year old and reading my Serendipity books, separated from the world by a few inches of shrubbery.

After I grew a bit and was able to climb the tree, I spent even more time in it, adding gymnastics and acrobatics (you gain a very unique perspective of the world when you hang by your knees in a tree) to the more peaceful activities of writing and reading. During the school year, when the weather was warm, I would do my homework sitting in my tree and enjoying a snack.

Once I reached middle school, I spent almost as much time in my tree as I did in my bedroom. My writing now included short stories and haikus, usually about nature and animals, and my reading had grown to books with several chapters and little or no pictures (a sacrifice I was forced to make in the effort to find more challenging books). Homework was done at the base of the tree since it was a bit difficult to drag the textbooks up into the branches.

Now, however, at the end of my high school career, I am no longer able to enjoy the comfort and serenity of my apple tree - unless, of course, I want to be prosecuted for trespassing. When my family and I moved from our home in the country, we left behind many things pertinent to the first thirteen years of my life, but my apple tree is what I miss the most.

My apple tree was more than just a refuge from the unbearable boys of the neighborhood. For years, it was my best friend. It was the best listener, with its trunk leaning companionably against my back and its branches hanging above, and it would never reveal any of my feelings or secrets. It was always there for me, strong and dependable, soothing and peaceful.

See page 330 to find out where this student got in.

MEREDITH S. KNIGHT

During high school Meredith was on the varsity swim team for four years, was a member of the band, was a regional finalist in UIL literary criticism, and acted in many drama productions.

Stats

SAT I: 1490
High School GPA: 4.0
High School: Temple High School, Temple, TX
Hometown: Temple, TX
Gender: Female
Race/Ethnicity: White

Applied To

Massachusetts Institute of Technology

Please note: Meredith doesn't remember the admissions decisions or essays used for other schools.

Essay

The essay instructions were to choose your own essay topic. Meredith chose "*Describe your hair.***"**

Impossible to answer. My hair can't decide if it wants to be dirty blonde with golden highlights or light brown. It looks like I have streaks of every color, from baby blonde baby hairs at the nape of my neck to chestnut brown at the roots of the broadest part of the back of my head. My hair is both dry from chlorine exposure and oily from over-enthusiastic teenage glands. There is a window of fourteen hours after washing in which my hair decides it will look healthy and clean. Then, our glands cycle through again, and the hair slicks down and mats to a slightly sweaty forehead. When down, my hair tickles my neck and falls in my face while I feverishly erase answers to physics tests. But, if I twist her up in a hurried bun or pony tail, she starts to work herself loose. My hair resents the confinement. First, she sticks her ends out in disarray, then strands fall around my face and whole chunks block my vision. When up, my hair wants to come down. When down, I want it up. My hair is straight at top and bottom, but kinky in between. After a blow-dry, it's smooth and lustrous until its owner walks into the Central Texas humidity between the house and the Volvo. Somewhere around the garage door the kink comes back. My hair is knotted by driving with the windows down and loud music on cold days and frizzed by walking into a muggy hospital lab late in the afternoon. My hair is part everything: wispy and straight, blonde and brown, flowing and harnessed, loved and hated. My hair is as much of a spectrum as I am.

I don't think I can be defined by a few words like blonde, smart, or honest because I am part these words and part their opposites. Just like my hair, I am between definite color and can not decide who I want to be. I am easily knotted by wind and a wild side, always with loud music in the background. I struggle to get loose from the confinement of a tight ponytail. I like my hair because everything she is relates to me. I can cut her, just as I shape aspects of my self. I can curl or dye here, but there are some constants that I can never get way from, like humidity and people. I have sensitivity, a wanderlust, a curiosity, and a drive that no trim or dye job can take away. My hair and I are attached by roots. Every time a single strand tickles the edge of my nose or wraps itself around an eyelash, I am reminded of our strength.

See page 330 to find out where this student got in.

MEREDITH NARROWE

Meredith was a one-meter springboard diver for all four years of high school, placing third her freshman year, second her sophomore and junior years, and first her senior year in the state diving championship. She served as National Honor Society president, played in the band, and twirled flags with the color guard.

Stats

SAT I: 1370 (710 Verbal, 660 Math)
SAT II: 800 Writing, 730 American History, 650 Math IC
ACT: 29
High School GPA: 4.138
High School: King Kekaulike High School, Pukalani, Maui, HI
Hometown: Pukalani, Maui, HI
Gender: Female
Race/ Ethnicity: Caucasian

Applied To

Brown University
Columbia University
Occidental College
Pomona College
Scripps College
Stanford University

Essay

Meredith used the following essay in her application to Stanford and modified it for Pomona.

How has the place in which you live influenced the person you are? Define "place" any way that you like . . . as a context, a country, a city, a community, a house, a point in time.

Da Kine Diversity

He sauntered over from the neighboring display at the National History Day competition at the University of Maryland with an air of superiority.

"So," he drawled, "you three won this category last year? Refresh my memory; what was your project's title?" We turned our attention away from our current History Day display and focused on our competitor.

"It was called *Da Kine Talk: Migration to Hawaii Creates Pidgin English . . . And Controversy*," I replied.

"That's right," he conveniently remembered. "What does *da kine* mean, anyway?"

"It's a word you use when you don't know the actual word," I explained. "If you can't remember what color your shoes are, you would say their color is *da kine*."

"It's vague, kind of like 'stuff' or 'whatever,'" interjected my teammate. "For example, when asked what your day's activities will be, your answer would be, 'I'm gonna go *da kine*."

"It's kinda like 'whatchamacalit'," added my other teammate. "If you are frantically searching for your homework assignment and someone asks, 'What are you looking for?' you could reply, 'I can't find my *da kine*!'"

"Oh, I get it," he sneered. "You won last year without knowing what your title means." Haughtily, he turned away. We looked at each other and raised our eyebrows. Although we had given three different answers, each was correct and symbolic of a language that sprouted from Hawaii's unique cultural diversity. Designed as a means for the *lunas* (overseers) of the canefields to communicate in general terms with laborers of different ethnicities, cultures, and languages, Hawaii's Pidgin English often fails to yield the clear definition our fellow competitor expected.

Hawaii is known as the ethnic and cultural melting pot of the Pacific. It is a place where my parents are Mainland "immigrants," and, I suppose, a place where as a *haole* (Caucasian),

I am a minority in my public high school. After growing up in Hawaii, I can discern a thick line between our "island style" and Mainland "normalcy." Like a *keiki* (child) of split custody, I experience both worlds regularly. Sure, I have no clue how to operate a rice cooker, but I do know the difference between Island sticky rice and Uncle Ben's. A good luck cat figurine is absent from my home, but my family follows the custom of removing our rubber slippers before stepping onto our linoleum floor. When I speak with my local friends, I end statements with, "Yeah?" — the customary request for affirmation that your opinion is valid. While attending a three week summer writing program at Carleton College in Minnesota, however, I was surprised to learn that this habit was noticeable and thought of as a Hawaiian "accent" by Mainland students.

Few of my Maui friends would have elected to spend a month of their summer in Minnesota doing *more* schoolwork. In fact, even fewer of my schoolmates, when confronted with the lure of palm-tree lined beaches, would have opted to spend seven months of sunny Sunday mornings enclosed in a house analyzing the effects of Pidgin English on a century of Hawaiian history as my two teammates and I did. By taking advantage of our unique, isolated culture and the abundant amount of information available, we discovered that history is not old and stale, but is a living, personal part of every society. The possibility of supplementing this discovery in a place where everybody has a similar intellectual curiosity and where a never-ending pool of information exists is mind-boggling and exciting. Imagine a child —whose only video viewing experience has been a black and white silent movie — suddenly allowed an unlimited selection of cartoons at the local video store. Stanford is my ultimate video store, an institution in which my beliefs and ideas will be challenged and augmented by more developed views from different backgrounds and perspectives, both inside and outside the classroom. I will find a new *ohana* (family) of people who, like myself, crave new experiences and diverse intellectual pursuits. Again, there will be a variety of answers to any question, all describing *da kine* (truth).

See page 330 to find out where this student got in.

MICHAEL

Michael was actively involved in a computer science program where he won the USA Computing Olympiad's Junior First Prize and created award-winning autonomous robots. He was also actively involved in developing and implementing a pilot project to teach Visual Basic to at-risk kids. In addition, he volunteered at engineering camps for children, owned his own computer business, played varsity rugby, and was a downhill ski instructor.

Stats

SAT I: Initial score submitted with applications: 1410 (660 Verbal, 750 Math). January scores submitted late to all schools: 1470 (680 Verbal, 790 Math).

SAT II: 800 Math IIC, 700 Writing, 690 Physics

High School GPA: In Canadian terms, grade 13 (OAC) average was 94.8%

High School: Woburn Collegiate Institute, Scarborough, Ontario, Canada

Hometown: Scarborough, Ontario, Canada

Gender: Male

Race: Chinese Canadian (born in Canada)

Applied To

Brown University

Columbia University

Cornell University

Dartmouth College

Harvard College

Massachusetts Institute of Technology

Princeton University

Stanford University

University of Pennsylvania

Yale University

Essay

Michael used the following essay in each of his applications.

Write an essay which conveys to the reader a sense of who you are. Possible topics may include, but are not limited to, experiences which have shaped your life, the circumstances of your upbringing, your most meaningful intellectual achievement, the way you see the world—the people in it, events great and small, everyday life—or any personal theme which appeals to your imagination. Please remember that we are concerned not only with the substance of your prose but with your writing style as well.

Childhood Dreams

When I was a little boy, I really wanted to be a professional baseball player. Who didn't? In the glory days of the Toronto Blue Jays, life revolved around baseball for us 7 year olds. Everyone knew Roberto Alomar had 53 steals and Joe Carter had 33 home runs. I dreamed of being at bat on the 7th game of the World Series, in the bottom of the 9th inning with the bases loaded and 2 outs. I dreamed of the millions of dollars I would make playing a game I loved. Then, the baseball players went on strike, and the baseball craze died. So, I decided that I would become the next best thing – a *rocket* scientist. Of course, I had no clue as to what this entailed, but my interest in screw drivers, vacuum cleaners and lawn mowers was enough to have me convinced that I was destined for that career.

Ever since I started to walk, I loved everything that moved or made sounds. For that matter, I loved everything that helped build or fix anything that moved or made sounds. This was an early indicator of things to come, but my *dream* became closer to reality with the European godsend: Lego. Year after year I would write letters to Santa for the newest and greatest Lego kits. And year after year I would sit down and spend hours on end assembling and disassembling my prototype spaceships. My love for Lego eventually developed into a love for robotics. It started in the beginning of the seventh grade. I picked up a book at the local bookstore that had an interesting looking cover. Little did I know that this would spark the beginning of a six year *quest*. The book described how to build a simple robot out of cheap Radio Shack parts. Eager to move on from the realm of Lego, I dragged my dad out to five different Radio Shack stores to buy all of the required components. I struggled with building the robot for a few weeks on my own, as no one in my family had the experience to help me. Finally, after I had my first functional prototype, I realized that I had found a genuine interest in building things that moved and acted independently. Having the robot avoid crashing and emulate humanlike behavior were two basic things I worked on. After two years and many different iterations and ideas, I deemed my project complete and submitted it for review in our City's science and technology fair. The judges were impressed with the simple collision avoidance and behavioral functions I had built into the robot – it won the Institution of Mechanical Engineers' *Engineering Excellence* award. This was the first major accomplishment towards my rocket science/engineering goal.

Throughout high school I continued to experiment with different aspects of robotics. I joined my school's FIRST Robotics team, and have been a key contributing member in the development of our team's robot. My continued interest in small robots has led to my current senior year Computer Science project on autonomous robots. For my school project I hope to enter the Trinity College Fire-Fighting Home Robot Competition in Hartford with a good chance of success having built in all of the optional robot features. This ongoing project is proving to be a complicated test of both my knowledge of hardware and my programming skills. Operating quite nicely in parallel with my school project is my developing mentorship with the University of Toronto Institute for Aerospace Studies studying robotics for space exploration. At the Institute, I will be exposed to more current approaches that are used to tackle large scale robotics problems. I will work with other graduate students developing things like cellular automata and neural networks that will eventually be implemented on the Institute's robots. It will be a very exciting and valuable experience to be able to work with some of the most technologically advanced equipment with the country's brightest researchers.

It may not exactly be *rocket science* just yet, but robotics has played a large role in my intellectual development. It has showed me just how virtuous patience really is through solving problems systematically and logically. It has provided me with a vehicle to apply and enrich my abilities in creativity, maths, and sciences; robotics has become one of my passions. I may not have built a Mars Rover (yet), but the realization of this dream is something I will definitely pursue further in college.

See page 331 to find out where this student got in.

MICHELE CASH

Michele was president of her high school's Interact Club and Latin Club, and she organized schoolwide canned food drives and blood drives. She played tennis and ran cross-country, and she was an attorney on the school mock trial team for three years. Michele attended the California State Science Fair twice, winning first place her junior year. She also worked as a research assistant at NASA Ames Research Center the following summer.

Stats

SAT I: 1450 (690 Verbal, 760 Math)

SAT II: 710 Math IC, 750 Math IIC, 720 Physics, 670 U.S. History, 720 Writing

ACT: 29

High School GPA: 4.0

High School: Abraham Lincoln High School, San Jose, CA

Hometown: San Jose, CA

Gender: Female

Race/Ethnicity: White

Applied To

Harvard College

Harvey Mudd College

Princeton University

Rice University

Stanford University

University of California—Berkeley

University of California—Davis

University of California—San Diego

University of Rochester

Essay #1: Stanford

Talk about a place in which you have lived and how it has influenced you.

I gaze with contentment at the crisp, cool world around me. Hugging a shawl to my body, I look down the rows of uniform white canvas tents. The sun has begun to peek over the glistening golden hills and the makeshift town comes alive. The men, in their nightshirts, gather in groups and talk about the events planned for the day. The women start fires for breakfast and the children scurry to the water pump with metal buckets to get water for oatmeal. Morning is my favorite part of the day when the entire day spans endlessly before me, and I know I can spend it however I want.

One weekend a month I relieve the Civil War era. Wearing period attire, I stay in a canvas tent and sleep on the ground with my grandparents. The reenactment represents a place were I can run wild with my friends and participate in activities like those portrayed in Little House on the Prairie books. All my cares dissolve along with the twentieth century, as I inhabit the world of 1863. I pick berries - staining my pinafore with the dark juice - catch tadpoles in a nearby creek, and run like a banshee through the wide-open fields. Life becomes simple, free, and magical as familiar conventions disappear. At night, the world shimmers in the soft glow of candlelight, as flashlights do not exist. The lanterns make late night trips to the outhouse an exciting adventure into the unknown. The entire environment is so different, so foreign. I savor the freedom, the adventure, and the challenge of living in this simple time period.

The Civil War reenactments afford me time to learn forgotten skills which my busy schedule at home never allows. I sit with the women and learn to embroider, crochet, and spin yarn with a spinning wheel as I listen quietly to their conversations. I enjoy afternoon tea in the shade of an awning, following proper social protocol and etiquette while I carry on light conversation with the other ladies who talk gleefully of marrying me off. Knowing the proper etiquette of the 1860's has given me greater confidence in social settings of the 1990's. I have learned the lost language of the fans, and often walk through camp communicating in this secret form with my friends. Learning these past arts fascinates me, and with persistence I spend entire afternoons trying to fill a spinning wheel bobbin with perfect, even yarn. At home my life is hectic and busy, organizing school-wide canned food drives, working at NASA, and participating in sports. At camp I can take the time to learn these forgotten crafts. The reenactments are a place where life is uncomplicated, where I can retreat from my self-imposed, academic discipline, where I can let go and focus on life in a simpler time.

Essay #2

The following essay was used in all applications, with the exception of Stanford (and as an optional essay for Princeton). Michele responded to a question that was along the lines of *"Tell us something about yourself."*

I came home from summer camp to find another foster child in our home. Noel had returned to his parents and Christian had replaced him. He was a quiet, shy, four-year-old who never made a sound. His past rendered him scared of adults, and when he spoke, it was barely an audible whisper. When I first met him, Christian did not faze me as anything other than another foster kid, with whom we would be sharing our home and love until a more permanent home could be assigned by the court. My parents were emergency foster parents and I had seen foster children come and go, some stayed only two days, others lived with us for several months. In the end, they all left.

At first Christian's presence did not impact me. With my busy schedule it was easy to let the cowering child who wanted to be left alone go unnoticed. But Christian's sad face and puppy dog eyes sang to me. Before long I found myself reading If You Give a Mouse a Cookie to him every night before tucking him into the little miniature bed in my brother's room. The dark held monsters which scared Christian. Every night I made sure that the soft yellow nightlight beside his bed was casting its friendly glow on the walls, protecting him from the monsters concealed in the dark. I did not want Christian to wake up scared and frightened; he was so fragile and sweet I could not stand to see him upset.

Weeks passed and Christian found comfort in my active and compassionate family, slowly he shed his shell of fear and insecurity and transformed into an assertive four-year-old demanding attention. Christian willingly tried new activities. There were many common childhood experiences Christian never had. I taught him how to hold a crayon and color imaginative pictures, how to throw a softball and kick a soccer ball. We sat together on the family room floor and built Lego towers. We explored the mysterious corners of the backyard, creating secret magical lands for us to play in. I enjoyed Christian's inquisitive mind and loved watching his reactions to the surrounding world.

Christian fit perfectly into the makeup of our family. He even continued the pattern set by our ages: 16, 13, 10, 7, 4; obviously he was meant to be part of our family. In every way Christian became my little brother. I protected him from harm and held him in my arms if he was ever hurt or upset.

In August of that summer my family went on a trip to Washington where we hiked up a steep trail toward the glaciers on Mount Rainer. Even Christian and my youngest sister, Gayle, made it most of the way up without whining to be carried; but before we reached the desired glacier, more than half our party decided they would rather rest than continue up the steep ascending path. Christian anxiously sought to play in the glistening snow, but he was too tired to climb any higher. I wanted him to encounter the cold softness of snow, so my brother, Stephen, and I plodded up the steep slope on a mission to bring back snow for Christian. Hiking up the mountain was not as difficult as coming down. The icy snow burnt my hands and soaked my heavy sweatshirt. I didn't mind the stinging numbness in my fingers; the pain dissipated upon seeing Christian laugh as he built three-inch snowmen and participated in our miniscule snowball fight. The genuine happiness Christian displayed that day playing with snow made my trek to the glacier one of my most meaningful achievements.

Christian stayed with my family through Halloween and Christmas and into February of the next year. Once school started I no longer had countless hours to imagine marvelous kingdoms and explore hidden worlds with Christian, but I still managed to read to him and tuck him in bed on a regular basis. One cold Friday in February I came home from school to find a Polaroid picture of Christian on my desk with the caption, "To Michele" written in his shaky writing. The authorities had taken Christian away and I had not even had the opportunity to say good-bye. The loss of Christian devastated me. He fit so logically, so perfectly into our family; he made it balanced and whole. Christian's deep inquisitive mind and genuine shyness reminded me of myself at his age. I wanted Christian to have all the opportunities life held open for him, but circumstances snatched him away from me.

When people find out that my parents are foster parents they often ask how we can take care of foster kids, don't we get attached to them? I only have one answer for their question: I have loved them all, and have cared for them all, but some have left an aching hole in my heart.

See page 331 to find out where this student got in.

NATALIE ANN SCHIBELL

Natalie was the varsity swimming captain her junior and senior years, varsity track captain, varsity field hockey captain, and a member of the varsity softball team. She was also a member of Team USA, competing in the Rescue 2000 World Lifesaving Championships in Sydney, Australia, and a member of the U.S. Team in the Japan Surf Carnival (another lifeguard competition) in Chiba, Japan. Natalie received the Frank Catabilota Sportsmanship Scholarship Award, was a Jersey Sports News Swimmer of the Year nominee, and was a double gold and silver medallist in the lifeguard nationals. In addition, she attended the National Youth Leadership Forum on Defense, Intelligence, and Diplomacy in Washington, D.C.; was an SPCA volunteer; and won the Pax Christi Student Peacemaker Award.

Stats

SAT I: 1070 (560 Verbal, 510 Math)
SAT II: 640 Writing
High School GPA: 3.5
Washington College GPA: 3.4
High School: Red Bank Catholic, Red Bank, NJ
Gender: Female
Race/Ethnicity: Caucasian

Applied To

United States Naval Academy

Essay

In a well-organized essay of 300 to 500 words, please discuss the following: (1) Describe what led to your initial interest in the naval service and how the Naval Academy will help you achieve your long range goals, and (2) Describe a personal experience you have had which you feel has contributed to your own character development and integrity.

"Leadership is based on truth and character. A leader must have the force of character necessary to inspire others to follow him with confidence. Character is knowing what you want to do and having the determination to do it, in a way which will inspire confidence in those around you for whom you are responsible." -Unknown-

With intention, I have been training for the US Naval Academy and a future career as a naval officer since I was a very small child. All that time, my life, my longing has been the sea. As a lifelong resident of the Jersey Shore, I developed a passion for the ocean. Under the compelling influence of my parents, I learned to swim long before I could even walk. The discipline of twelve intense years of competitive swimming has dictated a life of strict regimentation, instilling in me the proper ethics of conduct and work. Consequently, I have developed superior time management and organizational skills along with an extreme desire, courage, confidence, humility, and stamina necessary to be a successful naval officer. Over the years, from the myriad of local, national, and international competitions in which I have participated, a strong sense of healthy patriotism has evolved, accompanied by an abiding calling to serve my nation. As a result, I naturally gravitated toward the Naval Academy.

The event that gave birth to my initial desire to be in the military was at the 1997 National Jr. Lifeguard Championships in San Diego where I placed 2nd in the flexed arm hang contest sponsored by the Marines. Impressed by my enthusiasm and fierce never-quit attitude, the Marines present encouraged me to pursue a military career. Later that same year, my freshman history teacher, Mr Rafter, who is a former USNA recruiter and diehard Navy fan, excitedly encouraged me to apply. After visiting Academy admissions, attending crew camp, and speaking to midshipmen of every class, I knew that being a Naval Academy midshipman had been my destiny. I took honors in math in science, accumulated a 3.5 GPA, was a five-sport varsity athlete and captain of three, a Christian Service volunteer, national lifeguard champion, and an international competitor. As a winner of multiple academic and athletic awards, I obtained a senatorial nomination, passed the medical, and upheld the physical requirements to the highest standards. I was truly prepared to be a valuable asset to the Brigade of Midshipman. In March of my senior year, I traveled to Australia to compete in the Rescue 2000 World Lifesaving Championships in Sydney. There, I placed 10th out of a field of both Olympic and professional competitors from 28 countries of the world. My excitement quickly dimmed, however, when I called my brother at home from Sydney who read me "the letter" over the phone.

When I did not gain an appointment; however, the last thing I wanted to do was give up my dream. To satisfy the plebe academic requirements, I enrolled in the challenging premed program at Washington College in Chestertown, MD, where I attended on academic scholarship and rowed on the varsity level. As a student athlete, I had scheduled my classes, activities, and dedicated all efforts towards my sole intention of gaining admission to the Naval Academy. I received a primary nomination from my congressman, passed the medical, and exceeded the maximum physical standards. The repeat of devastation inflicted tremendous heartache that no few words can describe. Nevertheless, upon visiting Colonel Vetter in his office, I instantly mustered the perseverance and the willpower to follow his advice and "Try again." That semester I studied even harder, improved a whole grade from chemistry I to chemistry II, and finished with a 3.3 GPA. I knew I would soon see the light at the end of the tunnel. Shortly after, based on my second and first place finish at the 1999 Lifeguard Nationals, I was selected to become a member of team USA to represent the US in an all expenses paid lifeguard competition in Chiba, Japan. It was a thrilling, unforgettable experience as I placed sixth and ninth among a total field of 650 Japanese competitors. Unlike the year before, I was welcomed home with some outstanding news, an acceptance letter to The George Washington University. I instantly pursued the NROTC program to be a member of a new US team, the United States Navy. I was certain that the superior unit would help me establish a professional military background and most importantly, gain an appointment to the Naval Academy. That summer, my beach supervisor selected me to coach the junior lifeguard team, a leadership experience in which I have had the opportunity to teach eleven and twelve year olds not only how to save lives and to win competitions, but how to believe in themselves. My summer closed with a fourth place performance at the Lifeguard Nationals in South Beach, Miami in the beach flag competition. One week later, I would leave on the bus from George Washington University for Orientation in Quantico, bidding farewell to competition, my junior lifeguards, the beach, and a civilian life. I was overwhelmed with excitement in anticipation of the challenge that lied ahead.

When the bus departed from George Washington on August nineteenth, my ship suddenly set sail. My journey began with the midshipman instructors testing my knowledge. Sitting at attention, head up, eyes on knowledge, and getting drilled on what I had mastered beforehand, I was in my glory. I even got reprimanded for my smiles. When the instructors tested me on new knowledge, however, I immediately learned the importance of military bearing. In the days ahead, I felt the constant sweat marching on the drill field, the chills aboard a CH-46 as it maneuvered through the air, and the assurance that I belonged in the military. Each day began with reveille at 0515 and ended with taps at 2200. During the activities in between, I sounded off unforgettable cadences, mastered physical training, the swim test, close order drill, obstacle courses, pugil sitck fighting, watch detail, sailing, and the completion of required tasks with military bearing and a great "sense of urgency."

On the last day, each platoon got the opportunity to ride aboard a CH-46 helicopter. Fueled by excitement, we sprinted out to and boarded the helo. By this time, I was exhausted, starving, and filthy. When glancing over at my squad mates, their bobbing heads and pale faces told similar stories. While looking out the window at the base, my mind flashed back to the experiences of leading them in attack assaults over the NATO course, cooperatively swabbing the decks, and cheering them on during the PRT and PT sessions. I recalled my shipmate and I hurriedly lifting each other's racks off the floor after they were ripped apart and thrown by a midshipman instructor who ordered us to have the hospital corners remade. For inspection, together we shined each other's belt buckles, polished each other's shoes, ironed and creased each other's whites, looked one another over, simultaneously exited the room, and stood at attention side by side against the bulkhead. Some of the highlights were: being a member of the winning squad at drill competition, maxing out the pushup require-ment, hearing stories of Naval and Marine Corps heroes, as well as the exhilaration of my platoon's roaring cheers after knocking the helmet off of my opponent's head. In the words of William Bulger, "There is never a better measure of what a person is than what he does when he is absolutely free to chose." As a college programmer, I came to Quantico, joined the NROTC program, and entered the Navy on my own free will. Standing proudly in my whites at graduation, I confidently raised my hand and took the Oath. On that very day, I made a commitment to continuously display a relentless perseverance and an unremitting dedica-tion to the goal of further strengthening the unit, gaining a Naval Academy appointment, becoming superior naval officer upon commissioning, and to improving the Self. In response to the recent terrorist attacks, I hold fast to this commitment more now than ever before.

One week after the World Trade center and the Pentagon attacks, the sirens still fill the atmosphere by day and I fall asleep to the sound of a helicopter circling above my DC apartment by night. The events of the past week have only made me more willing to become a Naval Academy midshipman and to better serve the United States. To me, there is no greater honor than to carry out the mission of safe guarding this nation and its people than to doing so in uniform. President Bush told this glorious nation, "We will not tire, we will not falter, and we will not fail." I have followed his advise and will continue to do the very same. A willingness to be commissioned is what brought me here to George Washington University and what keeps me in this relentless pursuit of the worthy goal of becoming a Naval Academy midshipman.

Charles Sima said it best when he stated, "Inside my empty bottle I was constructing a lighthouse while all the other were making ships." Looking back on my life, I look to the sacrifices that define me as the person I am. This is for my first ocean mile I swam in Bermuda at the age of six, the twelve years of competitive swimming, the 0530 practices, the broken thumb I kept playing with in an eight grade soccer game on the all boys soccer team, the dirty laundry I cleaned for the animals for which I also helped find a safe home as a volunteer for the SPCA. This is for the winning goal I scored at a championship field hockey game, going from a muddy track meet to getting ready for the high school prom, the lives I have saved at the beach, and the junior guards I cheered across the finish line. This is for the time I was the only student present at extra instruction when there was a concert on the Washington College campus and for the terrorist victims to whom I donated my blood. This is for my family, faculty, and friends who support me and for every prayer that keeps me going. I know they will all be answered. Clark H. Minor once stated, "No sacrifice short of individual liberty, individual respect, and individual enterprise is too great a price to pay for permanent peace." Through my experiences, I as well as many others have come to know the extreme motivation, dedication, and perseverance that I continuously exhibit. I will display this same commitment to the Naval Academy and to he Naval service. As a graduate of the Class of 2006 I will indeed, be well on my way to realizing my dream of both serving God and country with distinction and honor and to representing USNA as well as the United States Navy to the very best of my ability. I began this journey through my initial desire to be more than I ever thought I could be and I have done just that. It is one that has made me a better student, athlete, candidate, and person for "Patience and perseverance have a magical effect before which difficulties disappear and obstacles vanish." Still, "I have not yet begun to fight" and the very best is yet to come.

John Paul Jones once said, the Naval Officer "should be the soul of tact, patience, justice, firmness, and charity." I feel I have demonstrated these qualities by dedicating my mind, body, and spirit to the tenacious pursuit of this endeavor. As the fourth-class commanding officer, vice president of the Surface Warfare Club, and member of the Special Warfare and Pistol clubs, I anticipate some very exciting activities. Whether it be leading my fellow shipmates, field training, war gaming, getting hands on experience in damage control, live fire exercises, or laying wreaths at the Arlington National Cemetery, I will bring these experiences to the Naval Academy and positively contribute as a leader among the Brigade of Midshipman As I aspire to follow in the footsteps of the many notable men and women who have taken this same path before me, I also look forward to joining this extraordinary group of leaders.

In a thank you letter addressed to me, the Bradley Beach Junior Lifeguards wrote: "You have made an important difference in each of our lives, you have taught us and strengthened us as individuals. The lessons we learned the past few weeks and the experience we had, will stay in our hearts. We have all benefited from your efforts."

I have no doubt that I will do the very same for my future sailors and superiors. I once read, "The beginning of leadership is a battle for the hearts and minds of men." Thank you from the heart for your serious and thoughtful consideration of my application.

See page 332 to find out where this student got in.

NEENA ARNDT

Neena Arndt danced with a small ballet company while in high school. She was also on the Math Team and Student Council and was active in music and drama.

Stats

SAT I: 1420 (770 Verbal, 650 Math)
High School GPA: 3.93
High School: St. Mary's School, Medford, OR
Hometown: Medford, OR
Gender: Female
Race/Ethnicity: White

Applied To

Pomona College (applied early decision)

Essay

Who is your hero? Describe a person, real or fictional, who has influenced you.

Everyone, especially children, should have a hero. I am not sure who decided this but it must be true because I was asked, "Who is your hero?" or similarly themed questions at least once annually throughout my formative years. These questions came on surveys that were handed out on the first day of school, and were reviewed the following June to see if anything had changed. By third grade, I had learned that the best response to the hero question (known by those most familiar with it as the "HQ") was to print, in one's best handwriting, "My teacher." This response assured me that a.)My teacher would be reminded of her ability to influence the world's future leaders and act accordingly b.)I would spell my response correctly because in the late 1980s there apparently was a trend toward elementary school teachers keeping large wooden apple-shaped sculptures on their desks bearing the word "Teacher," which gave students a convenient reference and c.)My teacher would like me best.

These surveys were intended to help our educational providers get to know us better. I fail to see how questions such as "What is your favorite food?" will, from a strictly educational standpoint, give our teachers an advantage. ("Well, Mrs. Fettuccini, it's not surprising really that your little Alfredo has trouble reading. According to this survey his favorite food is pasta with a creamy cheese sauce, which has been linked with all kinds of developmental delays…") In my case, the surveys could not have been helpful at all, since I lied about the HQ every time.

Quite truthfully, nobody ever interested me to the extent that I considered them heroic. Still the HQ persisted into middle school, where I began to answer it humorously. At least I tried."My dog, because she sleeps all day" is one answer I remember writing. "The Jolly Green Giant" is another.

In high school, the get-to-know-you surveys stopped, so teachers were spared my lies and caustic remarks. Now, however, the ol' HQ has come up again. Who has impacted me in a special way? I've had so many fine teachers, read the works of so many great authors, and heard about so many selfless acts of sacrifice. But the person who has inspired me the most is Dave Barry, the humorist. Why else would I have peppered this essay with Barry-style writing?

Dave Barry is able to create humor without insulting its object. It is obvious that his statements are all in fun, for they are a combination of gross hyperbole and half-truths. I, too, want someday to be able to make people laugh at no-one's expense. I love to imitate Dave Barry. Maybe I should let him know that, because they say imitation is the sincerest form of flattery. Unless you're an elementary school teacher, in which case the sincerest form of flattery is having a student tell you that you're her hero.

See page 333 to find out where this student got in.

NITIN SHAH

Nitin went to public school in California, where he was editor-in-chief of his high school newspaper and president of its Amnesty International chapter.

Stats

SAT I: 1590 (800 Verbal, 790 Math)
SAT II: 800 Writing, 800 Math IIC, 760 American History
High School GPA: 4.60 weighted
High School: La Costa Canyon High School, Carlsbad, CA
Hometown: Carlsbad, CA
Gender: Male
Race/Ethnicity: Indian American

Applied To

Harvard College
Stanford University
University of California—Berkeley
University of California—Los Angeles
Yale University

Essay

Nitin used the following essay in his applications to Harvard and Yale.

Evaluate a significant experience, achievement, or risk that you have taken and its impact on you.

Christmas in India

I never understood how my culture and background were different from everyone else's until a visit to my parents' mother country of India opened my eyes. Before that, I was just another kid in Southern California's suburban wilderness, in which parking spaces, large backyards, BMWs, and a strange sense of surrealism abound.

As I, age nine, stared out of the jumbo jet's window at the puffy white cloud tops and into the pale blue late December sky, I pondered back over the intense activities of the previous few days, including Christmas. That holiday was always perplexing for me as a child. Judging by what I could gather from my primary source of reliable information, cartoons, this

Christmas thing involved a confused fat man forcing a bunch of moose to be his partners in crime as he broke into people's homes only to leave things, instead of take them. The most puzzling feature of all to me, as a San Diegan, was that white substance everyone was walking in and building real live snowmen out of.

It was all oddly interesting, but what did all this have to do with me? I asked my mother, my backup data source. Christmas, she told me, can mean certain things to certain people, but to most people, it's a religious day. Is that what it is for us? I asked. No, she said flatly. Upon further pressing, all she would say was that we believed different things than some people. She would not explain those different things, though. My parents never did much explaining; they preferred rather that my sister and I figure things out for ourselves in our own way.

Things in India were a far cry different from back home. This was apparent from the moment we departed from the airport into a hot Bombay night so muggy there was no need to stop for a drink; I need only open my mouth to take in all the moisture I would need.

It was like this, with my mouth and eyes and ears wide open, that I took in the tastes and sights and sounds of India, conscious for the first time of my background and identity. I watched from a filthy, rust-covered train as a tiny cross-section of Indian life passed me by, a virtual slide show of the people here and their way of life, much removed from my own.

Dozens of dark-skinned naked children, many about my age, engaged in a playful shoving match in a waist-high brown-colored river. They cared not about getting dirty or sick or about the passing train they undoubtedly saw many times a day; their only care was about the moment. On an overlooking hill, old and wrinkled women watched them coolly in the sweltering heat as they milked cows and swiftly unleashed words that I could not have understood even had I been able to hear them over the train's drone and the children's screaming. Nearby, the women's husbands repaired the proud yet cramped dried-mud homes that stood chipped and battered from a recent earthquake. The men functioned as a single unit, concentrating completely on one building before moving on to the next. The entire village had perhaps twenty of these constructs, and the cows and bulls grazing in the surrounding pasture seemed to outnumber the people 2-to-1.

I realized that this place, not the life back home, was where I really came from, yet I was still awed with the people's contentment. They had so little in the way of material possessions, yet were so happy. They didn't need a car, or fence, or swanky home to be satisfied. Every day was their Christmas, and the gift was life.

See page 333 to find out where this student got in.

PETER DEAN

Peter Dean was a baseball and football player and was captain of both teams senior year. He was involved with Student Government all four years, and during senior year he was a member of the Executive Committee of the school.

Stats

SAT I: 1340 (650 Verbal, 690 Math)
SAT II: 600 American History, 680 Math, 530 Writing
High School GPA: 3.9
High School: James Madison High School, Vienna, VA
Hometown: Vienna, VA
Gender: Male
Race/Ethnicity: Caucasian

Applied To

Davidson College
Gettysburg College
Rhodes College
University of Virginia
Valparaiso University
Vanderbilt University
Wake Forest University
Washington and Lee University
Wheaton College (IL)

Essay

The following essay was used in each of Peter's applications.

Common Application Question 1: *Evaluate a significant experience, achievement, or risk that you have taken and its impact on you.*

No underarm hair, no facial hair, baby fat, and a mouthful of baby teeth is how I spent my first two years at James Madison High School. In the middle of my sophomore year, when most of my peers had begun shaving, I was getting the last of my baby teeth removed, because at age 16, I had "the mouth of a 12 year old," my dentist told me.

My older brother was big, strong, mature, and only a year ahead of me. Therefore, I was continuously asked, "what happened to you?" I always tried to answer the question optimistically - as I tried to do with the question, "do you shave your legs?" After long anticipation, Mr. Puberty finally arrived at the end of my sophomore year. Since that time I have grown at least eight inches, lost my baby fat, gained some underarm hair, and become the starting quarterback on the Varsity football team. Starting my senior year I can now look back and appreciate the lessons I learned before puberty, and I am glad that puberty did take so long.

Delayed puberty helped build my character. It taught me a lot about humility. In the halls during my freshman and sophomore years I was always looking up to, or being pushed around by, everyone. Now that I am bigger than most of my peers, I do not feel that I am better than they are. Lacking appearance, size and strength I was also forced to develop other character traits such as friendliness, a sense of humor, and kindness to attract friends - especially those of the opposite sex.

Delayed puberty eliminates many worries that usually are associated with entering high school. In the morning I did not need to shave, because the peach fuzz was still sparse. I did not worry about my wisdom teeth having to come out, because I had just lost all my baby teeth. I did not need to worry about braces, because I was on pace to get them in graduate school. I did not have to worry about any girl problems, because I learned from experience that girls are not interested in guys that remind them of their younger brothers.

Delayed puberty also postponed and shortened my adolescent conflicts with my parents. Of course, I have tormented my parents with petty arguments about use of the car and curfew. However, my adolescence has been efficient. My brother tortured them for four full years, but I achieved the same results in a few short months.

As I look back on my pre-puberty days there are many reasons why I am glad Mr. Puberty visited me late. I realize that there is no way to control when he comes, but if he ever chooses to visit you later than your peers you should be thankful. Even though you might spend a few years on the "short" end of jokes, in the end it will only make you better.

See page 334 to find out where this student got in.

PHILIP JAMES MADELEN RUCKER

Philip lived away from home in Lake Arrowhead, California, between the ages of ten and sixteen to pursue competitive figure skating training. Following his sophomore year of high school, he moved home to Savannah, Georgia, to be with his family. In school, Philip was actively involved in the yearbook, National Honor Society, Rotary Interact Club, and many other organizations. In the Savannah community, Philip was a Junior Block Captain with his local neighborhood association and a staff writer for his local newspaper, and he held a part-time job as a legal assistant at a small law firm.

Stats

SAT I: Did not include score in any applications
SAT II: 740 Math IC, 700 Writing, 650 U.S. History
ACT: 30
High School GPA: 94% out of 100%
High School: St. Andrew's School, Savannah, GA
Hometown: Savannah, GA
Gender: Male
Ethnicity: Bi-racial (African-American/Caucasian)

Applied To

Boston College

Brown University

Emory University

Georgetown (applied early action)

Harvard College (applied early action)

Tufts University

Tulane University

University of Chicago (applied early action)

University of Rochester

Yale University

Essay

Philip used the following essay in his applications to Yale, Harvard, Brown, BC, University of Chicago, Georgetown, and University of Rochester. The question was different for each, but he provided the question from his three top-choice schools.

Yale: *There are limitations to what grades, scores, and recommendations can tell us about any applicant. We ask you to write a personal essay that will help us to know you better. In the past, candidates have written about their families, intellectual and extracurricular interests, ethnicity or culture, school and community events to which they have had strong reactions, people who have influenced them, significant experiences, personal aspirations, or topics that spring entirely from their imaginations. There is no "correct" response. Write about what matters to you, and you are bound to convey a strong sense of who you are. (As with the first essay, observe the 500-word limit.)*

University of Chicago: *In a pivotal scene of a recent American film, a videographer— a dark and mysterious teen-aged character—records a plastic bag blowing in the wind. He ruminates on the elusive nature of truth and beauty, and suggests that beauty is everywhere—often in the most unlikely places and in the quirky details of things. What is something that you love because it reflects a kind of idiosyncratic beauty—the uneven features of a mutt you adopted at the pound, a drinking glass with an interesting flaw, the feather boa you found in the Wal-Mart parking lot? These things can reveal (or conceal) our identity; so describe something that tells us who you are (or aren't).*

Harvard College: *Supplemental essay on a topic of your choice.*

My Moment of Reckoning

The blistering sun shines through the tall fir trees onto a mound of frosty snow that sparkles like diamonds. As the heat of the summer day melts the snow, the snow forms a stream that curls down the hillside onto the quiet road below. I walk up the hillside with my skates over my shoulder, the sun shining on my black pants. It is hot. I enter the rink to the familiar sounds of sharp blades etching the ice to the beat of Beethoven. Indoors, the air is chilly; the ice is glistening; the heat from outside meets the icy coolness of the rink at the tall, wide windows.

Hour after hour, day after day, the same Zamboni brings white snow from inside the rink to the outside, dumping it into the same spot, creating the same flowing stream down the hillside. Seen from outdoors, the mound of snow is an aberration in the summer heat, but seen through the windows from indoors the same snow, framed by the trees, suggests a crisp, sunny, winter day. Even though the snow has been there every morning since I started coming to this rink, it struck me on this particular morning both how lovely and how strange it appeared.

The snow is clean and fresh, the residue of the early morning practice of young, promising, and often famous, figure skaters. Not yet sullied like most snow by the time that it is taken away, it is still pristine. It clings to its frostiness in the hot sunshine – a futile effort. This snow has lived a short life. It began as the smooth, shimmering ice that first catches one's eye and then catches the edges of the skaters' blades. As the skaters worked harder, the ice became snow, and within an hour or two of its beginnings it was removed. The snow rests now in this mound like millions of tiny diamonds, vulnerable to the rays of the sun and awaiting its fate.

As I stop to notice the incongruous beauty of the snow, the evergreens, and the glaring summer sun, I reflect on an affinity that I feel towards this snow. I, like the snow, am a bit misplaced. It has been wonderful to be a part of the life at this beautiful rink, this elite training center that grooms champions, but it is not really my element. I long to be with my family and have a more "real" life, not the sheltered, specialized one that this rink offers, where one's purpose is so limited. I stare at the snow for a moment and consider that soon it will melt into water and flow down the hillside to regions uncertain. Yet, perhaps, it will land where water and snow naturally belong and where the season of its life fits the season of its setting. As I watch, I realize that, perhaps, it is time for me also to leave, to leave this rink and this rarefied life of competitive skating, to go down the hillside and return to my roots.

See page 334 to find out where this student got in.

PHILIP TIDWELL

Philip was a member of the National Honor Society, president of the Key Club, treasurer of the Fine Arts Club, and vice president of the Wildlife and Backpacking Club.

Stats

SAT I: 1470 (770 Verbal, 700 Math)

SAT II: 600 Physics, 600 Writing, 600 Math IIC

ACT: 31

High School GPA: 3.77

High School: Emporia High School, Emporia, KS

Hometown: Emporia, KS

Gender: Male

Race/Ethnicity: White

Applied To

Arizona State University

Columbia University

Stanford University

University of California—Berkeley

University of Kansas

Washington University in St. Louis

Essay

Philip used the following essay in his applications to Washington University in St. Louis and UC Berkeley. The prompt was *"Write your own question and answer it."* Phillip's question was *"Perseverance is a valuable asset for any person pursuing a college education. How have you developed such perseverance in your high school career?"*

Though my life has only just begun, I have already collected a wealth of experiences to aid me in my future ventures. It is these experiences that define each and every individual; our personality, goals, and character are direct results of the situations that we encounter and the actions we take when faced with them. The greater the collection of experiences that a person possesses, the better prepared they will be to confront those obstacles that will inevitably obstruct their path to success. My experiences have come from many different areas, but few have had greater impact than those challenges I have faced as an athlete. One particular run has been permanently etched in my mind, an event on which I often reflect for strength, determination, and perseverance; it reminds not of success or triumph but rather of the bitter taste of failure and defeat.

The run began like most; my legs fell in to their familiar, rhythmic stride while my arms swung loosely at my sides. After the fifth mile my body began to show signs of fatigue. My abdominal muscles began to tighten, my stride grew heavier and my breathing shortened. This discomfort was not unusual so I pressed on, confident that the pain would subside shortly, yet the pain continued to mercilessly pound my body. Each step became an extraordinary exertion of force, sending a harsh pain through my entire body and begging my mind to cease this torturous punishment. My legs, my chest, my entire body cried for release, and in an instant I quit. I dropped my arms, stopped my legs and stumbled to the ground. I knelt there, sweat dripping from my chest as blood ran from my knees, and regained my breath. I stood slowly and began walking along the road toward my destination, whose distance was now immeasurable in my mind's eye. After a few moments of walking, I regained my familiar stride and continued on until I reached my destination. That day, that moment will remain forever in my mind as the day I quit, the day I allowed myself to be beaten, and gave up. In the four years following, rather it be in running, in school, or in life I have not yet, nor will I ever, give up again.

See page 335 to find out where this student got in.

REBECCA YAEL BACK

Rebecca was actively involved in both the Gay-Straight Alliance and Amnesty International in high school. She participated in theatre as both cast and crew and she graduated first in her class. Rebecca went to Israel for a semester abroad during her junior year of high school, and she held internships at Human Rights Watch and a New York–based grassroots political party.

Stats

SAT I: 1370 (710 Verbal, 660 Math)

SAT II: 800 Writing, 760 American History, 720 Biology E

High School GPA: 4.0

High School: Guilderland Central High School, Guilderland, NY

Hometown: Guilderland, NY

Gender: Female

Race/Ethnicity: White/Jewish

Applied To

Wesleyan University (applied early decision)

Essay

Common Application Question 2: *Discuss some issue of personal, local, national, or international concern and its importance to you.*

Six months ago, I was living in Jerusalem, near what is now a battleground in the Israeli-Palestinian conflict. While there was always an underlying current of tension, my semester abroad was entertaining, educational, and never scary. Today, as the casualties of this "conflict" (such a neutral term for bloodshed) rapidly increase, the situation *is* scary.

Throughout my life, during the Gulf War attacks on Israel and after the assassination of Prime Minister Yitzhak Rabin, I knew that I was supposed to worry about what was happening in the Middle East. After all, I was Jewish, had Israeli relatives, and had learned from Hebrew day school that everything happening in Israel somehow affects Jews all over the world. I did worry, or at least I tried to worry, but it always seemed like yet another bloody conflict happening in some exotic location on the other side of the world.

Living in Israel, even for just four months, made me feel like I was a part of this conflict. In Jerusalem, I took a class dealing with the history behind the Israeli-Palestinian conflict. While some of the lessons were held in the classroom, most were conducted on the streets. One day, we were sent out to interview Israelis and Palestinians about their views on the issue. I was most shocked by the responses from a group of Israelis my age. When I asked them, in my faltering Hebrew, whether the Palestinians should have their own country, they told me that the Palestinians should just be kicked out. I countered with the question as to where they *could* or *should* go, but these teens just shrugged and replied, "It's not our problem." I wanted to scream at them that this apathetic attitude is what causes the tension to increase and that the Israelis and Palestinians need each other, even for purely economic reasons. I wanted to ask them *who* is to say that Israel is just a Jewish country? Unfortunately, my struggle with the Hebrew language impeded my attempt at dialogue.

The current situation is much more vivid to me than ever before. When newspapers report on yet another battle, it is likely that I have traveled to that area. I may have even been just ten feet away from the spot now stained by death. I am not just reading the smudgy black letters of the *New York Times*; I can picture the rocky hills in the background and feel the hot dry air.

This summer, when I interned in the Middle East division at Human Rights Watch, I had to archive hundreds of documents from the early nineties. I was fortunate to be able to read the personal testimonies stuck in those folders, many of which were never released to the public. These testimonies were filled with horrid accounts of torture and murder, but the victims, both Israelis and Palestinians, weren't just mere statistics. They had names and histories, they had families and careers, they had interests and loves and hobbies. These testimonies put a personal touch on the conflict. As the current violence continues to escalate, many more of these testimonies will unfortunately emerge. And I realize that while I am interested in everything, from history to creative writing, from anthropology to politics, from women's studies to archaeology, I will always make sure that my interests coincide with human rights work. The Babylonian Talmud best explains my motive: "If you save a single person, it is as if you saved the entire world."

See page 335 to find out where this student got in.

SAMANTHA CULP

In high school, Samantha explored her interests in art, photography, writing, and filmmaking and had works displayed in local art galleries and festivals. Her passion for writing led her to produce four small, independent magazines filled with art and prose and to a job writing film reviews for an online magazine. In her senior year Samantha and three other students formed an advertising firm that completed graphic design and advertising commissions for local companies and won national recognition in graphic design competitions. Each summer during high school she did internship work with museums, advertising firms, and film productions to further explore her interests.

Stats

SAT I: 1450
SAT II: 800 Literature, 800 Writing, 720 World History,
    720 French, 720 Math
High School GPA: 4.17
High School: Marlborough School for Girls, Los Angeles, CA
Hometown: Los Angeles, CA
Gender: Female
Race/Ethnicity: White

Applied To

Brown University

Columbia University

Wesleyan University

Yale University

Essay: Sent to each school

There are limitations to what grades, scores and recommendations can let us know about an applicant. Please use this space to let us know something about you we might not learn from the rest of your application. There is no correct response to this essay request, in writing about something that matters to you, you will convey to us a sense of yourself.

The Beauty of Impermanence

One day I learned about the universe and I began to cry. Well, I didn't cry right *away*, probably an hour or three later. It took a while to sink in, as things that smack of the profound tend to do. I was about nine years old and taking a summer biology class under rather harsh conditions at the museum downtown. It was long hours slicing formaldehyde-infused flesh and narrow unstable tables with peeling "wood-grain" surfaces, but at that time my career plans were to become the world's first archaeologist/paleontologist/zoologist/ballerina, so I weathered it all with equanimity as just another mile on the long, hard road of science.

This fateful day our teacher, Tim (a slightly distracted UCLA premed), told us about the Big Bang: stars being born, masses of rubble getting sucked into orbit and turning into spheres, lava and saltwater giving rise to land and sea on one such sphere, itty-bitty creatures starting to multiply in that sea, and how these creatures got bigger and more complex until here we were in late-80s South Central Los Angeles learning about it all, scuffling our Keds under the table and yearning for the Bugs Bunny Pop that the suddenly-audible music of a nearby ice cream truck brought to mind. A Brief History of Time, but far more *Highlights for Children* than Hawking. After finishing, he gestured for us to begin our dissection of the earthworm. But before we could make the first incision, some kid asked if we, as human beings, were still evolving.

"Yes, for all evidence it appears that we still are evolving," Tim replied (impatient to get us started).

"Well, then we could still get extinct as a species, right?" the kid continued. The teacher sighed.

"Possibly. But we've mastered our environment so well that it's unlikely. Now, worms."

"So we'll continue for eternity?" the kid kept on.

"Listen, even if we don't go extinct, eventually the gravity of the universe will pull together all matter, the Big Bang will happen in reverse, crunch everything together into one tiny point and nothing will be left. OK? OK, go, worms!!"

He looked out on the rows of tiny horrified faces, each pair of eyes bulging like quail eggs. He backpedaled.

"But don't worry. It'll be another many billion years before that happens. You'll be long dead, your children and grandchildren too. Now, for the love of god, cut your worm."

The other kids seemed placated by his assurance, and so took their scalpels in hand and got busy. But I paused a moment, the sweat on my skin suddenly cold. I had already known about the Big Bang and evolution, but the fact that in some billion years it might all come crashing in together again was horrifying news to me. I sat there on the orange plastic chair, now putting on my rubber gloves and piercing into the poor, smelly dead worm splayed out in my tin tray, and the realization began to sink in, that all this knowledge, civilization, progress, art, worms, heck, even these rickety tables and fierce formaldehyde, would someday be gone and there wouldn't even be anyone to remember it.

This idea stayed with me the remainder of the day, stayed with me as firm and sharp as a mist of salt lodged in my throat until we arrived home and I could go to my special little place in the backyard where this dilute promptly flooded out my tear ducts. I sat leaning against a rock at the bottom of the slope, hidden so well by the overgrown ivy that the air was simply heat and green, and I cried because I felt that the most fundamental notion of life was now violated, the concept that everything we as human beings did worked toward progress that made the world better in a never-ending tradition of strife and grandeur. All this dissolved, leaving behind the void that echoed in every shadow and every death, the absolute death of memory and the ceasing of existence.

This basic postulate of general relativity profoundly affected the way I would view the world from that time onward. I sat there for quite a bit longer that day, saline smudging my cheeks, in utter desperation and awe. And for much time after, the fear and sadness clung to my subconscious. My focus remained riveted to how everything would be gone.

As time went on, however, my attention shifted. When driving the canyons at night, feeling the cool air through the open window, I would suddenly catch a glimpse of the carpet of stars that is Los Angeles, and instead of simply mourning its eventual absence, it became all the more beautiful for its fleeting nature. I could go to the Central Marketplace downtown in the early morning and buy cactus fruits and tamarind powder, drink coffee by the crumbling Angel's Flight tramway, talk to the old woman sweeping out the gutter, feel the first raindrops after months of drought, and I was okay. Everything in this world is finite; ends are inevitable; but knowing this from an early age helped me reconcile this cessation with the immediacy and beauty everywhere. Every once in a while I still feel that pang of future void, and stop a minute to really see how perfectly earth and sky are stitched at the eastern horizon. And then I snap out of it, and start laughing hysterically with my friends.

See page 336 to find out where this student got in.

SCOTT DAGGETT

While in high school, Scott was a four-time varsity swimmer and team captain his senior year. He was also active in the high school Honor Society, senior class play, and the local Boy Scout troop.

Stats

SAT I: 1250 (600 Verbal, 650 Math)

ACT: 31.25

High School GPA: 3.81

High School: Hardee Senior High School, Wauchula, FL

Hometown: Wauchula, FL

Gender: Male

Race/Ethnicity: Caucasian

Applied To

Embry Riddle Aeronautical University

United States Air Force Academy

Essay: United States Air Force Academy

Why do you want to come to the Air Force Academy?

The moment that I read the brochure about the challenges and educational opportunities at the Air Force Academy, I wanted to attend. The thought of serving my country in the Air Force excited my mind, causing me to think of the possibilities that are available within the Air Force Academy.

Reading the material that I received about the Air Force Academy made me want to attend with a passion. I was impressed by the quality of the challenges the military training offers an exceptional chance to strengthen my desire to succeed. The excellent athletic programs offered at the academy will prepare me for service in the Air Force. The Air Force Academy's swimming program interests me, because I wish to continue with my swim training as I attend college.

The Air Force Academy's exceptional educational program offers a challenge to my mind. The educational challenges offered would keep me thinking when I am not involved with the athletic activities. The Air Force Academy's educational program can allow me to look towards one of the best educations in the nation. The engineering program at the Air Force Academy will allow me the education to become an exceptional part of society.

The training opportunities at the Air Force Academy will allow me to successfully serve my country to my fullest ability. The leadership skills that I will develop while attending the Air Force Academy shall allow me to gain the knowledge I need to become an exceptional member of society. The exceptional training and education that I will receive will prepare me for the future. The service that I will be able to accomplish after attending the Air Force Academy will be better than if I attend a less challenging school.

The knowledge, leadership skills, and education that I will receive at the Air Force Academy makes me wish to attend. The opportunities that I will also receive from the Air Force Academy will help me in my service to society. To be able to serve appropriately, I will need the education and training that the Air Force Academy can offer me.

See page 336 to find out where this student got in.

STANLEY SONG

Stanley trained with and raced on a cycling team and worked at a bike shop. Stanley has also been playing the violin for over a decade, performing several times each year.

Stats

SAT I: 1450 (660 Verbal, 790 Math)

SAT II: 640 Writing, 800 Math IIC, 780 Chinese with Listening, 730 Biology M

High School GPA: ~3.78

High School: Taipei American School, Taipei, Taiwan

Hometown: Taipei, Taiwan

Gender: Male

Race/Ethnicity: Taiwanese

Applied To

Brown University

Case Western

Cornell University

Northwestern University

Rice University

Stanford University

University of California—Berkeley

University of California—Davis

University of California—Los Angeles

University of California—San Diego

Please note: Stanley applied to the engineering school at each of the above universities.

Essay

Stanley used the following essay in all of his applications, modifying them slightly for Northwestern and Stanford.

What do you believe the capabilities of technology hold?

The biggest mistake in the history of evolution is the development of testicles for the human species. The sole function of the testicles is to produce sperm for reproduction. For humans, testicles do not fully develop their roles until puberty – around teen age. However, in our society where having children after marriage is the norm, testicles are usually superfluous until twenty or thirty years of age. In fact, they can be quite a nuisance in men's daily life. As a result of my strong belief in the capabilities of technology, allow me to present a proposal.

I am certain that most men can attest to the fact that their testicles have dangled in an uncomfortable position at one time or another, whether during an executive meeting, or on a bus ride, or at a date. I am more confident that almost all men have experienced a loathed infliction of pain on their testes. I must say, the placement and vulnerability of human testicles are mistakes on the part of Mother Nature.

I am far from knowing exactly what biotechnological capabilities we have. Sure, from my own readings and research I understand the basic mechanics of pacemakers and prosthetic limbs, but can I claim to know the details? Heck, no! However, the understanding and awareness of present day technology have shaped my imagination and creativity towards dreaming up solutions we can incorporate into our future. With biotechnology advancing at such a rapid pace, we are free to go in *any* direction.

Since testicles are simply a protrusion connected by the scrotum, a few nerves, and the vas deferens, surgically removing and maintaining a way to reattach them are fully feasible. In transplants, organs are removed from one body and implanted into another. Don't get me wrong; I am by no means implying we trade testicles from one person to another. I'm simply saying that we *are* capable of detaching and reattaching organs. In sperm banks, we are also capable of keeping cells and tissues that are no longer part of the body alive. My proposal is merely an extension.

As with most developing ideas, there are complications. In this case, the testes function in the release of hormones that develop male secondary characteristics. However, I'm sure we can overcome the problem with injections, medications, or other twenty-first century inventions.

Imagine how males would benefit if testicles were detachable and could be stored away until needed. Carrying around this extra lump of flesh would cease to be an inconvenience. Furthermore, since ninety percent of the semen normally ejaculated is not produced in the testicles and thus do not contain sperm, people can still take pleasure in sex and simultaneously avoid unwanted pregnancy. Physical birth control methods such as condoms and diaphragms will become obsolete as will surgical sterilization, vasectomy.

Without a trace of doubt, I believe that the incorporation of our creativity and rapidly advancing biotechnology will soon allow us to juggle ideas as bizarre as this proposal into new inventions and realities. In fact, I see this as our future. In a few generations, carrying testicles around will no longer be the fashion. Please, don't dismiss this idea as absurd. When telephones were first introduced, men were shocked and afraid to think of their wives talking to other men they couldn't see!

Forty years ago, a burly linemen bashes out quarterback Joe Namath's right knee during an AFL game. A spectator wonders, "What if Joe can replace his knee?" Ten years later, a child sits at her grandfather's funeral thinking, "If only there were a metronome to keep my grandfather's heart beating steadily..." Ten more years later, a man lies in bed thinking, "Isn't there a pill to rid my wife of her depression?" Now in 1998, when prosthetic knees, defibrillators, and Prozac pills have all become realities, I sit in a couch at school watching a friend curled up in agony, and I think, "What if testicles..."

See page 336 to find out where this student got in.

STEPHANIE CROSS

Stephanie played for the varsity softball team for two years (following one year on JV), spent two years on the varsity bowling team, and participated in numerous summer leagues for both sports, including ASA and YABA. She was a member of the National Art Honor Society (treasurer), the National Spanish Honor Society, and the National Honor Society. Stephanie was also awarded the Bausch and Lomb Science Award and earned both the Silver Award and Gold Award in Girl Scouting (she was a member for eleven years). She played the viola for nine years and went to District and Regional Pennsylvania State Orchestra three years in a row.

Stats

SAT I: 1510 (710 Verbal, 800 Math)
SAT II: 690 Writing, 700 Math, 720 Biology
High School GPA: 103.5
High School: Lewisburg Area High School, Lewisburg, PA
Hometown: Lewisburg, PA
Gender: Female
Race/ Ethnicity: Caucasian

Applied To

Swarthmore College (applied early decision)

Essay

Write an essay about people who have influenced you, situations that have shaped you, difficulties or conflicts with which you have struggled, goals and hopes you may have for the future, or something else you consider significant.

At times I hated Mrs. Shambaucher, at times I admired her, but to this day I thank God that she was my fourth grade teacher. I didn't know at the time how much she would influence me as a student or as an individual, but Mrs. Shambaucher provided me with more aggravations and realizations than anyone else I have ever met. Many view her too authoritarian and too tough, but she has a great sense of humor and a great understanding of what is needed in our youth for them to succeed in the future. She instills great ethics and habits in her students, but she can also cause the most frustration.

As I soon learned, Mrs. Shambaucher wasted no time. I remember entering her classroom for the first time and being given a small notebook. It was the first day of school and our make-shift classroom had no black board but she was teaching within the hour. Our first science lesson was on cell structure and organization, terms I wouldn't see again until sixth grade. I was confused, lost, and overwhelmed. What kind of person would expect a fourth grader to know what a nucleus was or what cilia did? I was scared for my life on that first day but I know I am better because of it. Other science lessons of the year would include rocks, Moh's scale of hardness, the development of a chicken, and the solar system. The other fourth graders never had to study so much or complete so many worksheets, but they also never even heard of some of the terms I knew until they reached high school. Mrs. Shambaucher was the first person to ever teach me history. I was always interested in the Erie Canal and I had limited access to information on topics I had only scarcely heard of before. The brief overview of Pennsylvanian and American history that I had that year was better than what I received in eighth and ninth grade. I often found myself looking through my tattered notebook to find facts that I had learned over five years earlier.

Another area that I grew to love was literature. Up until this point we had never read a book over one hundred pages long in school, unless it was for a personal book report. I still remember O'Henry's short stories, The Secret Garden, Black Beauty, Amos Fortune, The Witch of Blackbird Pond, The Adventures of Tom Sawyer, and The Westing Game (one of the best books I have read to this day). Most of these classics are never taught in my school and I don't know how I would be today if it hadn't been for the passion for reading that Mrs. Shambaucher instilled in me. She also taught me how to write a biography and how not to write an essay. These helpful hints are never considered in most curricula yet the students are expected to know it. The work load was atrocious when it came to reading and writing. Most students complained, but we continued to read in class as well as at home. My reading skills were sharpened dramatically during that year. One assignment we had was to write instructions for making a peanut butter and jelly sandwich. A classmate would then follow the instructions and we would have to eat the result. Lets just say that I never forgot to include every last step in the future after I was presented with a mass of peanut butter and jelly on one piece of bread.

She had a great sense of humor and learning was supposed to be fun. There were always contests to find an answer to a math problem or research facts on famous people. We were the only class to perform school plays, complete with costumes, sets, and pages of memorized lines. Worksheets were assigned to sharpen our reasoning and spark creativity. I learned so much in that year and because of her I have developed a greater appreciation for all aspects of life and learning. The skills that she fostered have been so useful throughout my schooling and in my interactions with other people. I know that I would have been unable to handle so many situations and assignments if it had not been for her emphasis on study habits, attention to detail, and that everything be your personal best. My drive and the quality of my work all stem from her teachings and influence. If it had not been for her, I would never have valued the classics so highly or learned about African American history, algebra, or the stage until at least eight grade.

Despite the effects of her teachings, there were times where I was ready to scream. The homework was intense and there were no excuses for not completing or trying what was taught. Numerous projects and reports were assigned in addition to regular classroom work. The automatic A was no longer a reality and everything that was handed in was expected to be of your best caliber. Instructions had to be followed and just about everything was expected to be typed. She would almost always point out your flaws, even though she could have been reprimanded if a student were to complain. She knew what we were capable of and she would never settle for less. Although a great philosophy when applied to the future of the child, it made life a little more difficult. At times I would think her so unfair and so strict, especially when other classes had two recesses or extra time to talk and play Connect Four. I hated when my name would go on the board for talking in class, or when I wasn't allowed to go to recess because I had missed a quiz. Through it all she would shrug off any complaints and continue teaching at a rate she knew we could handle if we would apply ourselves.

Politicians today often complain about the state of our public educational system and I would have to agree with them most of the time. However, no amount of money or state regulated guidelines will fix the problems that exist in our schools. I personally feel that we need more Mrs. Shambauchers in the elementary schools. Children should see what they can accomplish and be pushed to their limits time and again until they too desire to learn and yearn for knowledge. I have been shaped in ways I can't fully comprehend by one teacher who taught what she felt was important and at a rate that even parents were questioning. No principal could have forced her to change a lesson or teach ridiculous state courses without a fight. She knew how to work with children and bring out the best in them in a hope for the future. I admire her so much for changing the world one child at a time. Its a noble goal that no politician can achieve through laws and the fact that she continues to influence over twenty-five children a year is reassuring when faced with so many ill-prepared students. She is one of a kind and her spirit is unparalleled to any teacher I have had thus far. Mrs. Shambaucher influenced me in so many ways outside of education that I know I would not be who I am today if it hadn't been for her constant prodding and high expectations.

See page 337 to find out where this student got in.

STEPHANIE LUH

Stephanie was president of the math club and class treasurer during her senior year. She also dedicated her time in high school to community service.

Stats

Please note: All test scores listed here are approximations.
SAT I: 1330 (620 Verbal, 710 Math)
SAT II: 730 Math IC, 770 Math IIC, 760 Writing, 630 Chemistry
High School GPA: 3.3
High School: Westridge School For Girls, Pasadena, CA
Hometown: San Marino, CA
Gender: Female
Race/Ethnicity: Asian

Applied To

Wellesley College (applied early decision)

Essay

Evaluate a significant experience or achievement that has special meaning to you.

As I was traveling home on Orange Grove Boulevard, I was so ecstatic that school had ended and summer had arrived. All I wanted to do was to sit back, relax, and bask in the California sun. Junior year was finally over and I didn't have to look at another page of biology. Biology was a class that I would never forget. The workload was tough, and the language was unfamiliar and secret. I longed for essay tests as I struggled with grueling multiple choice exams covering minor scientific details. My fantasy was to avoid opening a biology book for the rest of the summer. Shattering this dream later that day, the mailman delivered a white, crisp letter from the U.S.C. School of Medicine:

Dear Stephanie,

We are very happy to announce that you have been accepted to the U.S.C. Edmondson Summer Fellowship. Out of more than two hundred students who applied, twenty-three were selected to study at this internship in pathology. . . .

Okay, so I took the risk of encountering biological sciences again, possibly humiliating myself in front of an omniscient team of expert doctors. Given the fact that I had never backed down from a challenging opportunity, I decided not to do so now. What I had initially anticipated to be the revival of learning countless biology facts turned into a learning experience that revitalized my intellectual curiosity.

For the next few days, I was exposed to what pathologists do every day. I had the opportunity to look at real specimens taken out of patients from surgeries, and I was quickly amazed when I handled warm, fresh human organs. Even though I only had a meager background, I could actually comprehend much of the doctors' work. After several weeks, I evaluated slides independently, giving my opinion to doctors and listening to their views. I found myself engrossed and had the urge to learn more.

One day, as I was looking at a slide, a doctor casually asked, "Wanna see a *brain*?" I enthusiastically replied, "Sure, why not." It's not every day that you see someone's brain, and I surely did not want to miss this opportunity. I followed two doctors to the "Lower Level." We were going to the *MORGUE* (part of me heard—doom-doom-dooooom, the m-word, Frankenstein's sanctuary, the home of the "stiffs," the "*basement*"). As the doctor opened the door with a key and a punch code, I took deep breaths. We entered the silent, cold room with long refrigerators against the walls. "Okay," I assured myself, "it's just the morgue. I'm fine, it's not like the dead people are going to resurrect. We'll just get in and get out in two or three seconds. No sweat." My inner voice smirked at me two hours later when we were still in the morgue.

The room was ice cold, and I was extremely tense. I have to say that I have never seen so much stainless steel in my life. I remember staying behind the doctors, watching them work, as if the whole experience were a dream. As I stood there, wearing an itchy blue mask to prevent intoxication by the formaldehyde fumes, the doctors sliced the brain like a chunk of Thanksgiving ham. After cutting the brain stem into thin sections and sending them to the department of histology, the doctors later examined the slides of the brain microscopically. Every little groove or bump of the specimen imprinted on the slide was crucial to the evaluation. I went home and opened my biology book to discover what function each part of the brain performed. I had read about the brain structure before, but now I was able to actually see the shiny brain and feel the slimy texture with my hand. The experience of dissecting the brain left me in awe for weeks.

As the summer went by, I felt more mature in my attitude toward trying new things. A few weeks earlier, I had been apathetic about the internship, but then I gave biology a second chance and discovered another side of it. What had begun as a summer retreat from biological sciences turned into an invigorating experience—one that I will never forget. I was reassured by how much easier it was to learn from people than from textbooks and by how much more I was motivated about biology after I saw organs, malignant tumors, a half-open eyeball, amputated limbs, and a lot of fat from liposuctions. Visiting the library and various websites, I pored over countless pages, trying to find any information relating to any organ that I had seen in its entirety or under a microscope—its function, its role, and its location. I absorbed all of the facts on my own, knowing that nobody was assigning me the research. I will now apply this same intellectual curiosity toward all opportunities in life, including a future challenge—going to a university and exploring a different life on my own.

See page 337 to find out where this student got in.

STEPHANIE WUN-LEE CHOW

Stephanie was president of the Spanish National Honor Society of her high school for two years and vice president of the Science Club her senior year. She was named Most Valuable Player for her school's Mathematics League two years in a row and captained her high school tennis team senior year.

Stats

SAT I: 1480 (690 Verbal, 790 Math)

SAT II: 720 Writing, 800 Math IIC, 730 Chemistry,
740 Molecular Biology

High School GPA: 3.88/4.00

High School: Wethersfield High School, Wethersfield, CT

Hometown: Wethersfield, CT

Gender: Female

Race/Ethnicity: Asian American

Applied To

Massachusetts Institute of Technology

Boston University

Brown University PLME Program

Columbia University

Cornell University

Harvard College

Princeton University

Rensselaer Polytechnic Institute

University of Connecticut

Yale University

Essay #1: MIT

Essay instructions were to make up your own question and answer it. Stephanie posed the question *"Which more describes your personality, a Cheerio or a Snickers bar?"*

Drawing parallels between both Cheerios and Snickers bars and myself is no problem; I find both foods agreeable to my personality quirks. Pressure to select one, however, favors the chocolatey Snickers bar over the wholesome Cheerio. The former's multitude of ingredients, physical structure, and rise to fame bear a stronger resemblance to the circus of thoughts entertained in my mind.

Cheerios sports the healthier nutrition label; having this cereal's "healthy, whole-grain" personality marks an untiringly responsible, straightforward individual content to live an ordinary life, free from wild excitement. The simpleton Cheerio, lacking the domineering clutter of flakes and raisins, connotes a humble and uncomplicated life. These qualities portray a very stable and worldly individual.

Snickers cannot compete with the nutritional "virtuosity" of its opponent but combatively wields wonder weapons of its own. The ingenious combination of Snickers's delectable ingredients: chocolate, caramel, and peanuts, evokes strong sensations of pleasure in the blissful consumer.

The chocolate coating washes the restless soul like morning tides over a sun-baked sandcastle, problems and concerns reconciled with each passing mouthful. Likewise, my mind bears the task of extinguishing problems, my own and of others.

My imagination finds representation in the caramel, rich and flexible. Leisurely pulling each bite of Snickers from the origin and watching the gooey strands stretch their fullest, glistening in the light with sticky, sweet happiness, ensures maximum exposure of the golden luxury.

The highlight of my Snickers adventure lies largely in the presence of the crunchy peanuts, sharp contrast to their creamy confectionery counterparts. These crispy hidden treasures rejuvenate my optimism and jocularity by replenishing my mind with imaginative ideas and perspectives. I also entertain the thought that the peanuts allude to my slightly "nutty" personality.

One may elect to analyze the physical structure of the two foods to draw additional comparisons; Cheerios sport the infallibly circular doughnut shape while the Snickers take on a more rectangular prismatic skeleton. Circles commonly serve as symbols of perfection and complete unity; presumably, the Cheerio's circular shape as a representation of the personality of an individual implies a continuing contention for a life of perfection. Nevertheless, I do not care to fall victim to a life of endless struggle in achieving and maintaining a state of utopia; I prefer the company of the natural, reliable, Snickers figure, so mundane and simple yet an ingeniously constructed idea; countless architectural structures utilize the strength and practicality of the rectangular prism.

The much famed Honey Nut Cheerio flaunts an attractive honeybee mascot; Snickers relies simply on rewards of its taste for promotion through the ambitious ladder of success. While the Cheerios are the more publicized and celebrated, Snickers has managed to make a name for itself through simple hard work and strife for excellent taste.

Although Cheerios embodies the qualities of the ideal and perfect individual, to possess such a resume of virtues leaves no room for improvement and consequently offers no fire for motivation. Thus I select the Snickers candy bar as the better representative of my personality.

Essays #2-5: All essays sent to Princeton

What one class, teacher, book, or experience can you point to as having really changed the way you think?

I discovered one of my favorite books, *The Westing Game,* by Ellen Raskin, in fourth grade. I read it because I was looking for something to read and my teacher had recommended it to the class, and because he had told us that those students whom he knew had read the book needed to reread the story a few years later before completely understanding the complex plot. I admit now that I bought the book more for the second reason than the first although I still maintain that I was a mystery-love-struck fourth grader with a voracious appetite for reading.

The plot revolves around the "murder" of the eccentric millionaire Samuel W. Westing and the challenge the "deceased" man poses to his sixteen potential heirs to uncover the identity of his killer. In the end, it is the neglected thirteen-year old Turtle Wexler who deciphers the Westing Game riddle and wins the inheritance. Her triumph was especially important to me because it instilled in my pliant young mind a strong belief of succeeding in areas where one is not expected to succeed. Westing's meticulously planned "murder" and "game" confounded all the heirs but young Turtle, whose clever thinking and resourcefulness enabled her to piece together the complicated mystery.

Turtle's spunky character also left a deep impression in my mind. In reading of her smart-alecky mouth, her flaring temper, and her independence, I felt myself applauding her "un-girl-like" behavior so shunned in other children's novels. I did not believe that I would begin kicking people in the shins when someone provoked my temper, but I did treasure the idea that I did not have to bear the sweet, obedient facade of the "classic ladylike girl" as I had witnessed in *The Babysitters' Club* series or in stories like *Little Women*. As a girl with a burning spirit of independence and resolve, *I* believed that I could outwit Supreme Court judges, doctors, and private eye detectives if I was brave and clever enough for the task!

Discuss something (anything) you just wished you understood better.

I wish I understood the workings of a juvenile mind and what qualities in a toy or style appeal to the youthful masses. In elementary school I remember the Cabbage Patch Kid dolls with their stringy hair and round belly buttons. I had thought them ugly, but because "everyone else had it," I felt I needed a doll to prove that I too was a "normal" child. Youthful fads also included but were not limited to pet rocks, wrist slapping bracelets, Fimo necklaces, and horizontally striped shirts. As I aged and began realizing an innate call for independence, my "lifeline link" to the World of Fads quickly faded until I scorned association with stylistic crazes of any kind.

Yet I find that I still cannot escape the World of Fads! My nine year old sister boasts a collection of over forty Ty Beanie Babies and can spout trivial facts about more Pokemon characters than I care to acknowledge exist! The childhood Fad Web snares early and deep, and I would like to comprehend just what stimulates the rush of excitement, the unrelenting desire and obsession to motivate a child to declare, "I MUST have that toy!"

A friend once drew the conclusion that if a toy company slaps its product into the waiting hands of "the coolest kid in school" and its product wins the approval of the child, that toy will inevitably become the school's newest fad. Like a nuclear reaction, other children will begin bringing the toy to school and the obsession will spread to other school systems in the town by family or by media. If powered enough with enough child-market appeal, the toy might spread across the nation, a nuclear chain reaction of toys and youthful whims!

Where is this chain reaction ignited? What lights the fuse to begin the craze? If I ask my sister I am not given a straight answer. She doesn't know but follows the masses because "she likes what everybody else likes." I harbor a belief that in childhood, a person unwittingly seeks a role model, a person of whom to idolize and pattern him or herself after. In a way, children resemble young animals with instincts to copy other members of their species; yet for wild animals, this imitation is important for survival. Don't tell me that children's fads exist to ensure survival of the world's youth!

If you could hold one position, elected or appointed, in government (at any level), which one would you want it to be and why?

In my opinion the most important and nationally influential position of government is one that affects the economic structure and stability of the country. The United States of America relies on the strength of its booming economy to bolster the nation's wealth and prosperity, hence establishing the health and survival of the nation's economy as an item of utmost importance. With this perspective in mind, to be appointed Federal Reserve Chairman of the United States would bring me the greatest honor and personal satisfaction.

As chairman of the Federal Reserve, I head the organization that controls the flow of money through the economy; by raising or lowering the nation's interest rates I can cut down on inflation or encourage businesses and individuals to invest. I wield the executive axe that influences levels of employment and stabilities of prices, interest rates, financial, and foreign exchange markets. The Federal Reserve System serves as the "central bank and monetary authority of the United States" in that it has the power to regulate and set the interest rate standards for the nation's banks.

I see the position of Federal Reserve Chairman as an office existing for the survival of the nation, dictating economic growth and prosperity, or possible financial disasters dating back to the period of the Great Depression. The Federal Reserve System supports the United States of America like a shell protecting an egg; without the Federal Reserve to reinforce and "calcify" the shell of the economy, the economy would crack and shatter. With America relying so heavily on the economy for employment and living, a ruptured economy would invariably result in a formless and withering nation, weak and easy prey to be exploited by other countries. As appointed chairperson I would make it my duty to protect the nation from such misuse and guide the United States into a new millennium of prestige.

What one or two suggestions would you have if asked about how to improve race relations in this country and around the world?

In improving any relationships, the best way for individuals to accept one another is to understand the background, culture, and beliefs of the other person; I believe that this "ethnic comprehension" is best conveyed through education. In a broad sense, such education encompasses both actual classroom learning of the culture and incorporation of that foreign race into the student body. Schools around the world should practice the concept of desegregation, breaking down ethnic barriers and establishing "homogenous student mix-ture-type" school systems. Foreign exchange student programs should be encouraged as well as the integration of inner city schools into more "well-rounded" school systems. My high school currently enrolls approximately ten to fifteen foreign exchange students and I would like to see the numbers increase as we move into the next century. Wethersfield High to my knowledge does not practice integration, but this concept too would play an influential role in spreading awareness of different ethnic cultures.

One cannot expect an immediate change in race relations by simply instigating a few measures. Aside from exposure to the different ideas and beliefs of foreign cultures, one must accept the difference psychologically; wars and friction always begin "in the minds of the people." By incorporating ethnic diversity into the daily life of a young student, society is molding the child into a bastion for racial tolerance. Teachers claim that "students are the future," and I must agree. When the youth of the world is exposed to a multitude of racial differences as a part of everyday life, discrepancies become the norm and any and all prejudices and stereotypes will hopefully melt away. We are all different only by mindset; once we learn to accept others on basis of their humanity and character, we will unlock the secret to the planet's racial tolerance.

See page 337 to find out where this student got in.

TAMAR KORNBLUM

Tamar was editor of her senior yearbook and captain of the varsity volleyball team. She was an active member of a religious youth group, various singing groups, and the National Honor Society, and she also performed volunteer work and tutored other students. Tamar was a finalist in the Governor's School of Science and earned a National Merit Commendation and the Bausch & Lomb Honorary Science Award.

Stats

SAT I: 1430 (710 Verbal, 720 Math)
SAT II: 790 Writing, 730 Physics, 720 Chemistry, 760 Math IIC
High School GPA: 3.83
High School: Solomon Schechter Day School, West Orange, NJ
Hometown: Mendham, NJ
Gender: Female
Race/Ethnicity: White

Applied To

Barnard College
Binghamton University
Boston University

Columbia University

Rutgers University—Rutgers College

Tufts University

University of Michigan

University of Rochester

Essay

The following essay was used in each of Tamar's applications.

Columbia: *Write an essay which conveys to the reader a sense of who you are. Possible topics may include, but are not limited to, experiences which have shaped your life, the circumstances of your upbringing, your most meaningful intellectual achievement, the way you see the world—the people in it, events great and small, everyday life—or any personal theme which appeals to your imagination. Please remember that we are concerned not only with the substance of your prose but with your writing style as well. We prefer that you limit yourself to one page of typed text.*

Tufts (Common Application Question 1): *Evaluate a significant experience, achievement, or risk that you have taken and its impact on you.*

What if life came with a guarantee, reassuring me that everything would be all right? I guess that is something that I just can't count on. I used to be able to depend on certain things: it's always warm in the summer, always cold in the winter, and fathers never cry. Until June 20, 1997, all of these things were true. On that day, the last day of my freshman year, I was forced to accept that not everything is guaranteed. That day, I saw my father cry.

I came home from school that Friday to find a note on the kitchen table explaining that my parents were to be home by 5 o'clock. No problem, I figured, as I went to go watch TV. By 5:30, I was more annoyed than concerned that my parents hadn't called, and by 6 o'clock I was starving. As I made myself a snack, my parents arrived, conveying the feeling that the world was about to end. I figured they were in the middle of a petty argument, so I went along my merry way, badgering my mother to tell me when dinner was going to be ready.

When her answer to me was silent tears, I proceeded to ask my father why everyone was so sad. "Today," he explained, "I saw the doctor because of the headaches I've been getting. They found some foreign cells . . ." At that point, I stopped listening to the words. School was over, I thought, why should I have a science lesson now? Then I noticed a tiny droplet of water forming in the corner of my father's eye. He continued, " . . . they think it's, it's cancer." Cancer? What was that? Wasn't that like AIDS or diabetes, or one of those things they can't find a cure for? By this time, there was a steady stream flowing down his stoic face. The words coming out of my father's mouth had little effect, but the beads rolling down his cheek said it all. Without a word, the tears told me that our lives were going to change.

Now, two and a half years later, I still feel the effects of that moment when I saw my hero reduced to human terms. At that moment my life was transformed from that of a child, where a broken toy is the tragedy of the century, to that of an adult, where misfortunes must be faced with courage. I have not discounted the circumstances which still loom over my high school years, but I have learned to deal with them, as I watch my father's heroic battle. My father's tears dissolved my "Daddy's little girl" disguise, and uncovered an emotionally mature individual. With the new sense of survival I have developed as a result of those previously unseen tears, I no longer expect, or need, guarantees for life.

See page 338 to find out where this student got in.

THOMAS JERDE

Thomas played the flute for two years in the senior orchestra of the world's largest youth orchestra organization, for two years in the All-State Band, and in several other orchestras and bands. During his senior year, he won second place in a multi-state flute competition, was named Minnesota's Young Composer of the Year, and won Most Improved on his high school track team.

Stats

SAT I: 1600 (best scores were 800 Verbal, 800 Math)
SAT II: 800 Writing, 800 Math IIC, 770 Chemistry
ACT: 35
High School GPA: 3.9/4.0
High School: Minnehaha Academy, Minneapolis, MN
Hometown: Burnsville, MN
Gender: Male
Race/Ethnicity: White

Applied To

Brown University (applied early action)

Essay

Tell us something about yourself that you think we should know. We ask only that whatever you write be honestly written in your own handwriting.

The debate rages. Science provides more and more of the answers, as busy technicians with consciences not nearly so clean as their lab aprons point to this gene and that, proclaiming these minute particles to be the causes of baldness, Alzeihmer's, and juvenile crime. An information age intoxicated with its own cleverness assures us that science will find a solution to every mystery of human function. What will be the last question unanswered? I think it will prove to be the very one that has been the longest asked: why are we here? And when science comes up against this inevitable thorn that has been abrading philosophers for centuries, what answer will it find?

The modern reductionist has proven that by studying the body bit by bit we can vastly increase our understanding of it works. Positron emission tomography can show us exactly what parts of the brain are working while we speak, read, and think. A drop of blood can be tested for any of a dozen genetic death sentences. Science tells us that what we are we cannot change, and was in fact determined before our conception, by chance, that over billions of years has accumulated into natural selection. Free will? An illusion: every creature is constrained to its own genetic predispositions, and when science reaches its Sisyphean zenith, every thought and deed will be predicted like a mathematical function.

Yet as I sit and listen to the second movement of Beethoven's Seventh Symphony, I cannot in that moment believe that the capacity for feeling which this music fills and overflows in me is a mere interaction of electrochemical components within my humble skull, a product of a vast and ancient chain of randomness in a universe devoid of meaning. This column of vibrating air pierces through all my mess of neurotransmitters, endorphins, and synaptic impulses, and melts my intellect into a sorrowful ocean that throbs with Beethoven's dying heartbeat. What series of interactions between neurons, no matter how many, could effect this? For me, a scientifically based source for these depths of feeling is inconceivable.

Other roots of our strongest emotions can be explained into existential oblivion by biological forces. Grief for a lost one may be a means of keeping communities together, which can better defend themselves against predators. Infatuation for an object of affection is a purely procreative urge. But what brute purpose of such base nature may have ascribed to it the sensitive appreciation of music, or for that matter, of any art? There is none; the ability to perceive that something is beautiful fits no grand biological scheme.

But it seems preposterous that a response this strong could be an artifact of a design that was guided by chaos alone. And what are we to make of the lack of this discretion in animals, the higher forms of whom seem otherwise to share our emotional capacities? As the proud owner of an Airedale terrier whose profound eyes have a broad spectrum of the simpler emotions, let me make it plain: even the lovely sounds of my own flute practice yield no artistic appreciation from the philistine mutt.

It thus seems that art is a purely human occupation that sets us on a plane above the animals. From this point of view, music seems for a moment a kind of proof of spirituality, a badge of humanity's transcendence of biological necessity towards a nobler universe. Or perhaps, music is not a bridge across the void, but merely our lonely searchlight, scanning the foggy depths in search of meaning; all it may represent is our vain wish that the universe would offer up the answer. Are we alone? Is there a reason? Why? Empty silence meets our technological squabblings, and no two religions agree, though each inspires magnitudes of contrary emotion strong enough to prove its particular divinity. What answer can resolve the dichotomy? The upwellings of religious fervor are indeed inspired—by the silence.

I stand looking into the blank night, and a warm wind meets my face from the north, potent with life. Is the fact that I question my own consciousness proof enough that it exists? Is my ability to appreciate beauty indicative of some meaning behind the senseless vastness of space? I am resigned to the uncertainty: I cannot possibly find the answer. But if it is the futile search that brings me music, art, and beauty, the doubts are a thousand times recompensed.

See page 338 to find out where this student got in.

TIMOTHY D. GIBEAU

Timothy was a four-year letterman in football, and during his captaincy senior year was selected for both the Herald News and South Coast Conference All-Star Teams. Also a four-year member of the JCHS Theatre Company, Tim earned acting honors from the Massachusetts High School Drama Guild while also serving as president and historian.

Stats

SAT I: 1340 (630 Verbal, 710 Math)

SAT II: 730 Writing, 660 Math IC, 600 Math IIC, 570 Chemistry, 550 Biology

High School GPA: 4.36 weighted

High School: Joseph Case High School, Swansea, MA

Hometown: Swansea, MA

Gender: Male

Race/Ethnicity: Caucasian

Applied To

Tufts University

University of Notre Dame

University of Pennsylvania

Yale University

Essay: Notre Dame and Tufts

Notre Dame: *Tell us how a particular book, play, film, piece of music, dance performance, scientific theory or experiment, or work of art has influenced you. If you choose a novel, film, or play, assume we know the plot.*

My love of films has influenced my life in many ways. Of all the movies I have viewed over the years, *Mr. Holland's Opus* has had the greatest impact on me. The passion, perseverance, camaraderie, and desire displayed by the characters have changed my life immeasurably.

Among the messages conveyed by this movie, the greatest are of perseverance and passion. Throughout his life, Glen Holland was faced with many obstacles. However, no matter how great the barrier, he made the best of the situation. Although he was never able to fulfill his dream, he found a way to become passionate about his work and consequently changed many people's lives. Due to the perseverance of Mr. Holland, I no longer allow myself to dwell in my misfortunes; instead, I endure life's obstacles and learn from them. If I discover that what I am doing is no longer invigorating, I find a way to become passionate about it. For example, when I think that I cannot withstand another minute of a nerve-racking play rehearsal, I remember the feeling of accomplishment a performance brings and rehearse with renewed vigor. Passion for a class or activity increases both my success and enjoyment. These are essential qualities that one must possess to prosper in life, and because of Glen Holland, I believe that I have acquired the tools necessary to succeed.

Another valuable lesson is that of friendship. Upon becoming a teacher in a school of unfamiliar faces, Glen Holland is befriended by the principal. This woman continually supports him, no matter how controversial or uncongenial his ideas may be. Over the years, their relationship strengthens, showing the importance of friends. Although my schedule often restricts the time I can spend with my friends, I always try to get as involved as I can because I now realize how important friends are. Without my friends, I would be a completely different person for the memories I share with them have molded me into the person that I am. The bonds I have established with my peers have greatly affected my life, and their influence will forever remain with me and be evident in my character.

The final lesson that can be learned from this movie is desire. Due to Lou Russ's poor academic performance, he is prevented from participating in sports and he is forced to join the band to make up lost credits. Although he has no musical ability, Lou Russ's tenacity shows that he wants to succeed no matter what the cost. That is desire. I have found that by committing myself wholeheartedly to a project, I can accomplish what I had never thought possible. For instance, although not the biggest, fastest, or strongest player on the football team, I had the desire to play. Through my determination and effort, I earned a position that I was not necessarily built to play. Were it not for the desire displayed by Lou Russ, I do not believe that I would have realized how to reach my goals.

The impact these lessons have had on my life cannot be easily quantified but are evident in many ways. My personality, point of view, and way of thinking have all changed because of the characters and situations portrayed in his film. I know that the passion, strength, relationships, and desire I now possess will help make my life meaningful and fulfilling. I no longer fear that I will look back and wish that I had lived my life a different way.

See page 339 to find out where this student got in.

TRACY SERGE

Tracy was involved in a wide variety of activities in high school, including forensics, where she specialized in original oratory and sales, and theater, both directing and performing in a number of plays.

Stats

SAT I: 1480 (780 Verbal, 700 Math)
SAT II: 800 Writing, 800 Literature, 690 Math IC
ACT: 35
High School GPA: 4.0
High School: Fairmont Senior High School, Fairmont, WV
Hometown: Fairmont, WV
Gender: Female
Race/Ethnicity: White

Applied To

Yale University (applied early decision)

Essay

Tell us something about yourself that we couldn't learn from the rest of your application.

Waltzing Over the Border With a Paintbrush in My Hand

One of my favorite books is The Little Prince by Antoine de Saint-Exupéry. The narrator of the novel states that adults never ask the important questions about a person, such as "What does his voice sound like?" or "What games does he like best?" Often, in applying for scholarships and, now, for college, I have felt that perhaps no one was asking the "important questions." I believe I have been shaped more by those profound experiences which have become my anecdotes, than I am of my grades and ACT scores, which reveal only one aspect of my life that is important to me. So, when asked to state something about myself that the admissions committee would not be able to gather from my application, I found I was unable to limit myself to just one interest or story. After all, twenty-four straight hours on a bus with twenty-one classmates has influenced my life far more than even a perfect score on the SATs ever could.

To elaborate on the above, my eighth grade class had only twenty-one students. We all knew each other as no one else could (eight hours a day, five days a week, for nine years, will do that) and decided to celebrate (or mourn) the impending graduation from our close-knit, sheltered group to the larger world of high school with a bus trip to Canada. As it happened, the bus broke down about twenty-five feet from the Canadian border. This was the greatest exercise in patience I have ever had to endure. It took four hours for our driver to realize the problem and inform us that we had run out of gas. I love absurdity...and truckstops.

The patience I learned in this situation has served me well in another area of my life: ballroom dancing. In the seventh grade, I decided that I preferred the beauty and grace of the stylized ballroom dances to the repetitive back-and-forth sway of the usual teen moves. My partner was a fellow student, and we weren't sure it was going to work out when we arrived at the first class and discovered that we were the only couple there not contributing to our retirement plans. However, the problem was soon solved when preference grew into passion. I have now been a avid ballroom dancer for nearly six years and have learned much more than just the proper sequence of steps in a samba. Aside from the obvious self-discipline of many hours a week spent in training, learning dance requires patience. Everyone learns at a different speed and in different ways. A dancer must understand that while she has trouble with the waltz, her partner may be equally perplexed by the fox-trot. The two must then cooperate to become comfortable and confident. From dancing, I have learned the incomparable value of teamwork. After all, it does take two to tango.

Another experience that has had a lasting impact on my view of myself has been painting murals. From the time I was three and couldn't color inside the lines, through the many days in geometry I spent trying to draw at least a respectable imitation of a circle, I was certain I had no artistic talent. It's amazing how an overabundance of white walls will bring out the artist in anyone. I don't know exactly what made me decide to paint the girl's dressing room in our theater department, but my friend and I decided that it had to be done, and we were the ones to do it.

We started the day after the idea occurred to us, deciding that a sunset over mountains must be respectably simple. It wasn't. Within the first ten minutes, we realized we were in way over our heads. We did manage to make the sun somewhat circular, but could not get it any color resembling nature's pale yellow. Of course, we'd started and we knew we couldn't stop—not until walls, floor, and ceiling were completely transformed. In my head, I often likened the painting of a mural to the stages of grief: denial (This certainly wasn't my idea!); anger/rage (Why did you pick mauve? Any fool knows the sky is never mauve!); envy (Why can't I be as talented as Michelangelo?); resentment (You started this because you knew it would make me look bad!); bargaining (If I mow your lawn, will you finish my mural?); depression (What's the use? It's never going to look good.); and acceptance (Wait a minute...this actually does looks good!).

We struggled for weeks, teaching ourselves art basics such as shading, blending, and highlighting. We began to absorb ourselves into the painting. The excited chatter of the first days died down, replaced by the soothing sound of brush strokes from the hands of two teenaged girls in meditative concentration. Slowly, the mural began to take form and our confidence began to grow. The room brightened, and the harsh fluorescent lighting seemed to fade into the background behind our luminous sun. The last part, the ceiling, was perhaps the most difficult. We spent hours a day, heads at 90-degree angles to our necks, trying not to be so presumptuous as to compare ourselves to Michelangelo.

Finally, it was complete: sun, valley, mountains, and the sprawling colors of the sunset. As the first freshman walked into the room this year and said, "Oooh...that's really good. Who painted it?" I realized that there is an additional stage beyond acceptance: wisdom. The painter is rewarded not only with pride, but with a sense of the power of passion and perseverance.

These activities and events have contributed substantially to the person that I am. With every decision I make, every responsibility I am given, and every strange circumstance in which I find myself, I gain a little more wisdom. Academic learning is central in my life, but it is only one aspect of the person I am. I haven't told you what games I like best, and you may still not know what my voice sounds like, but I think I have begun to, at least partially, answer the important questions.

See page 339 to find out where this student got in.

USMAN O. AKEJU

Usman was the 1998 National Speech and Debate Champion in the category of Declamation, and a three-time qualifier for the national tournament. He was also an editor and contributor to his school's county-recognized literary magazine, as well as co-president of his school's drama and Internet clubs.

Stats

SAT I: 1420 (680 Verbal, 740 Math)

SAT II: 750 Math IIC, 580 Biology (taken in ninth grade), 580 Writing

High School GPA: 3.76/4.00

High School: Iona Preparatory School, New Rochelle, NY

Hometown: Mt. Vernon, NY

Gender: Male

Race/Ethnicity: African American/Black

Applied To

Massachusetts Institute of Technology (applied early decision)

Essay

The instructions were to write one of two essays, A or B. Essay A was a prompt a la *"Write about a meaningful even in your life and how it changed you."* Essay B was something like *"Think of a question you think we should've asked and answer it."* Usman chose Essay B and posed the question *"Why did you choose Essay B?"*

My decision to choose Essay B was mainly influenced by the fact that it opened to me an infinite amount of other choices. Each one posed a new possibility and another way to present myself. If everyone were to have the same thought processes, the world would be too predictable, nothing would be new, and you would be reading the same essay 8,676+ times. And that's just no fun.

Being a teenager in a society where "the thing" at my age is to be different (like everyone else), I saw the option to choose my own question as a very enticing one. Every day, I am reminded of the various rules and regulations that I must follow; going to a private Catholic school and having to abide by a dress code every day doesn't give much room for freedom. Although I know that these doctrines are mostly for the students' own good, I look at the chance to attempt something that has no bounds or limits as a gift and take it wholeheartedly.

Freedom of choice is one of the most important things in my life when it comes to expressing my individuality. I love to use my imagination to explore all of the possibilities that lie in any given situation, and I feel that being creative in solving problems is one of my gifts. When I first looked at Essay B, several ideas and options came to mind which, for a moment, made it difficult for me to see where to start — and this new challenge motivated me even more.

Though I can't say that I'm the greatest fan of the new computer recently introduced by Macintosh, the iMac, I can say that I truly do believe in their advertising slogan — "Think Different." Even as some may see this phrase as grammatically incorrect, I believe otherwise. There is a distinction between thinking different and thinking differently. I think that they are trying to portray "different" as a frame of mind, as a "what," and not just a "how"; and I can relate to that.

See page 339 to find out where this student got in.

VICTORIA MARIEL BARONE

Victoria was the editor of her school newspaper, played water polo for three years, and helped her parents take care of three foster babies while living at home.

Stats

SAT I: 1410 (700 Verbal, 710 Math)
SAT II: 770 Math IIC, 730 Writing
High School GPA: 4.35 weighted, 3.83 unweighted
High School: Lauralton Hall Academy, Milford, CT
Hometown: Stamford, CT
Gender: Female
Race/Ethnicity: Caucasian

Applied To

University of Michigan
University of Notre Dame
University of Southern California

Essay #1: Main Essay for Notre Dame

The essay question asked applicants to tell the admissions committee something interesting about him or herself that could not be revealed anywhere else in the application.

Don't Worry About the Girl

I looked around as I walked into the unfamiliar pool area and spotted "the guys" from my team sitting in the bleachers. I felt a hand on my shoulder and heard someone say, "Excuse me, you have to pay to get in." Trying to stay calm, I looked at the woman and politely explained that I was playing in the tournament, which meant I did not have to pay for a ticket. Confused and embarrassed, she mumbled, "Oh, good for you." I knew I would be the only female player that day so I understood her mistake; however, I was still annoyed that I had to explain my presence.

When I play water polo, both my teammates and my opponents are members of the opposite sex. On most occasions, I am the only woman, refreshingly unlike the all-female environment at my school. Although I am regularly a starter for the B-team, I have been selected to join our A-team this year for most of the games. I do not play much during the toughest matches, but I enjoy cheering for my teammates from the bench.

Three years ago, I was an unlikely water polo player until my older brother suggested I join his team, in the Eastern High School Water Polo League. I was sore and tired when I first started practicing. I was lost in the water and afraid to ask the older boys on my team for help, but I was enjoying myself. On the third night of practice, I was hit in the face by a pass from one of the boys. My nose began to bleed profusely. I cried from pain and embarrassment. I thought that would be the end of my water polo career, but my coach convinced me to get back in the water. Once I recovered from that incident, I knew I had finally found a sport I loved.

Over the years, I have learned to deal with being different. During games, opponents overlook me as not being a threat. There are few feelings more satisfying than scoring a goal or stealing the ball after hearing them say, "Don't worry about the girl, go guard someone else." I capitalize on the ignorance of boys who feel I am not good enough to play with them. I do not let it bother me when some opponents do not respect me enough to shake my hand after a game. These experiences have taught me how to handle narrow-minded people.

Being on the team has become a very important part of my life. I have proven myself capable to my coach and my teammates. Without being a tomboy, I found my place among the men and maintained my femininity. My self-confidence has grown with the knowledge that I can play such a rough sport. Water polo has taught me to be aggressive, both in and out of the water. I am not be intimidated by people who look bigger or stronger. I have learned not to be too sensitive and to accept a certain amount of teasing. Water polo has been a great source enjoyment for me while helping me develop into a well-rounded person.

Essay #2: Supplemental Essay for Notre Dame

The essay question that prompted this response involved reading a brochure about the Catholic Church's views on abortion and euthanasia.

A Winning Alternative

When a young woman made the courageous decision not to abort her unplanned baby girl, my life was enriched. My family, a licensed foster family, was chosen to care for Madelene, who lived with us from the day after she was born until she was adopted ten weeks later. I formed a special bond with our baby, as I was deeply involved in caring for her. I loved to feed her and rock her to sleep on my chest. Wherever I was out with Madelene, I faced many questions from both strangers and acquaintances. I explained that my family takes in foster babies to do our part in offering women an alternative to abortion. We have had three foster babies so far, and each one still has a special place in my heart.

Madelene has already positively affected the lives of many people. I cannot imagine my life without her in it. When she lived with us, she became a part of our family. Each of my five siblings, my parents, and my cousin, who also was living with us, loved Madelene and will never forget her. When I saw her new parents at her Christening a few months after she was adopted, I realized what a wonderful gift she was. Madelene brought untold happiness to the young couple, unable to have children of their own. Viewing the Christening, I was moved by my mother's dedication and commitment to supporting life. I realized that my mother must have a boundless amount of love to give.

My mother has been an inspiration to me. She has taken into our home both old and young to show her children how important it is to respect life at these fragile times.

When I was eleven years old, my grandmother was ill and confined to a wheelchair. My mother insisted that she live with us when she was no longer able to care for herself. I remember how special it was when I came home from school and my grandmother would be there. I was still small enough to cuddle on her lap in the wheelchair. It was difficult near the end of my grandmother's life to watch her mental and physical health deteriorate and feel the strain on the relationship between my mother and her mother, but I knew that my mother felt good about her decision. She taught me to be there for those who need me no matter how difficult the situation.

The message in the statement of the Bishops, Faithful for Life, coincides with my personal belief that life of any kind deserves respect. My experiences with Madelene and my grandmother taught me much about this. Caring for these individuals has given me a means of tapping into my heart to share the love that I have. I realize that some people do not share my feeling on these issues, but everyone should be aware when making a moral decision that there are options.

See page 340 to find out where this student got in.

WENJUN JING

Wenjun was a tri-varsity athlete in volleyball, squash, and crew and was voted captain of the volleyball team her senior year. She sang soprano in the school's concert choir, and the group produced a CD and went on a singing tour of France.

Stats

SAT I: 1500 (740 Verbal, 760 Math)

SAT II: 760 Writing, 700 Math IIC, 720 Chinese with Listening, 660 French, 620 Biology

High School GPA: N/A; school graded with a "group" system, student had an A average

High School: St. Andrew's School, Middletown, DE

Hometown: Cherry Hill, NJ

Gender: Female

Race/Ethnicity: Chinese

Applied To

Barnard College

Carnegie Mellon University

Columbia University

Connecticut College

Harvard College

Massachusetts Institute of Technology

Rice University

Rutgers University

Tulane University

Washington University in St. Louis

Wellesley College

Yale University

Essay

Wenjun used the following essay in her applications to Wellesley, Harvard, Rice, and Washington University in St. Louis.

Common Application Question 5: *Topic of your choice.*

Personal Statement: Coming out of the Cave

When I left for boarding school, Sasha and I promised to write to each other and keep in touch through email. She and I had become best friends ever since she rescued me from an empty seat on the school bus in the beginning of 7th grade. About a week into my new high school, after I finally learned how to use the email system, we started emailing each other every day. She would update me on things going on at home, and we would trade stories about our schedules. She was horrified at my Saturday classes and the fact that we were required to play sports. We found it ironic that our schools could be so different, and yet we were so much alike. We exchanged the normal amount of silly emails—complaints about homework, lack of sleep, guy trouble, etc. I assumed that her life back at home was about the same as it was last year.

Then, one evening, as I was checking my email, there was a message from Sasha. It began, "Wenjun, there's something I have to tell you. I'm gay." I was shocked. I was scared. I thought, this is a joke. Sasha? Gay? My best friend of three years was gay and I hadn't had a clue. In that email, the longest I've ever read, she told me everything. She had known she was gay for almost two years, and she had told very few people, only those she could trust would support her. She hadn't told her parents, and wasn't planning to. She said she couldn't bring herself to tell me in person because she couldn't be sure of my reaction so she was doing it over email. I thought to myself, where have I been for the past two years? On another planet? I had been totally oblivious. I was in shock. How could I not have known? There were so many clues. She never wore skirts or dresses. Never wore makeup. Never crushed on the same guys that we crushed on.

All this time, I had been in the dark to Sasha's identity. Either through assumption or deception, I had never thought that she was gay. As Plato, in his Allegory of the Cave, spoke of those in the cave who mistook shadows for reality, I mistook Sasha's true self. I only saw her shadow, the outward appearance of the Sasha that *I* knew, and not the Sasha that *she* was. With this email, I was drawn into the "light", and I felt blinded. But I realized that I wasn't friends with Sasha simply because she was a heterosexual person. No, I was friends with her because she was funny, witty, kind, generous, and sweet. As I got used to the "blinding light", my eyes adjusted, and I wrote back to her, telling her I didn't care if she was gay. The next time I saw her I wouldn't treat her any differently, I said.

I also was drawn into the light about her mental problems. She had been having such a hard time keeping her secret to herself, on top of having family problems, that she had been contemplating suicide. I had no idea. The entire time that I knew her, I never once thought she was anything but happy and stable.

Presently, our friendship is strained by this new revelation, and I worry about being PC around her. Many times, I wish I were back in the cave, mistaking shadows for reality. It is so easy to just overlook the difficult issues or pretend things don't exist if it's advantageous for yourself. However, I know that had I been kept in the dark, Sasha and I would have always had a chasm between us. Now, we both work hard to remain best friends, knowing that a friendship built on truth is stronger than one built on shadows.

See page 340 to find out where this student got in.

WILL

Will was a letterman in soccer and earned the rank of Eagle Scout while in high school, and he enjoyed helping out regularly at a local food bank. In his sophomore year Will began weightlifting often and became a bowling advocate. He worked a variety of minimum-wage jobs, from cooking at a small bar and grill and working as a cashier at Arby's to working in retail sales at an Abercrombie and Fitch clothing store.

Stats

SAT I: 1530 (730 Verbal, 800 Math)

SAT II: 800 Math IC, 800 Math IIC, 770 Chemistry, 730 Writing, 720 Biology

High School GPA: 4.0

High School: Porter-Gaud School, Charleston, SC

Hometown: Charleston, SC

Gender: Male

Race/Ethnicity: Caucasian

Applied To

Clemson University

Davidson College

Duke University

Princeton University

Essay: Duke

Although he does not remember the exact essay question, Will said that he chose the most open-ended option.

We had hiked for over five miles and were getting close to our campsite when it began to rain. The younger Boy Scouts had packed too much gear and were getting very tired. We needed to get to our campsite before dusk, so we could not afford to slow down. After I draped my poncho over my backpack so that my tent and sleeping bag would stay dry, I helped the new scouts cover their backpacks and offered to help carry some of their excess gear. After I had taken some of the weight off two scouts' backs, we continued the trek, looking forward to a break at the end of our hike and hoping that the rain would stop. Once we had reached our campsite and set up camp, we were able to find enough wood to have a small campfire before we retired for the night. My membership in the Boy Scouts has been full of similar challenging and rewarding experiences.

I started out as a Cub Scout at age seven, following in the footsteps of my father who had been an Eagle Scout and wanted me to join the scouting organization as soon as I could. The Boy Scouts of America is an institution that promotes trustworthiness, loyalty, reverence, service, and spirit. I was attracted to this organization immediately, and I am still active in the scouting program to this day.

The goal that I set for myself when I joined the Boy Scouts was the same as the hope that my parents had for me: to earn the rank of Eagle Scout. Throughout my climb through the ranks of scouting, I had to "live" the Scout Law in my activities and service. I had to prove my trustworthiness and determination as well as my eagerness to help others. I went on many camping trips with my troop where I learned various skills to complete merit badges. As I began to prove myself, I became a leader in the troop. As a patrol leader, I had to help plan camping trips and determine what supplies would be needed. I had to set an example for the younger scouts in my troop as well.

As I grew older, I began to widen my participation with the Boy Scouts. I took part in Eagle Scout service projects as well as other service opportunities such as food drives and working in a soup kitchen. I have continued my community service with the scouts and outside of scouting through my entire high school life. Finally, after going on many hikes and earning over 21 merit badges, I was ready to become an Eagle Scout. All that was left was my Eagle Scout service project. After much thought, I decided to build eight benches near an outside basketball court at my school. I had to plan the dates of the project, get the materials, make a design for the benches, and get other Boy Scouts to help me in the undertaking of this project.

My Eagle Scout project was the most important part of my life in scouting. It allowed me to prove my skills as a planner, an organizer, and a leader. After the project had been planned and organized, I continued by buying the materials that we would need and planning the dates that the project would take place. The younger scouts volunteered to help me with my project, and when the time came to begin, I delegated the individual jobs to my fellow Boy Scouts. We built the benches during the summer before my ninth grade year and secured them in poured concrete the following fall. The project was completed without a hitch, and I am proud of that accomplishment, especially when I see students using the benches.

Throughout my years as a Boy Scout, I came to understand and love the ideals that the scouting organization stresses. The environment that this organization provides gives me a wonderful feeling. I can be around honest, kind people who respect each other and who are energetic and involved. For these reasons, I have continued in the Boy Scouts and I have actually expanded my participation. While in the eleventh grade, I was elected President of the Venturer Scouts, a branch of scouting for older Boy Scouts. I have continued to work on extra merit badges to earn palm awards to add to my Eagle Award. Recently, I was elected as my troop's Junior Assistant Scout Master. Having this position allows me to help the adult leaders of my troop to plan events, meetings, and campouts.

For as long as I can remember, my parents have taught me how to distinguish right from wrong. They taught me how to have good morals and a high ethical standard. I learned from them the great feeling that comes from helping others in need. My parents always urged me to complete any challenge I had accepted. Since I had this wonderful foundation of love, morals, service, and determination, the Boy Scouts of America was perfect for me.

One of the rewards of staying in the Boy Scouts is seeing younger scouts advance in the program. As an Eagle Scout, I enjoy helping the younger scouts complete requirements for higher ranks and merit badges. I know how demanding the trail to the Eagle Scout Award is, so I am always happy to help potential Eagle Scouts strive to achieve their personal goals. My future goal is to continue to be involved in my community as a volunteer and a leader.

See page 341 to find out where this student got in.

PART 4

WHERE THEY GOT IN

ADAM BERLINSKY-SCHINE

Cornell University, Class of 2005

Applied to:

Cornell University .... accepted

Please note: Adam did not disclose information on other applications.

What He's Doing Now:

Adam is a computer science major and electrical and computer engineering double minor at Cornell's College of Engineering.

ALISON KAUFMANN

Amherst College, Class of 2003

Applied to:

Amherst College .... accepted

Brown University .... accepted

Stanford University .... accepted

Swarthmore College .... accepted

Wellesley College .... accepted

Wesleyan University .... accepted

Yale University .... accepted

What She's Doing Now:

Alison is majoring in psychology with an emphasis on conflict resolution and plans to attend graduate school for social psychology.

AMANDA JORDAN

United States Naval Academy, Class of 2004

Applied to:

Louisiana State University .... accepted

Tulane University .... accepted

United States Air Force Academy .... accepted

United States Naval Academy .... accepted

University of Mississippi .... accepted

University of Texas—Austin .... accepted

What She's Doing Now:

Amanda received an ROTC scholarship to UT, LSU, Tulane, and Ole Miss. She is currently an economics major and a member of the Naval Academy track team, and she sings in the Protestant Church Choir. After graduation, she will be commissioned in the United States Navy as a surface warfare officer.

ANDREA SALAS

Dartmouth College, Class of 2004

Applied to:

Amherst College .... waitlisted, removed name
Bates College .... accepted
Bowdoin College .... accepted
Dartmouth College .... accepted
Tufts University .... waitlisted, removed name
University of California—Berkeley .... accepted
University of California—Los Angeles .... accepted
University of California—San Diego .... accepted
University of California—Santa Barbara .... accepted
University of California—Santa Cruz .... accepted
Williams College .... accepted

What She's Doing Now:

Andrea is currently an English major at Dartmouth, with a minor in French. She is a staff writer for *The Dartmouth*, plays club tennis, volunteers in the Big Brother Big Sister program, and is also an active member of Kappa Kappa Gamma sorority. She will be working as an intern for *Glamour* magazine in the winter of 2003.

ANDREW COLLINS

Duke University, Class of 2005

Applied to:

Duke University .... accepted
Georgetown University .... accepted
Harvard College .... denied
Princeton University .... denied

Stanford University .... denied

University of California—Berkeley .... denied

University of Virginia .... accepted

Vanderbilt University .... accepted

What He's Doing Now:

Andrew is an associate editor for Duke's daily newspaper, *The Chronicle,* and he continues to play and compose for the piano. He studied abroad in France in the summer of 2002 and plans to major in political science. As is the case with most twenty year olds, he enjoys a good pick-up basketball game.

ANDREW P. SCHRAG

Tufts University, Class of 2004

Applied to:

Boston University .... accepted

Brown University .... denied

Cornell University .... waitlisted, denied

Georgetown University .... waitlisted, denied

Lafayette College .... accepted

Tufts University .... accepted

University of California—San Diego .... denied

University of Southern California .... accepted

What He's Doing Now:

At Tufts, Andrew is a double major in economics and international relations, and he is also an Eagle Scout. He currently works during the school year as director of operations at an Internet startup company. Andrew has strong aspirations to go to business school.

ANNA HENDERSON

Applied to:

Carleton College .... accepted early decision

What She's Doing Now:

At Carleton, Anna was involved in the campus ministries and started a Bible study with one of her friends. After the spring of 2002, she withdrew from Carleton; she decided to spend the fall term in London studying at L'Abri, a missionary study center, as it will be a great asset to her future plans for seminary. She is applying to larger schools such as the University of Virginia and has been accepted to Emory University.

ANONYMOUS

Wesleyan University, Class of 2006

Applied to:

Wesleyan University .... accepted early decision

What She's Doing Now:

The applicant took poetry classes at the University of Virginia the summer before starting her education at Wesleyan University. She has been accepted to the university symphony orchestra and is considering majoring in African American studies.

ANYA MANES

Barnard College, Class of 2002

Applied to:

Barnard College .... accepted

Boston University .... accepted

Claremont McKenna College .... denied

Columbia University .... denied

Duke University .... denied

New York University .... accepted

University of California—Santa Barbara

(College of Creative Studies) .... accepted

Vassar College .... denied

What She's Doing Now:

Anya applied in 1997, but deferred admission for a year to see what the world was like for those who didn't go on to college. What did she learn during her year off? "My conclusion was that college is essential, and I'm a better student now than I ever was in high school."

AUDREY NATH

Rice University, Class of 2005

Applied to:

Harvard College .... denied

Massachusetts Institute of Technology ..... accepted

Rice University .... accepted

What She's Doing Now:

Audrey is majoring in bioengineering and cognitive sciences at Rice University, where she DJs at Rice Radio, performs in theatre productions, and is basically having the time of her life.

BENJAMIN SPATZ

Wesleyan University, Class of 2001

Applied to:

Amherst College .... accepted

Brown University .... accepted

Hampshire College .... accepted

Sarah Lawrence College............................ accepted

Vassar College .... accepted

Wesleyan University .... accepted

Yale University .... waitlisted, denied

What He's Doing Now:

Ben is currently living in New York City, searching for the overlap and synthesis of radical politics and experimental performance art.

BRANDON MOLINA

Harvard College, Class of 2004

Applied to:

Columbia University .... accepted

Elon University .... accepted

Harvard College .... accepted early action

Stanford University .... rejected

Tulane University .... accepted

University of Pennsylvania .... rejected

United States Military Academy .... accepted
What He's Doing Now:

Brandon spent the summer of 2002 as a registered stockbroker after interning with a financial company the previous summer. At Harvard, he is an honors biology concentrator and plays varsity football.

Brian Tracy

University of Notre Dame, Class of 2005
Applied to:
University of Notre Dame ... accepted early decision
What He's Doing Now:

Brian is a civil engineering major and is currently the liturgical commissioner of his residence hall at Notre Dame.

Brooke Paul

Georgetown University, Class of 2003
Applied to:
Carleton College .... waitlisted, removed name
Colgate University .... accepted
Columbia University .... denied
Cornell University .... waitlisted, removed name
Georgetown University .... accepted
Middlebury College .... accepted
Northwestern .... waitlisted, removed name
Oberlin College .... accepted
What She's Doing Now:

Brooke is a government major at Georgetown and spent her junior year abroad in Scotland. She plans to attend law school and possibly join the Peace Corps after graduation.

Caroline Ang

Brown University, Class of 2004
Applied to:
Brown University .... accepted
University of California—Berkeley .... accepted

University of California—Los Angeles .... accepted
University of California—San Diego .... accepted
Please note: Caroline did not disclose information about other applications.

What She's Doing Now:

During her first two years at Brown, Caroline wrote for student publications and served as the recording secretary and Panhellenic delegate for the Alpha Epsilon chapter of Kappa Alpha Theta sorority. She spent her junior year abroad at Oxford University and is majoring in English.

CAROLINE HABBERT

Brown University, Class of 2004

Applied to:

Brown University .... accepted
Stanford University .... accepted
Yale University .... accepted
University of Michigan .... accepted
Washington University in St. Louis .... accepted

What She's Doing Now:

Caroline is currently pursuing a B.S. in psychology. She is also involved in a variety of nonacademic activities: she is coordinator of the Hillel Eldercare program, co-chair of the Brown University Mediation Project, and a member of the yearbook staff.

CASEY NEWTON

Northwestern University, Class of 2002

Applied to:

Northwestern University ..... accepted early decision

What He's Doing Now:

Casey Newton graduated cum laude from Northwestern University in 2002 with majors in English and journalism. He covers government and politics for *The Times,* a daily newspaper based in Munster, Indiana, with a circulation of 90,000.

CHARLES LIGHT

Dartmouth College, Class of 2004

Applied to:

Bowdoin College .... accepted

Cornell University .... accepted

Dartmouth College .... accepted

Johns Hopkins University .... accepted

Massachusetts Institute of Technology ..... accepted

Northeastern .... accepted (full scholarship)

Swarthmore College .... accepted

What He's Doing Now:

Charles is an economics major at Dartmouth. In the spring of 2002 he worked at the Federal Reserve Bank of Boston as a research assistant, and he is currently doing an independent study in economics at Oxford University.

CLAUDIA GOLD

Massachusetts Institute of Technology, Class of 2006

Applied to:

Brown University .... denied

Cornell University .... accepted

Massachusetts Institute of Technology ..... accepted

New York University .... accepted

Rice University .... waitlisted, removed name

University of Chicago .... accepted

Yale University .... denied

What She's Doing Now:

Claudia is currently attending MIT and plans to double major in music and physics.

CONNIE TAYLOR

Harvard University, Class of 2006

Applied to:

Boston University .... accepted

Harvard College .... waitlisted, accepted

Massachusetts Institute of Technology ..... accepted

University of Chicago .... accepted
University of Maryland—College Park .... accepted
Yale University .... accepted

What She's Doing Now:

Connie is currently a sophomore at Harvard, where she concentrates in honors neurobiology. She plans to graduate in 2006 and continue onto graduate or medical school.

DANIEL FREEMAN

Yale University, Class of 2004

Applied to:

Yale University .... accepted early decision

What He's Doing Now:

Upon arriving at Yale, Dan studied organic chemistry and classics before settling into a double major in political science and international studies. He spent his spare time at Yale singing and touring the globe with his a cappella group, the Yale Spizzwinks, leaving some time for theater and campus activism as well. During the summers Dan has dedicated himself to political campaigns, though he still makes sure to find time to escape to the wilderness to go climbing, hiking, and canoeing as often as possible.

DAVID AUERBACH

Carleton College, Class of 2004

Applied to:

Carleton College .... accepted
Dartmouth College .... accepted
Macalaster College .... accepted
Willamette University .... accepted

What He's Doing Now:

David is happy at Carleton where he is majoring in geology. In his spare time he hikes, plays ultimate Frisbee, climbs, kayaks, and enjoys life as a college student. Future plans include studying geology in Italy, traveling to Alaska, and eventually going on to graduate school.

DAVID JOSEPH ESTREM

United States Air Force Academy, Class of 2005

Applied to:

Embry Riddle Aeronautical University .... accepted

St. Louis University .... accepted

United States Air Force Academy .... accepted

University of North Dakota .... accepted

What He's Doing Now:

At the Air Force Academy, David is a meteorology major, following his interest in climate and weather and his position as a weather spotter for a TV station during high school. David aspires to be a pilot after graduation.

DIANA SCHOFIELD

Northwestern University, Class of 2004

Applied to:

Boston College .... accepted

Cornell University .... accepted

Emory University .... accepted

Georgetown University .... denied

Harvard University .... denied

Northwestern University .... accepted

University of North Carolina—Chapel Hill .. accepted

University of Pennsylvania .... denied

Washington University in St. Louis .... accepted

What She's Doing Now:

Diana is a member of the Alpha Lambda Delta and the Gamma Sigma Alpha honors fraternities in addition to being on the Dean's List. She is also in the Chi Omega sorority, in which she was pledge educator for 2002–2003 rush. Diana also volunteers at a nursing home and assists physical therapists in rehab. She is majoring in human development and psychological services at Northwestern, which requires a practicum internship in her chosen field of study. At the time of this writing, she looks forward to interning at the Children's Memorial Hospital in the psychiatric in-patient unit. Upon graduation, she plans to earn a master's degree in social work.

Diandra Lyn Bobé

Haverford College, Class of 2003

Applied to:

ROUND ONE

Columbia University .... waitlisted, removed name

Duke University .... denied

Georgetown University ... waitlisted, removed name

New York University .... accepted

Northwestern (journalism school) .... denied

Pomona College .... accepted

Swarthmore College .... accepted

Washington University in St. Louis .... accepted

Yale University .... waitlisted, denied

ROUND TWO

Barnard College .... accepted

Columbia University .... denied

Haverford College .... accepted

New York University .... accepted

Wesleyan University .... accepted

What She's Doing Now:

Diandra attended Pomona College from August 1999 to May 2001 and then sent out transfer applications. She is currently an English major and a comparative literature minor at Haverford. Diandra is a member of the all-female a capella group and works with incoming transfer and exchange students as a Student Resource Person as well as working as a mentor through the Minority Scholars Program. One of her biggest responsibilities this year will be serving on the Haverford College Commencement Committee for the class of 2003. Diandra plans to get her master's after traveling around Europe.

ELIZABETH KEMNITZER

University of Kansas, Class of 2005

Applied to:

Boston University	accepted
Brown	deferred early action, then denied
Johns Hopkins University	accepted
University of Chicago	accepted early action
University of Southern California	accepted

What She's Doing Now:

When Elizabeth received her acceptance from the University of Chicago, the admissions office also sent her a hand-written note telling her how much they enjoyed her essay. Elizabeth transferred to the University of Kansas in the fall of 2002. She spends her time studying and watching the wheat grow.

ELLISON WARD

Princeton University, Class of 2004

Applied to:

Brown University	accepted
College of William & Mary	accepted
Connecticut College	accepted
Duke University	accepted
Johns Hopkins University	accepted
Harvard College	waitlisted, denied
Princeton University	accepted
Yale University	waitlisted, removed name

What She's Doing Now:

At Princeton, Ellison is intending to major in sociology and minor in Latin American studies. She is also a captain of the women's ultimate Frisbee team, and she participates in Sustained Dialogue, a race discussion and action group.

EMILY PETRONE

Northwestern University, Class of 2004

Applied to:

Northwestern University ..... accepted early decision

What She's Doing Now:

Emily is a film major at Northwestern's School of Speech, where she works on the crews of several student films each year and is directing a short film she wrote.

EMMA FRICKE

Smith College, Class of 2004

Applied to:

Mount Holyoke College .... accepted

Smith College .... accepted

Sweet Briar College .... accepted

Vanderbilt University .... accepted

Wellesley College .... waitlisted, removed name

What She's Doing Now:

A senior at Smith College, Emma is majoring in early childhood education and plans to teach kindergarten in the inner city after graduation.

ERIC OSBORNE

Amherst College, Class of 2004

Applied to:

Amherst College .... accepted early decision

What He's Doing Now:

Currently, Eric is serving as class representative to the College Council, the committee in charge of setting policies on student life; President of SEAS (Students Engaged in Active Service); and an officer on the school's Social Council, which plans social activities for the campus. He is also involved in the Christian Fellowship, runs track, works at the admissions office, and was the formal dance committee chairman his sophomore year.

Eric Weingart

University of Pennsylvania, Class of 2002

Applied to:

Brown University .... denied
Bucknell University .... accepted
Colgate University .... accepted
College of William & Mary .... accepted
Duke University .... waitlisted, removed name
Princeton University .... denied
University of North Carolina—Chapel Hill ...... denied
University of Pennsylvania .... accepted

What He's Doing Now:

Eric was a psychology major at Penn. He currently works in public policy research at the American Enterprise Institute, a think tank in Washington, D.C.

Gaurav P. Patel

University of Pennsylvania, Class of 2004

Applied to:

Dartmouth College .... accepted
Harvard College .... denied
Princeton University .... waitlisted
University of Pennsylvania .... accepted
Yale University .... denied

What He's Doing Now:

Gaurav is currently a pre-med student at the University of Pennsylvania, double-majoring in the biological basis of behavior and French.

Gianna Marzilli

Williams College, Class of 2004

Applied to:

Amherst College .... waitlisted (not used that year)
Brown University .... waitlisted, accepted
Carleton College .... accepted
Colby College .... accepted

Macalester College .... accepted
Skidmore College .... accepted
Smith College .... accepted
Tufts University .... accepted
Washington University in St. Louis .... accepted
Wellesley College .... accepted
Williams College .... waitlisted, accepted

What She's Doing Now:

A studio art and psychology double major, Gianna sings in her college's concert choir and is a co-coordinator of a progressive religious organization on campus. She is also a student mediator, serves on two student-faculty committees, and works in the college's media labs. Gianna's artwork has been displayed at the Smithsonian. She plans to write a psychology thesis during her senior year and eventually attend graduate school in the fine arts or social sciences, with an eye toward teaching at the college level.

HALEY A. CONNOR

Washington University in St. Louis, Class of 2005

Applied to:

Washington U. in St. Louis .. accepted early decision

What She's Doing Now:

Haley hopes to major in painting or illustration with minors in business and music.

HEATHER FIREMAN

Massachusetts Institute of Technology, Class of 2004

Applied to:

California Institute of Technology .... accepted
Massachusetts Institute of Technology ..... accepted
Stanford University .... waitlisted, removed name
University of California—Berkeley .... accepted

What She's Doing Now:

Heather is now a materials science and engineering student at MIT. In the summer of 2002 she interned at the Naval

Undersea Warfare Center in Newport, Rhode Island, as part
of her industrial internship program.

HEATHER HERMANN

Cornell University, Class of 2003

Applied to:

Cornell University	**accepted**
Johns Hopkins University	**denied**
Michigan State University	**accepted**
Northwestern University	**accepted**
University of Michigan	**accepted**
Yale University	**denied**

What She's Doing Now:

Heather was admitted to the College of Arts and Sciences as a
chemistry major, but she is now majoring in applied economics and management with a business management concentration in Cornell's College of Agriculture and Life Sciences.

JAMES ROBERT COOLEY

United States Coast Guard Academy, Class of 2003

Applied to:

American University	**accepted**
SUNY College at Fredonia	**accepted**
U.S. Coast Guard Academy	**accepted**
U.S. Military Academy	**denied (for poor eyesight)**
U.S. Naval Academy	**denied (for poor eyesight)**
University of Hartford	**accepted**
University of Miami	**accepted**

JAMES SAMUEL FLETCHER

United States Naval Academy, Class of 2003

Applied to:

Hillsdale College	**accepted**
Samford University	**accepted**
United States Naval Academy	**accepted**

What He's Doing Now:

At the Academy, Sam rows crew and sings in the glee club and has chosen political science as his major with a minor in French.

James Gregory

Duke University, Class of 2004

Applied to:

Duke University .... accepted
Harvard .... waitlisted early action, then denied
Princeton University .... denied
University of North Carolina .... accepted
Yale University .... denied

What He's Doing Now:

James is a comparative area studies major with a particular interest in international health care systems and policy. He plans to study cultural differences in approaches to medicine and medical training and then attend medical school after graduation.

Jamie Manos

Cornell University, Class of 2004

Applied to:

Cornell University .... accepted early decision

What She's Doing Now:

Now a mechanical engineering major at Cornell University, Jamie still finds time for her music as the president of the Cornell University Jazz Ensembles and as a member of various other performance ensembles on campus.

Jason Freidenfelds

Harvard College, Class of 2000

Applied to:

Cornell University .... accepted
Harvard College .... accepted
Princeton University .... accepted

University of Pennsylvania .... accepted

Yale University .... accepted

What He's Doing Now:

Jason studied neuroscience at Harvard and continued his artistic and entrepreneurial pursuits. He currently works as a Web designer at a New York software firm.

Jessica Lau

Harvard College, Class of 2004

Applied to:

Brown University .... accepted

Dartmouth College .... accepted

Harvard University .... accepted

Pennsylvania State University .... accepted

Princeton University .... denied

Rutgers University .... accepted

Tufts University .... accepted

University of Pennsylvania .... accepted

University of Michigan .... accepted

University of Virginia .... accepted

What She's Doing Now:

Jessica is currently a student at Harvard, where she is an economics concentrator and participates in student government and community service activities.

Jessie Seymour

Dartmouth College, Class of 2004

Applied to:

Cornell University .... accepted

Dartmouth College .... accepted

Middlebury College .... accepted

University of Maine .... accepted

What She's Doing Now:

At Dartmouth, Jessie is a senior English major and education minor. She is on the student ski patrol and participates in other Outing Club activities.

Joseph A. Rago

Dartmouth College, Class of 2005

Applied to:

Brown University .... accepted early action

Dartmouth College .... accepted

Princeton University .... waitlisted, removed name

Yale University .... waitlisted, denied

What He's Doing Now:

At Dartmouth, Joe is on the crew team and will double major in economics and history.

Julia Hypatia Orth

New College of Florida, Class of 2003

Applied to:

New College of Florida .... accepted

Southampton College of Long Island U. .... accepted

University of California—Santa Cruz .... accepted

What She's Doing Now:

Julia majored in biopsychology and conducted dolphin research; she graduated in May 2003 after completing New College's senior thesis project requirement. She will marry her fiancé, whom she met in the first few weeks at college, and continue on to graduate work in dolphin research. Grad school possibilities include St. Andrews University in Scotland and the University of North Carolina at Wilmington.

Julie Yau-Yee Tam

Rice University, Class of 2003

Applied to:

Rice University .... accepted early decision

What She's Doing Now:

As of this writing, Julie was a senior economics major finishing her two-semester news internship at KHWB-TV (WB 39) Houston. She served for two years as news director/executive producer/anchor of Rice Broadcast TV's student news show. Julie was a Rice Ambassador and a member of three honor societies: Who's Who, Golden Key, and the National Society of Collegiate Scholars. As an active member of the Asian American Journalists Association, she anchored the student TV newscast at the 2002 national convention. She also produced, directed, and starred in a student film during her senior year.

KAREN A. LEE

Stanford University, Class of 2004
Applied to:

Duke University .... accepted
Johns Hopkins University .... accepted
Rice University .... accepted
Southern Methodist University .... accepted
Stanford University .... accepted

What She's Doing Now:

Karen is a biology major and a creative writing minor, and she hopes to study in Paris this winter. She has learned a lot since the day she wrote her application essay and is grateful for everything.

KATHARINE ANNE THOMAS

Haverford College, Class of 2005
Applied to:

Bucknell University .... accepted
Colgate University .... accepted
Emory University .... waitlisted, removed name
Georgetown University .... denied
Haverford College .... accepted
Johns Hopkins University .... accepted
Swarthmore College .... denied
Vassar College .... waitlisted, removed name
Wake Forest University .... accepted
Yale University .... denied

What She's Doing Now:

Katharine returned to Poland to teach English through UNESCO in the summer of 2002, and she is currently studying abroad in Europe. She will major in English.

KATHLEEN ANN MIRANDA

Princeton University, Class of 2002

Applied to:

Princeton University .... accepted

University of Notre Dame .... accepted

Please note: Kathleen withdrew all other applications.

What She's Doing Now:

A chemical engineering major at Princeton, Kathleen also found time to continue playing the flute and to take up figure skating. Currently, she is pursuing a Ph.D. in chemical engineering at the University of Pennsylvania.

KATRINA ERIN FLETCHER

Colby College, Class of 2003

Applied to:

Amherst College .... denied

Bowdoin College .... waitlisted, denied

Colby College .... accepted

Dartmouth College .... denied

Middlebury College .... denied

Wesleyan University .... denied

Williams College .... denied

What She's Doing Now:

After spending a semester studying literature in London, Katrina is back at Colby leading their fledgling equestrian team and hoping to secure a job in publishing after graduation.

Katrina believes she had a really weak essay. She explained, "The more I read this essay, the more I wonder how I got accepted at Colby. As you can see, there are plenty of other schools that I didn't get into. I used the same application essay for each of the colleges that I applied to as part of the

Common Application (a big no-no, I have since learned) along with supplementary essays where required."

KENDALL MORRELLY-BOTT

Cornell University, Class of 2004
Applied to:

Cornell University .... **accepted early decision**
What She's Doing Now:

Kendall is currently studying abroad in Italy before finishing her B.S. in neurobiology and behavior at Cornell's College of Agriculture and Life Sciences. She works as a student advisor to incoming freshman biology majors and in a research lab, studying dopamine and the motivational response. Kendall is also a member of STAND, a children's rights organization, and a sister in Alpha Phi. Kendall isn't sure what she'll do after graduation—she plans to attend graduate school and may get her M.B.A. so she can pursue a career in industrial organizational psychology.

KIM HAMMERSMITH

Duke University, Class of 2003
Applied to:

Duke University .... **accepted**
Johns Hopkins University .... **denied**
North Carolina State University .... **accepted**
University of North Carolina—Chapel Hill.. **accepted**
What She's Doing Now:

Now a women's studies major and chemistry minor at Duke, Kim plans to live abroad for a year following graduation and then pursue a career in pediatric dentistry.

KIMBERLY RITTBERG

University of Pennsylvania, Class of 2002
Applied to:

Penn .... **accepted early decision**

What She's Doing Now:

Kim graduated in May of 2002 with a major in communications and minors in art history and Spanish. She designs jewelry and plans to work in communications, marketing, or the art world.

KIMEN FIELD

Stanford University, Class of 2004

Applied to:

California Polytechnic State University—
San Luis Obispo .... accepted
Rice University .... accepted
Stanford University .... accepted
University of California—Los Angeles .... accepted
(full ride as Regents Scholar)
University of California—San Diego .... accepted
(full ride as Regents Scholar)

What She's Doing Now:

Kimen took a quarter off and backpacked through Europe last spring and will graduate in June 2004 as planned. At Stanford, she is active in her sorority, Delta Delta Delta, and works for the student government. She is majoring in product design and minoring in management science and engineering and hopes to blend her major and minor in a product management career.

KRISTI DERRICK

Johns Hopkins University, Class of 2004

Applied to:

Johns Hopkins University .... accepted
Swarthmore College .... denied
University of Rochester .... accepted

What She's Doing Now:

Kristi is currently a pre-med public health major at Johns Hopkins. She is a Resident Advisor and participates actively in the campus Emergency Medical System group called HERO.

KRISTIN SHANTZ

California Institute of Technology, Class of 2004

Applied to:

California Institute of Technology .... accepted
Claremont McKenna College .... accepted
Harvard College .... accepted
Pepperdine University .... accepted
Princeton University .... denied
Stanford University .... denied
University of California—Berkeley .... accepted
University of California—Los Angeles .... accepted
University of California—San Diego .... accepted

What She's Doing Now:

Kristin is currently majoring in electrical and computer engineering at Caltech. She is actively involved on campus as a dancer with the Caltech Dance Troupe, as a campus tour guide, and as the treasurer of the Society of Women Engineers. She is also the coordinator of youth mentoring programs for an on-campus community service organization. Kristin has performed cutting-edge research during a Caltech research fellowship in biophysics, developing microfluidic chips to study bacterial cells. Kristin hopes to pursue graduate studies in bioengineering and eventually earn her M.B.A.

LAUREN FONTEIN

Dartmouth College, Class of 2002

Applied to:

Dartmouth College .... accepted
Harvard College .... denied
Princeton University .... denied
University of Nevada—Reno .... accepted

What She's Doing Now:

Lauren graduated with honors in psychology from Dartmouth College. She is currently working as a paralegal in a New York law firm with plans to attend law school within the next two years. At Dartmouth, she sang with the Dartmouth Chamber Singers, participated in musical theater, and wrote an honor thesis on the cognitive appeal of contemporary music.

LILLIAN DIAZ-PRZYBYL

Williams College, Class of 2004
Applied to:
Williams College .... accepted early decision
What She's Doing Now:
Lillian is now majoring in English and Japanese, and is still playing the saxophone, although she has left the swim team for ultimate Frisbee.

LINDSAY CLAIBORN

Claremont McKenna College, Class of 2005
Applied to:
Claremont McKenna College .... accepted
College of William & Mary .... accepted
Emory University .... accepted
Pomona College .... waitlisted, removed name
Stanford University .... denied early decision
Yale University .... denied
University of Southern California .... accepted
USC School of Cinema-Television .... accepted
What She's Doing Now:
Lindsay is majoring in government and film studies, and she is currently studying abroad in London.

LISA BLUMSACK

Amherst College, Class of 2004
Applied to:
Amherst College .... accepted
Harvard College .... accepted
University of Florida .... accepted
University of Virginia .... accepted

What She's Doing Now:

Lisa was voted the 2002–2003 secretary of the Massachusetts Senior Classical League and the 2002–2003 vice president of the National Senior Classical League, so it should come as no surprise that she has declared a classics major. She is also involved with Amherst's ultimate Frisbee team and the Amherst College Concert Choir and is a Latin tutor in Amherst's peer tutoring program. Lisa is considering pursuing a law degree after graduation.

MARIA INEZ VELAZQUEZ

Smith College, Class of 2004

Applied to:

Connecticut College .... accepted
Elms College .... accepted
Smith College .... accepted
Trinity College .... accepted
Yale University .... accepted
University of Massachusetts—Amherst ..... accepted
Xavier University of Louisiana .... accepted

What She's Doing Now:

Maria is currently the editor-in-chief of *Mulch* (www.geocities.com/mulchzine), an e-zine she founded her sophomore year of college. She is also a Ron Brown Scholar and a Mellon Fellow.

MEGHAN BUTLER

Boston College, Class of 2003

Applied to:

Boston College .... accepted
Catholic University of America .... accepted
Colby College .... waitlisted, denied
Fairfield University .... accepted
Providence College .... accepted
University of Notre Dame .... denied

What She's Doing Now:

Megan's love for writing and speaking led her to become a double major in English and communication at BC. She has remained true to her passion for singing, however, by joining some music groups on campus, through which she has had the honor of singing mass in St. Peter's Basilica and performing the *Star Wars* theme with its composer, John Williams. She feels that going to BC was the best choice she ever made, and she looks forward to working in public relations and possibly pursuing a law degree.

MELISSA HENLEY

Dartmouth College, Class of 2005

Applied to:

Dartmouth College .... accepted
Lewis and Clark College .... accepted
Linfield College .... accepted
Stanford University .... denied

What She's Doing Now:

At the moment, Melissa is planning on double majoring in classical archaeology and psychology.

MEREDITH S. KNIGHT

Massachusetts Institute of Technology, Class of 2003

Applied to:

Massachusetts Institute of Technology ..... accepted
Please note: Meredith doesn't remember the admissions decisions or essays used for other schools.

What She's Doing Now:

Meredith is currently studying brain and cognitive science and linguistics at MIT.

MEREDITH NARROWE

Stanford University, Class of 2004

Applied to:

Brown University .... accepted early action

Columbia University .... waitlisted, removed name
Occidental College .... accepted
Pomona College .... accepted
Scripps College .... accepted
Stanford University .... accepted

What She's Doing Now:

Currently a communication and American studies double major at Stanford University, Meredith was the top student in her high school and was the first in the school's history to attend a prestigious university. As a Stanford student, Meredith was able to study archaeology in Switzerland and Italy after her freshman year. She attended the Stanford in Washington program in Washington, D.C., in the fall of her junior year, where she interned in the postproduction department of National Geographic Television. After graduation, she intends to backpack around the world with her friends before finding a job.

MICHAEL

Yale University, Class of 2006

Applied to:

Brown University .... accepted
Columbia University .... accepted
Cornell University .... accepted
Dartmouth College .... accepted
Harvard College .... denied
Massachusetts Institute of Technology .... denied
Princeton University .... denied
Stanford University .... denied
University of Pennsylvania .... accepted
Yale University .... accepted

MICHELE CASH

Stanford University, Class of 2004

Applied to:

Harvard College .... waitlisted, denied

> Harvey Mudd College .... accepted
> Princeton University .... denied
> Rice University .... accepted
> Stanford University .... accepted
> University of California—Berkeley .... accepted
> University of California—Davis .... accepted
> University of California—San Diego .... accepted
> University of Rochester .... accepted

What She's Doing Now:

During the summer of 2002, Michele participated in a twelve-week NASA Undergraduate Student Research Program where she spent six weeks performing rocket science in Huntsville, Alabama, and six weeks in Los Alamos, New Mexico, working on plasma physics. In January of 2003, she traveled to Ethiopia with a geophysics professor from Stanford to study the East African Rift as part of the Ethiopia-Afar Geoscientific Lithospheric Experiment. Michele is majoring in physics and minoring in feminist studies, and she is working on a grant proposal for a project that will look at women astronauts within the American space program.

NATALIE ANN SCHIBELL

George Washington University, Class of 2004

Applied to:

> **U.S. Naval Academy .... denied third year in a row**

What She's Doing Now:

Natalie has been rejected from USNA three times. She writes, "Here is a brief explanation: I failed to get an appointment to USNA out of high school. I attended Washington College for one full academic year. When I was turned down again, I transferred to George Washington University where I am an NROTC midshipman. The admissions process to the Naval Academy is the same for college students [as for high school students] so I had to write another essay and do the entire application over again for the third consecutive time. . . . I put a lot of hard work into gaining an appointment and put my heart and soul into the essay as well. The experience I have gone through has had a major positive impact on my life, so much so, that I am thinking about writing a book one day to encourage people to never give up their dreams. I will also be giving a speech at an awards ceremony for [a] local essay sponsored by a local newspaper in May, and I will be reading an excerpt from the essay there."

At the time of this writing, Natalie was a junior and third-class midshipman at The George Washington University School of Public Health and Health Services, majoring in exercise science. She was a midshipman instructor at freshman orientation; a lifeguard in Bradley Beach, New Jersey, during the summer; and the assistant athletics officer during the semester. She is pursuing a career in special operations (specifically, explosive ordinance disposal) and, later, involvement in the U.S. Navy's marine mammal training program. She was recently engaged to Tim Payne, Ensign USN on board the USS *Normandy* CG 60, which is in support of Operation Enduring Freedom.

NEENA ARNDT

Pomona College, Class of 2003
Applied to:

Pomona College .... **accepted early decision**

What She's Doing Now:

Neena is a linguistics major and theatre minor at Pomona and can sometimes be found in the dance and music departments as well. She is unsure of her future plans but is considering applying to graduate programs in dramatic criticism.

NITIN SHAH

Harvard College, Class of 2004
Applied to:

Harvard College .... **accepted**
Stanford University .... **waitlisted, removed name**

University of California—Berkeley .... accepted
University of California—Los Angeles .... accepted
Yale University .... accepted
What He's Doing Now:

At Harvard, Nitin's concentration is government. He is a researcher, editor, and spokesperson for *Let's Go*, a student-run travelguide series, and he spent the summer of 2002 participating in a public service law internship in the office of the Massachusetts Attorney General. After college, Nitin plans to attend law school.

PETER DEAN

Washington and Lee University, Class of 2004
Applied to:

Davidson College .... accepted
Gettysburg College .... accepted
Rhodes College .... accepted
University of Virginia .... accepted
Valparaiso University .... accepted
Vanderbilt University .... accepted
Wake Forest University .... accepted
Washington and Lee University .... accepted
Wheaton College (IL) .... accepted
What He's Doing Now:

Peter is pre-med while majoring in chemistry, and he plays baseball and football at Washington and Lee.

PHILIP JAMES MADELEN RUCKER

Yale University, Class of 2006
Applied to:

Boston College .... accepted
Brown University .... accepted
Emory University .... accepted
Georgetown .... deferred early action, then denied
Harvard .... deferred early action, then denied
Tufts University .... accepted

Tulane University .... accepted
University of Chicago .... accepted early action
University of Rochester .... accepted
Yale University .... accepted

What He's Doing Now:

Following his high school graduation, Philip held an internship at the Savannah Area Chamber of Commerce in the Workforce & Economic Development department. He plans to major in "Ethics, Politics, and Economics" at Yale.

PHILIP TIDWELL

Washington University in St. Louis, Class of 2004

Applied to:

Arizona State University .... accepted
Columbia University .... denied
Stanford University .... denied
University of California—Berkeley .... accepted
University of Kansas .... accepted
Washington University in St. Louis .... accepted

What He's Doing Now:

Philip is currently pursuing a double major in architecture and urban studies at the Washington University School of Architecture. He spent the 2002–2003 school year at Columbia University participating in their New York/Paris program for architecture and urbanism. In preparation for this program, he interned with the New York City Department of City Planning during the summer of 2002.

REBECCA YAEL BACK

Wesleyan University, Class of 2005

Applied to:

Wesleyan University .... accepted early decision

What She's Doing Now:

At Wesleyan, Rebecca still has not decided on her major, but is very interested in sociology, women's studies, and medicine, and she continues to be involved in social and political action.

SAMANTHA CULP

Yale University, Class of 2004

Applied to:

Brown University .... waitlisted, removed name

Columbia University .... waitlisted, removed name

Wesleyan University .... accepted

Yale University .... accepted

What She's Doing Now:

Samantha is a senior at Yale, double majoring in anthropology and film studies and pursuing some sort of career in cultural study, journalism, and/or filmmaking. At school, she is a writer and editor for the *Journal of Contemporary Culture*, and she works at the Film Studies Center. She is also studying Japanese and would like to travel and work abroad after graduation.

SCOTT DAGGETT

United States Air Force Academy, Class of 2003

Applied to:

Embry Riddle Aeronautical University .... accepted

United States Air Force Academy .... accepted

What He's Doing Now:

Scott majored in mechanical engineering and participated in the intramural program at the United States Air Force Academy.

STANLEY SONG

Cornell University, Class of 2003

Applied to:

Brown University .... denied

Case Western Reserve University .... accepted

Cornell University .... accepted

Northwestern University .... accepted

Rice University .... denied

Stanford University .... denied

University of California—Berkeley .... accepted

University of California—Davis .... accepted

University of California—Los Angeles .... accepted
University of California—San Diego .... accepted

What He's Doing Now:

Stanley continues to be a bicycle fanatic in college, racing on the Cornell Cycling Team. He's majoring in mechanical and aerospace engineering and electrical engineering, with a concentration in biological engineering, at Cornell's College of Engineering.

STEPHANIE CROSS

Swarthmore College, Class of 2004

Applied to:

Swarthmore College .... accepted early decision

What She's Doing Now:

Stephanie is currently an honors biology major with a chemistry minor. She wishes to go into a M.D./Ph.D. program after graduation.

STEPHANIE LUH

Wellesley College, Class of 2003

Applied to:

Wellesley College .... accepted early decision

What She's Doing Now:

Stephanie is a mathematics major and economics minor and enjoys Wellesley very much, despite how cold the winter gets.

STEPHANIE WUN-LEE CHOW

Massachusetts Institute of Technology, Class of 2004

Applied to:

Massachusetts Institute of Technology ..... accepted
Boston University .... accepted
Brown University PLME Program .... denied
Columbia University .... accepted
Cornell University .... denied
Harvard College .... deferred, then denied
Princeton University .... deferred, then denied

Rensselaer Polytechnic Institute .... accepted

University of Connecticut .... accepted

Yale University .... **waitlisted, removed name**

What She's Doing Now:

Stephanie is currently a pre-med sophomore at MIT, majoring in the brain and cognitive sciences and minoring in Spanish language.

TAMAR KORNBLUM

Columbia University, Class of 2004

Applied to:

Barnard College .... accepted

Binghamton University .... accepted

Boston University .... accepted

Columbia University .... accepted

Rutgers University–Rutgers College .... accepted

Tufts University .... denied

University of Michigan .... accepted

University of Rochester .... accepted

What She's Doing Now:

Tamar is majoring in psychology and enjoys working with children and adolescents during both the summer and the school year. She wrote, "Of all the schools I applied to, the only one where I was not accepted was Tufts University. I think it is because I chose not to do the optional/supplemental essay."

THOMAS JERDE

Brown University, Class of 2003

Applied to:

Brown University .... **accepted early action**

What He's Doing Now:

At Brown, Thomas plays in the orchestra, the New Music Ensemble, and chamber music groups, and he triple majors in neuroscience, music, and philosophy. After graduation, he plans to pursue a Ph.D. in cognitive neuroscience.

Timothy D. Gibeau

University of Notre Dame, Class of 2004

Applied to:

Tufts University .... waitlisted, denied

University of Notre Dame .... accepted

University of Pennsylvania .... denied

Yale University .... denied

What He's Doing Now:

Tim is currently a science-business major at Notre Dame and a member of the "Band of the Fighting Irish." His other extracurricular activities at Notre Dame include participation in the symphonic band and the Pasquerilla East Musical Company.

Tracy Serge

Yale University, Class of 2004

Applied to:

Yale University .... accepted early decision

What She's Doing Now:

Tracy has recently returned from studying abroad in Ireland. She is currently a psychology major and has a job transcribing the testimony of Holocaust survivors in the Fortunoff Archives of Yale University's Sterling Memorial Library.

Usman O. Akeju

Massachusetts Institute of Technology, Class of 2004

Applied to:

MIT .... accepted early decision

What He's Doing Now:

In 2002, Usman worked with a team of software developers at IBM Research in Yorktown Heights, New York, developing a performance analysis and management tool. Though Usman's major is electrical engineering and computer science, he has a passion for performance that shows in his extensive involvement in theater, performance poetry, and a cappella, both on and off campus. Usman plans to pursue a master's degree at MIT after he completes his undergrad requirements.

VICTORIA MARIEL BARONE

University of Notre Dame, Class of 2004
Applied to:

University of Michigan	accepted
University of Notre Dame	accepted
University of Southern California	accepted

WENJUN JING

Wellesley College, Class of 2005
Applied to:

Barnard College	accepted
Carnegie Mellon University	accepted
Columbia University	denied
Connecticut College	accepted
Harvard College	denied
Massachusetts Institute of Technology	denied
Rice University	**waitlisted, removed name**
Rutgers University	accepted
Tulane University	accepted
Washington University in St. Louis	accepted
Wellesley College	accepted
Yale University	denied

What She's Doing Now:

During the summer of 2002, Wenjun worked as an instructional technology intern at Wellesley College designing websites, which encouraged her to consider computer science as a possible major. She is on Wellesley's varsity squash team and plays intramural volleyball. Wenjun plans to study abroad during her junior year in either in France or China.

WILL

Duke University, Class of 2004

Applied to:

Clemson University .... accepted

Davidson College .... accepted

Duke University .... accepted

Princeton University .... denied

What He's Doing Now:

Will is a double major in computer science and economics and a minor in religion at Duke, where he is a member of the crew team.

INDEX OF ESSAY THEMES

Notes

NOTES

NOTES

NOTES

NOTES

NOTES

NOTES

NOTES

NOTES

Graduate School Entrance Tests

Business School

Is an MBA in your future? If so, you'll need to take the GMAT. The GMAT is a computer-based test offered year round, on most days of the week. October and November are the most popular months for testing appointments. Most business schools require you to have a few years of work experience before you apply, but that doesn't mean you should put off taking the GMAT. Scores are valid for up to five years, so you should take the test while you're still in college and in the test-taking frame of mind.

Law School

If you want to be able to call yourself an "esquire," you'll need to take the LSAT. Most students take the LSAT in the fall of their senior year—either the October or the December administration. The test is also offered in February and in June. The June test is the only afternoon administration – so if your brain doesn't start functioning until the P.M., this might be the one for you. Just make sure to take it in June of your junior year if you want to meet the application deadlines.

Medical School

The MCAT is offered twice each year, in April and in August. It's a beastly eight-hour exam, but it's a necessary evil if you want to become a doctor. Since you'll need to be familiar with the physics, chemistry, and biology tested on the exam, you'll probably want to wait until April of your junior year to take the test— that's when most students take the MCAT. If you wait until August to give it a shot, you'll still be able to meet application deadlines, but you won't have time to take it again if you're not satisfied with your results.

Other Graduate and Ph.D. Programs

For any other graduate or Ph.D. program, be it art history or biochemical engineering, you'll need to take the GRE General Test. This is another computer-based test, and, like the GMAT, it's offered year-round on most days of the week. The most popular test dates are in late summer and in the fall. Take the test no later than October or November before you plan to enter graduate school to ensure that you meet all application deadlines (and the all-important financial aid deadlines) and to leave yourself some room to take it again if you're not satisfied with your scores.

Understanding the Tests

MCAT

Structure and Format

The Medical College Admission Test (MCAT) is a six-hour paper-and-pencil exam that can take up to eight or nine hours to administer.

The MCAT consists of four scored sections that always appear in the same order:

1. Physical Sciences: 100 minutes; 77 physics and general chemistry questions

2. Verbal Reasoning: 85 minutes; 60 questions based on nine passages

3. Writing Sample: two 30-minute essays

4. Biological Sciences: 100 minutes; 77 biology and organic chemistry questions

Scoring

The Physical Sciences, Biological Sciences, and Verbal Reasoning sections are each scored on a scale of 1 to 15, with 8 as the average score. These scores will be added together to form your Total Score. The Writing Sample is scored from J (lowest) to T (highest), with O as the average score.

Test Dates

The MCAT is offered twice each year—in April and August.

Registration

The MCAT is administered and scored by the MCAT Program Office under the direction of the AAMC. To request a registration packet, you can write to the MCAT Program Office,
P.O. Box 4056, Iowa City, Iowa 52243 or call 319-337-1357.

GRE

Structure and Format

The Graduate Record Examinations (GRE) General Test is a multiple-choice test for applicants to graduate school that is taken on computer. It is a computer-adaptive test (CAT), consisting of three sections.

- One 30-minute, 30-question "Verbal Ability" (vocabulary and reading) section

- One 45-minute, 28-question "Quantitative Ability" (math) section

- An Analytical Writing Assessment, consisting of two essay tasks

  o One 45-minute "Analysis of an Issue" task

  o One 30-minute "Analysis of an Argument" task

The GRE is a computer-adaptive test, which means that it uses your performance on previous questions to determine which question you will be asked next. The software calculates your score based on the number of questions you answer correctly, the difficulty of the questions you answer, and the number of questions you complete. Questions that appear early in the test impact your score to a greater degree than do those that come toward the end of the exam.

Scoring

You will receive a Verbal score and a Math score, each ranging from 200 to 800, as well as an Analytic Writing Assessment (AWA) score ranging from 0 to 6.

Test Dates

The GRE is offered year-round in testing centers, by appointment.

Registration

To register for the GRE, call 1-800-GRE-CALL or register online at www.GRE.org.

Understanding the Tests

LSAT

Structure and Format

The Law School Admission Test (LSAT) is a four-hour exam comprised of five 35-minute multiple-choice test sections of approximately 25 questions each, plus an essay:

- Reading Comprehension (1 section)
- Analytical Reasoning (1 section)
- Logical Reasoning (2 sections)
- Experimental Section (1 section)

Scoring

- Four of the five multiple-choice sections count toward your final LSAT score
- The fifth multiple-choice section is an experimental section used solely to test new questions for future exams
- Correct responses count equally and no points are deducted for incorrect or blank responses
- Test takers get a final, scaled score between 120 and 180
- The essay is not scored, and is rarely used to evaluate your candidacy by admissions officers

Test Dates

The LSAT is offered four times each year—in February, June, October, and December.

Registration

To register for the LSAT, visit www.LSAC.org to order a registration book or to register online.

GMAT

Structure and Format

The Graduate Management Admission Test (GMAT) is a multiple-choice test for applicants to business school that is taken on computer. It is a computer-adaptive test (CAT), consisting of three sections:

- Two 30-minute essays to be written on the computer: Analysis of an Argument and Analysis of an Issue
- One 75-minute, 37-question Math section: Problem Solving and Data Sufficiency
- One 75-minute, 41-question Verbal section: Sentence Corrections, Critical Reasoning, and Reading Comprehension

The GMAT is a computer-adaptive test, which means that it uses your performance on previous questions to determine which question you will be asked next. The software calculates your score based on the number of questions you answer correctly, the difficulty of the questions you answer, and the number of questions you complete. Questions that appear early in the test impact your score to a greater degree than do those that come toward the end of the exam.

Scoring

You will receive a composite score ranging from 200 to 800 in 10-point increments, in addition to a Verbal score and a Math score, each ranging from 0 to 60. You will also receive an Analytic Writing Assessment (AWA) score ranging from 0 to 6.

Test Dates

The GMAT is offered year-round in testing centers, by appointment.

Registration

To register for the GMAT, call 1-800-GMAT-NOW or register online at www.MBA.com.

Dispelling the Myths about Test Preparation and Admissions

MYTH: If you have a solid GPA, your test score isn't as important for getting into a college or graduate school.

FACT: While it is true that admissions committees consider several factors in their admissions decisions, including test scores, GPA, work or extra-curricular experience, and letters of recommendation, it is not always true that committees will overlook your test scores if you are strong in other areas. Particularly for large programs with many applicants, standardized tests are often the first factor that admissions committees use to evaluate prospective students.

MYTH: Standardized exams test your basic skills or innate ability; therefore your score cannot be significantly improved through studying.

FACT: Nothing could be farther from the truth. You can benefit tremendously from exposure to actual tests and expert insight into the test writers' habits and the most commonly used tricks.

MYTH: There are lots of skills you can learn to help you improve your math score, but you can't really improve your verbal score.

FACT: The single best way to improve your verbal score is to improve your vocabulary. Question types in the verbal reasoning sections of standardized tests all rely upon your understanding of the words in the questions and answer choices. If you know what the words mean, you'll be able to answer the questions quickly and accurately. Improving your critical reading skills is also very important.

MYTH: Standardized exams measure your intelligence.

FACT: While test scores definitely matter, they do NOT test your intelligence. The scores you achieve reflect only how prepared you were to take that particular exam and how good a test taker you are.

Hyperlearning *MCAT Prep Course*

The Princeton Review Difference

Nearly 40% of all MCAT test takers take the exam twice due to inadequate preparation the first time. **Do not be one of them.**

Our Approach to Mastering the MCAT

You will need to conquer both the verbal and the science portions of the MCAT to get your best score. But it might surprise you to learn that the Verbal Reasoning and Writing Sample are the most important sub-sections on the test. That is why we dedicate twice as much class time to these sections as does any other national course! We will help you to develop superlative reading and writing skills so you will be ready to write well crafted, concise essay responses. And of course, we will also help you to develop a thorough understanding of the basic science concepts and problem-solving techniques that you will need to ace the MCAT.

Total Preparation: 41 Class Sessions

With 41 class sessions, our MCAT course ensures that you will be prepared and confident by the time you take the test.

The Most Practice Materials

You will receive more than 3,000 pages of practice materials and 1,300 pages of supplemental materials, and all are yours to keep. Rest assured that our material is always fresh. Each year we write a new set of practice passages to reflect the style and content of the most recent tests. You will also take five full-length practice MCATs under actual testing conditions, so you can build your test-taking stamina and get used to the time constraints.

Specialist Instructors

Your course will be led by a team of between two and five instructors—each an expert in his or her specific subjects. Our instructors are carefully screened and undergo a rigorous national training program. In fact, the quality of our instructors is a major reason students recommend our course to their friends.

Get the Score You Want

We guarantee you will be completely satisfied with your MCAT score!* Our students boast an average MCAT score improvement of ten points.**

*If you attend all class sessions, complete all tests and homework, finish the entire course, take the MCAT at the next administration and do not void your test, and you still are not satisfied with your score, we will work with you again at no additional cost for one of the next two MCAT administrations.

**Independently verified by International Communications Research.

ClassSize-8 *Classroom Courses for the GRE, LSAT, and GMAT*

Small Classes

We know students learn better in smaller classes. With no more than eight students in a Princeton Review class, your instructor knows who you are, and works closely with you to identify your strengths and weaknesses. You will be as prepared as possible. When it comes to your future, you shouldn't be lost in a crowd of students.

Guaranteed Satisfaction

A prep course is a big investment—in terms of both time and money. At The Princeton Review, your investment will pay off. Our LSAT students improve by an average of 7 points, our GRE students improve by an average of 212 points, and our GMAT students boast an average score improvement of 92.5 points—the best score improvement in the industry.* We guarantee that you will be satisfied with your results. If you're not, we'll work with you again for free.**

Expert Instructors

Princeton Review instructors are energetic and smart—they've all scored in the 95th percentile or higher on standardized tests. Our instructors will make your experience engaging and effective.

Free Extra Help

We want you to get your best possible score on the test. If you need extra help on a particular topic, your instructor is happy to meet with you outside of class to make sure you are comfortable with the material—at no extra charge!

Online Lessons, Tests, and Drills

Princeton Review *ClassSize-8* Courses are the only classroom courses that have online lessons designed to support each class session. You can practice concepts you learn in class, spend some extra time on topics that you find challenging, or prepare for an upcoming class. And you'll have access as soon as you enroll, so you can get a head start on your test preparation.

The Most Comprehensive, Up-to-Date Materials

Our research and development team studies the tests year-round to stay on top of trends and to make sure you learn what you need to get your best score.

*Independently verified by International Communications Research (ICR).

**Some restrictions apply.

Online *and* LiveOnline *Courses for the GRE, LSAT, and GMAT*

The Best of Both Worlds
We've combined our high-quality, comprehensive test preparation with a convenient, multimedia format that works around your schedule and your needs.

Online *and* LiveOnline *Courses*
Lively, Engaging Lessons
If you think taking an online course means staring at a screen and struggling to pay attention, think again. Our lessons are engaging and interactive – you'll never just read blocks of text or passively watch video clips. Princeton Review online courses feature animation, audio, interactive lessons, and self-directed navigation.

Customized, Focused Practice
The course software will discover your personal strengths and weaknesses. It will help you to prioritize and focus on the areas that are most important to your success. Of course, you'll have access to dozens of hours' worth of lessons and drills covering all areas of the test, so you can practice as much or as little as you choose.

Help at your Fingertips
Even though you'll be working on your own, you won't be left to fend for yourself. We're ready to help at any time of the day or night: you can chat online with a live Coach, check our Frequently Asked Questions database, or talk to other students in our discussion groups.

LiveOnline *Course*
Extra Features
In addition to self-directed online lessons, practice tests, drills, and more, you'll participate in five live class sessions and three extra help sessions given in real time over the Internet. You'll get the live interaction of a classroom course from the comfort of your own home.

ExpressOnline *Course*
The Best in Quick Prep
If your test is less than a month away, or you just want an introduction to our legendary strategies, this mini-course may be the right choice for you. Our multimedia lessons will walk you through basic test-taking strategies to give you the edge you need on test day.

1-2-1 Private Tutoring

The Ultimate in Personalized Attention

If you're too busy for a classroom course, prefer learning at your kitchen table, or simply want your instructor's undivided attention,
1-2-1 Private Tutoring may be for you.

Focused on You

In larger classrooms, there is always one student who monopolizes the instructor's attention. With *1-2-1* Private Tutoring, that student is you. Your instructor will tailor the course to your needs – greater focus on the subjects that cause you trouble, and less focus on the subjects that you're comfortable with. You can get all the instruction you need in less time than you would spend in a class.

Expert Tutors

Our outstanding tutoring staff is comprised of specially selected, rigorously trained instructors who have performed exceptionally in the classroom. They have scored in the top percentiles on standardized tests and received the highest student evaluations.

Schedules to Meet Your Needs

We know you are busy, and preparing for the test is perhaps the last thing you want to do in your "spare" time. The Princeton Review *1-2-1* Private Tutoring Program will work around your schedule.

Additional Online Lessons and Resources

The learning continues outside of your tutoring sessions. Within the Online Student Center*, you will have access to math, verbal, AWA, and general strategy lessons to supplement your private instruction. Best of all, they are accessible to you 24 hours a day,
7 days a week.

*Available for LSAT, GRE, and GMAT

www.PrincetonReview.com

The Princeton Review Admissions Services

At The Princeton Review, we care about your ability to get accepted to the best school for you. But, we all know getting accepting involves much more than just doing well on standardized tests. That's why, in addition to our test preparation services, we also offer free admissions services to students looking to enter college or graduate school. You can find these services on our website, *www.PrincetonReview.com*, the best online resource for researching, applying to, and learning how to pay for the right school for you.

No matter what type of program you're applying to—undergraduate, graduate, law, business, or medical—**PrincetonReview.com has the free tools, services, and advice you need to navigate the admissions process.** Read on to learn more about the services we offer.

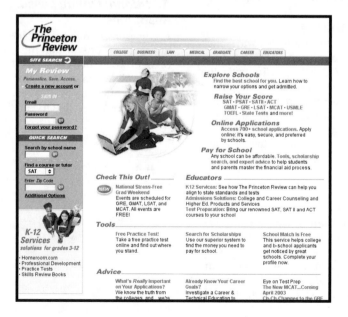

Research Schools
www.PrincetonReview.com/Research

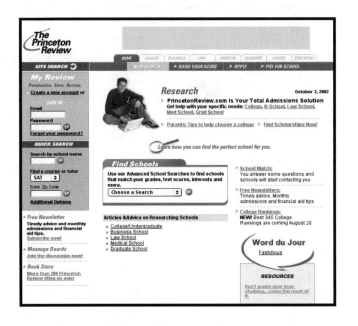

PrincetonReview.com features an interactive tool called **Advanced School Search.** When you use this tool, you enter stats and information about yourself to find a list of schools that fit your needs. From there you can read statistical and editorial information about thousands of colleges and universities. In addition, you can find out what currently enrolled college students say about their schools.

Our **College Majors Search** is one of the most popular features we offer. Here you can read profiles on hundreds of majors to find information on curriculum, salaries, careers, and the appropriate high school preparation, as well as colleges that offer it. From the Majors Search, you can investigate corresponding Careers, read **Career Profiles**, and learn what career is the best match for you by taking our **Career Quiz**.

Another powerful tool we feature is **School Match**. You tell us your scores, interests, and preferences and Princeton Review partner schools will contact you.

No matter what type of school or specialized program you are considering, **PrincetonReview.com has free articles and advice, in addition to our tools, to help you make the right choice.**

Apply to School
www.PrincetonReview.com/Apply

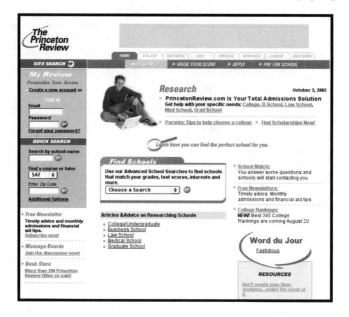

For most students, completing the school application is the most stressful part of the admissions process. PrincetonReview.com's powerful **Online School Application Engine** makes it easy to apply.

Paper applications are mostly a thing of the past. And, our hundreds of partner schools tell us they prefer to receive your applications online.

Using our online application service is simple:

- Enter information once and the common data automatically transfers onto each application.

- Save your applications and access them at any time to edit and perfect.

- Submit electronically or print and mail in.

- Pay your application fee online, using an e-check, or mail the school a check.

Our powerful application engine is built to accommodate all your needs.

Pay for School
www.PrincetonReview.com/Finance

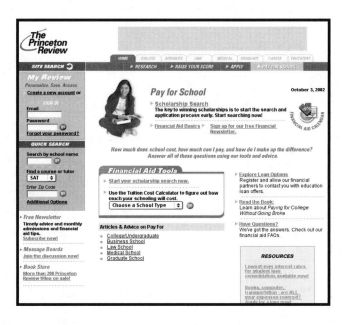

The financial aid process is confusing for everyone. But don't worry. Our free online tools, services, and advice can help you plan for the future and get the money you need to pay for school.

Our **Scholarship Search** engine will help you find free money, although often scholarships alone won't cover the cost of high tuitions. So, we offer other tools and resources to help you navigate the entire process.

Filling out the FAFSA can be a daunting process, use our **FAFSA Worksheet** to make sure you answer the questions correctly the first time.

If scholarships and government aid aren't enough to swing the cost of tuition, we'll help you secure student loans. The Princeton Review has partnered with a select group of reputable financial institutions who will help **explore all your loans options**.

If you know how to work the financial aid process, you'll learn you don't have to **eliminate a school based on tuition.**

Be a Part of the PrincetonReview.com Community

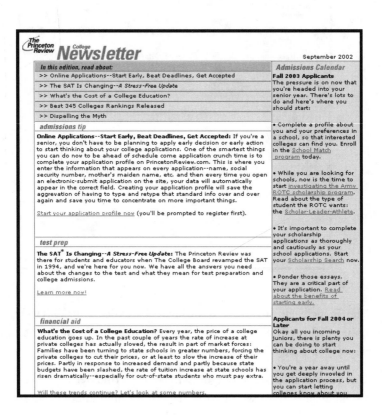

PrincetonReview.com's **Discussion Boards** and **Free Newsletters** are additional services to help you to get information about the admissions process from your peers and from The Princeton Review experts.

Book Store

www.PrincetonReview.com/college/Bookstore.asp

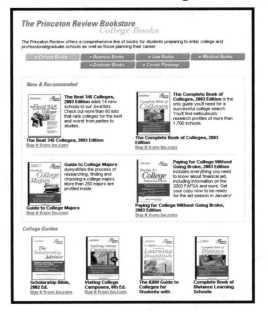

In addition to this book, we publish hundreds of other titles, including guidebooks that highlight life on campus, student opinion, and all the statistical data that you need to know about any school you are considering. Just a few of the titles that we offer are:

- Complete Book of Business Schools

- Complete Book of Law Schools

- Complete Book of Medical Schools

- The Best 351 Colleges

- The K&W Guide to Colleges for Students with Learning Disabilities or Attention Deficit Disorder

- Guide to College Majors

- Paying for College Without Going Broke

For a complete listing of all of our titles, visit our **online book store**:

www.princetonreview.com/college/bookstore.asp

Find the Right School

**BEST 357 COLLEGES
2005 EDITION**
The Smart Buyer's Guide to College
0-375-76405-4 • $21.95

**COMPLETE BOOK OF COLLEGES
2005 EDITION**
0-375-76406-2 • $26.95

**THE BEST MID-ATLANTIC
COLLEGES**
98 Great Schools to Consider
0-375-76341-4 • $14.95

**THE BEST MIDWESTERN
COLLEGES**
150 Great Schools to Consider
0-375-76335-X • $14.95

**THE BEST NORTHEASTERN
COLLEGES**
135 Great Schools to Consider
0-375-76334-1 • $14.95

**THE BEST SOUTHEASTERN
COLLEGES**
100 Great Schools to Consider
0-375-76329-5 • $14.95

THE BEST WESTERN COLLEGES
121 Great Schools to Consider
0-375-76338-4 • $14.95

Get in

**CRACKING THE NEW SAT
2005 EDITION**
0-375-76428-3 • $19.95

**CRACKING THE NEW SAT WITH
SAMPLE TESTS ON CD-ROM
2005 EDITION**
0-375-76429-1 • $31.95

MATH WORKOUT FOR THE NEW SAT
0-375-76433-X • $16.00

**READING AND WRITING WORKOUT
FOR THE NEW SAT**
0-375-76431-3 • $16.00

**11 PRACTICE TESTS FOR THE NEW
SAT & PSAT**
0-375-76434-8 • $19.95

CRACKING THE ACT, 2004 EDITION
0-375-76395-3 • $19.00

**CRACKING THE ACT WITH SAMPLE
TESTS ON CD-ROM, 2004 EDITION**
0-375-76394-5 • $29.95

**CRASH COURSE FOR THE ACT
THE LAST-MINUTE GUIDE TO
SCORING HIGH, 2ND EDITION**
0-375-76364-3 • $9.95

**CRASH COURSE FOR THE SAT
THE LAST-MINUTE GUIDE TO
SCORING HIGH, 2ND EDITION**
0-375-76361-9 • $9.95

Get Help Paying for it

**PAYING FOR COLLEGE WITHOUT
GOING BROKE, 2005 EDITION**
0-375-76421-6 • $20.00

HOW TO SAVE FOR COLLEGE
0-375-76425-9 • $14.95